VALOUR

RECONSIDERED

VALOUR
RECONSIDERED

INQUIRIES INTO

THE VICTORIA CROSS

AND OTHER AWARDS

FOR EXTREME BRAVERY

HUGH A. HALLIDAY

ROBIN BRASS STUDIO

Toronto

Published 2006 by Robin Brass Studio Inc.
www.rbstudiobooks.com

Printed and bound in Canada by Marquis Imprimeur, Cap-Saint-Ignace, Quebec

Library and Archives Canada Cataloguing in Publication

Halliday, Hugh A., 1940–
    Valour reconsidered : inquiries into the Victoria Cross
and other awards for extreme bravery / Hugh A. Halliday.

Includes bibliographical references and index.
ISBN-13: 978-1-896941-47-9
ISBN-10: 1-896941-47-8

    1. Victoria Cross. I. Title.

CR4885.H25 2006   355.1'342   C2006-903054-5

Canada Council   Conseil des Arts
for the Arts   du Canada

We acknowledge the support of the Canada Council for the Arts, which last year invested $20.0 million in writing and publishing throughout Canada.

Nous remercions de son soutien le Conseil des Arts du Canada, qui a investi 20,0 millions de dollars l'an dernier dans les lettres et l'édition à travers le Canada.

CONTENTS

I long ago gave up trying to spot potential VCs by their looks, but from experience, I should say that those who perform individual acts of the highest physical courage are usually drawn from one of two categories. Either those with quick intelligence and vivid imagination or those without imagination and with minds fixed on the practical business of living. You might almost say, I suppose, those who live on their nerves and those who have not got any nerves. The one suddenly sees the crisis, his imagination flashes the opportunity and he acts. The other meets the situation without finding it so very unusual and deals with it in a matter of fact way.

Field Marshal Sir William Slim (1891-1970)

MAJOR AWARDS FOR VALOUR

Victoria Cross

Victoria Cross – Canada

George Cross

Cross of Valour – Canada

Star of Courage

George Medal

Medal of Bravery

Cross of Valour – Australia

Distinguished Service Order

Conspicuous Gallantry Medal

Distinguished Conduct Medal

Medal of Honor – U.S.A.

INTRODUCTION

An author who speaks about his own books is almost
as bad as a mother who talks about her own children.

Benjamin Disraeli (1804-81), speaking in Glasgow, 1873.

The Victoria Cross, instituted by Queen Victoria in 1856, is probably the most famous gallantry decoration in the world. Few other
medals even rival it in reputation, the Medal of Honor (United
States) and the highest levels of the *Pour le Mérite* (Germany) being its only
close competitors. Tell a person that the *Param Vir Chakra* has been awarded
22 times and he will probably be baffled; inform him that it is India's post-
independence equivalent of the Victoria Cross (and that 13 of the awards
have been posthumous) and he will understand.[1] It is widely assumed that
the VC has always been on this pedestal, and that all Victoria Cross recipients
have risked dangers in equally hazardous circumstances. Both suppositions
are wrong. The history of the Victoria Cross is replete with contradictions.

The George Cross (GC), created in 1940, gradually superseded a number
of older gallantry medals that had been awarded to civilians and military
personnel for saving lives (the Albert Medal, Edward Medal and Empire Gallantry Medal, all discussed further). The principal distinction was that these
were for gallantry "not in the face of the enemy" whilst the Victoria Cross
was for gallantry in combat. Drawing a distinction between combat vs. non-
combat activities was not as simple as one might expect, but it was generally
recognized that from 1940 onwards a VC or GC action entailed an 85 per cent
probability (or worse) that the person involved would not survive.

This book arose from an earlier project, that of compiling lists of Royal
Canadian Air Force personnel decorated during the Second World War.

1

Many of these men and women had been Mentioned in Despatches (MiD) while overseas, and there was nothing in Canadian records to explain why they had been granted this seemingly modest honour. Successive visits to the Public Record Office in Britain provided many answers, but in a few cases those answers were startling. In rare instances, the men (they were exclusively men) had been recommended for a Victoria Cross but authorities had concluded that it should not be awarded. In the case of living nominees it was possible to substitute a lesser award, such as a Distinguished Service Order (DSO). However, policies of the day allowed posthumous awards of only three honours – the Victoria Cross, George Cross and Mention in Despatches. Thus, in the case of a recommendation for a posthumous Victoria Cross, there were only three choices available to those deciding – approve the award, approve a Mention in Despatches, or grant no award whatsoever.

Half way through the Second World War, authorities asked if the rules about posthumous awards should be relaxed, allowing lesser decorations to be granted to deceased personnel. The decision was reached that it would be unfair to change the rules at that point (see Appendix A). They remained unaltered until 1992 when Prime Minister John Major overhauled the British honours system. By that time, Canada and Australia had gone their own ways, creating service and gallantry awards distinct from those of Great Britain.

At times it appeared that the decisions of the approving authority were capricious, even political. In other cases there was evidence of measured debate before arriving at decisions. When one moved beyond the narrow range of RCAF personnel to a wider air force community, and then to army and navy awards, the subject became more interesting as comparisons could be made. The VC had been created by humans, and its bestowal was administered by humans. Its award was subject to policies – and politics – which varied with time and circumstance. From these insights, the idea of a book slowly developed to the present work.

The bulk of this work is drawn principally and without apology from Canadian and air force sources. They have been the most accessible to me and the records with which I have been most familiar. Nevertheless, I have attempted to include relevant non-Canadian cases, for it is only through comparison that we can understand some of the processes and pressures which have led to VC nominations and awards.

Having been at the fringes and then near the centre of Canadian military historical writing, I have heard many anecdotes. Some have been proven false. A story told to me about 1964 was that when Flight Lieutenant David Hornell was recommended for a Victoria Cross, his co-pilot, Flying Officer Bernard C. Denomy, was also put up for one. It has a certain plausibility; in the events of 24-25 June 1944, Denomy did almost everything that Hornell did except die. Nevertheless, the documents respecting these events are quite thorough, and there is nothing to indicate that Denomy was actually recommended for anything other than a DSO.

Another bit of historical gossip gathered in the late 1980s was that Lieutenant-Colonel Frederick A. Vokes was considered for a VC but that the process was halted because it would appear too much like favouritism, as his brother, Major-General Chris Vokes, was General Officer Commanding, 1 Canadian Division. Lieutenant-Colonel Vokes was in charge of the 9th Canadian Armoured Regiment (British Columbia Dragoons) and died heroically on 31 August 1944, leading his unit before Tomba di Pesaro (Italy). He was, in fact, serving in 5 Canadian Armoured Division, rather than his brother's formation, and the story of a possible VC recommendation is undocumented (although he was awarded a posthumous Mention in Despatches). Readers may wish to review the chapter on VC "standards," then compare it with the regimental history, and draw their own conclusions.[2]

Yet a further informal "historical briefing" came to me years ago from the late John Chown, ex-Royal Canadian Artillery and subsequently a dedicated employee of the Canadian War Museum. He told me that several instances occurred in the Second World War of Forward Observation Officers being about to be overrun by the enemy and calling down fire on their own positions, hoping that the artillery fire would spare them and kill the enemy. Impressed infantry officers were on the verge of recommending VCs, but senior artillery officers refused to sanction these because the process of calling down fire on one's own location was part of the training of artillery personnel and hence was a tactic and procedure well known within that arm. I did not press Chown for specifics at the time, but it is one of those cases where one senses that if it is *not* true then it *should* be true.

Although I have adopted a scholarly approach to most portions of this book, I confess to certain strongly held views. Readers will have no trouble in distinguishing between the detached observer and the passionate advocate. I have non-conformist opinions about the propriety of William Avery "Billy" Bishop's Victoria Cross. I believe that many brave men who may have merited a VC went unrewarded or were recognized by honours less than they deserved. Nevertheless, I am opposed to any movements that would retroactively bestow the VC (or any other decoration) on heroes who have passed into history. I recognize that at times there has been some unfairness in awarding Victoria Crosses, yet I believe that no system can be perfect. The only guarantee of equity would be to award nothing to anyone.

Even as author I find it hard to describe this book. It is not a history of the Victoria Cross. Rather, it is a series of studies of recommendations for the Victoria Cross, George Cross and related awards, some of which succeeded and some of which did not. I have re-entered the debate about Billy Bishop's VC because to ignore that controversy would be tantamount to ignoring the proverbial elephant in the room. I have also included a critique of the current Canadian awards system (gallantry and service awards alike) because, quite simply, the book provides an opportunity to do so, even if the discussion of these distinctive national honours seems to be a long way from an analysis of more historical rewards for valour.

This book raises many questions – and offers only a few answers. Its primary purpose is to entertain and stimulate, to focus attention on such issues as the definition of valour and if (or how) it can be quantified. When the reader is finished, he may discover that the Victoria Cross and related awards have lost some of their iconic status – but conversely, he may have found that those recommended, whether or not they received these honours, will have grown in stature.

CHAPTER 1

THE VICTORIA CROSS:
AN OVERVIEW

For it's Tommy this, an' Tommy that, an' "Chuck him out, the brute!"
But it's "Saviour of 'is country" when the guns begin to shoot.

Rudyard Kipling (1892)

Notwithstanding its name, the Victoria Cross was not exclusively Queen Victoria's idea. The Crimean War (1854-56) was the first major war covered for the newspapers by the modern equivalent of war correspondents, and the reports were devoured by a public that was increasingly literate. Along the way, British readers discovered the heroism and humanity of their soldiers and demanded better for them, whether in medical attention or formal recognition. Rudyard Kipling wrote his famous passage in 1892 but it was truer before the Crimean War than after.

Officers had many rewards open to them – knighthoods, appointments, promotions – but the common soldier had none. This was not true elsewhere; even French and Russian troops could aspire to decorations for valour. The idea of a prestigious British award for valour was first proposed in the House of Commons on 19 December 1854 by a Member of Parliament, George T. Scobell. It quickly became a joint project of the Queen, her consort Prince Albert, the Duke of Newcastle (Secretary of State for War), Lord Panmure (his successor) and Lord Palmerston (the Prime Minister), with advice from many others. The mountain laboured and brought forth the warrant of 29 January 1856 which created the Victoria Cross and laid down the first regulations governing its issue. The first investitures followed in Hyde Park on 26 June 1857 with the Queen herself on hand to bestow the decoration on 62 recipients.[3]

The Victoria Cross was remarkable for being in one grade only and open to all ranks, from private to general officer. This contrasted with other major British awards, which were generally in several grades and had a class bias. The Order of the Bath, for example, was for higher officers and had three levels (Companion, Knight Commander, Knight Grand Cross). In Russia the St. George Cross rewarded valour by enlisted men (but not officers) and had four levels (Class I, II, III and IV). In 1918 a recreated Poland revived the *Virtuti Militari* (which had existed from 1792 to 1831); both the old and new versions had five classes, of which only the highest could be equivalent to the Victoria Cross.* Moreover, the Victoria Cross was to be for valour alone – staff officers need not apply.

It is difficult to say why or when the Victoria Cross achieved its mythic status. It was awarded generously until 1914, largely because for much of that time it was the *only* award available for bravery alone and open to all ranks. No fewer than 522 were awarded between 1856 and 1913, often in quantities. Fighting on 16 November 1857 during the Second Relief of Lucknow (Indian Mutiny) resulted in the award of 16 VCs (a one-day record) distributed among four regiments plus land-based members of the Royal Navy. Eleven went to defenders of Rorke's Drift (Zulu Wars, 22/23 January 1879). Seven VCs were awarded in the Battle of Colenso (15 December 1899) – one to a doctor and six to officers and men for saving field pieces from imminent capture. Preventing artillery from being captured was at the heart of another VC action at Korr Spruet, South Africa (31 March 1900, five Victoria Crosses awarded) while three VCs went to Canadians saving artillery pieces from capture by Afrikaaners (Komati River, 7 November 1900).[4] Indeed, at various times authorities wondered if the Victoria Cross was being awarded too liberally. As early as 1864, Lord Lugard wrote that the VC was "losing its value … being looked upon in the light of a medal from the Royal Humane Society." The many awards for Rorke's Drift drew a protest that the VC was being awarded with "lavish prodigality." Even Queen Victoria questioned as to whether "the award might become too common."[5]

---

* John Kent, a Canadian who served in the Royal Air Force from 1935 to 1956 and was associated with Polish squadrons, has been described as having received "the Polish equivalent of the Victoria Cross," when he was awarded only the *Virtuti Militari*, Fifth Class.

The Queen might have had further reservations had every purported Victoria Cross recommendation succeeded. In February 1857, following the Battle of Khushab (an obscure engagement in an equally obscure campaign), Major-General James Outram recommended no fewer than 15 men for the VC, writing, "After the fullest inquiry, I am myself quite satisfied that the undermentioned officers and men of the 3rd Regiment of Bombay Light Cavalry are well deserving of the high distinction of the Victoria Cross...." Even in an age when the Victoria Cross was more easily won, Outram was deemed to have considerably "overdone" his recommendations, and only two of his nominees received the coveted decoration.[6]

Some reports of VC submissions are vague. Lieutenant William Thomas Mills, Bombay Native Infantry, was reportedly recommended for a VC following actions on 1 and 3 April 1858 which involved storming fortified positions and rescuing a soldier under fire. How far it went up the chain of command is not known, but in the absence of lesser gallantry awards this officer had to settle for an Indian Mutiny campaign medal and eventual promotion to lieutenant-colonel.[7]

Eligibility for a Victoria Cross evolved. Although officers and enlisted men alike could receive the VC, other distinctions were raised, then eliminated, often by the logic of events. Troops of the East India Company were made eligible, thanks to the Indian Mutiny and an amendment to the warrant (29 October 1857). Civilian volunteers bearing arms but under military direction were added (the Indian Mutiny again, plus an amendment dated 13 December 1858). The honour was extended to members of colonial militias, provided that they were serving alongside British troops and under command of an Imperial officer (warrant amendment, 1 January 1867, a result of the Maori Wars in New Zealand).[8] Clerics serving in India (and hence potential chaplains to Imperial forces) were added (warrant amendment, 6 August 1881), and personnel of the Indian Army became eligible as of 21 October 1911.[9] The first mention of female eligibility came with a revised warrant (22 May 1920).

Formal changes to the warrant were accompanied by informal adaptations in practice. A British officer recommended for a VC in 1891 was not given this honour because he was commanding Egyptian troops nominally under the jurisdiction of the Khedive of Egypt. In spite of the constitutional situation, his valorous act was recognized with a DSO. Eight years later, in another case involving virtually identical circumstances, the War Office changed its mind, recognized the true vassal status of Egypt and supported a VC nomination [10]

Surprisingly, the Victoria Cross was *not* initially awarded posthumously. Authorities nevertheless adopted a curious formula for gallantry demonstrated at the cost of one's life. Thus, the *London Gazette* of 27 May 1859 reported the award of Victoria Crosses to four soldiers – Private Michael Murphy (Military Train), Lance Corporal Alexander Thomson, Quartermaster-Sergeant John Simpson and Private James Davis (these last three from the 42nd Battalion) – for actions performed on 15 April 1858 during the Indian Mutiny. It then carried the following remarkable entry:

> *Private Edward Spence, 42nd Regiment, would have been recommended to Her Majesty for the decoration of the Victoria Cross,* had he survived. *He and Lance Corporal Thomson of that Regiment volunteered at the attack on the Fort of Ruhya, on the 15th April 1858, to assist Captain Groves, commanding the 4th Punjab Rifles, in bringing in the body of Lieutenant Willoughby from the top of the Glacis. Private Spence dauntlessly placed himself in an exposed position, so as to cover the party bearing away the body. He died on the 17th of the same month, from the effects of the wound he received on the occasion.* [11]

This acknowledgment of supreme valour which could not be accompanied by a Victoria Cross continued throughout the 19th century. A departure from this practice came on 8 August 1902 when the *London Gazette* announced that the King had approved delivery of the Victoria Cross to representatives of six soldiers killed in recent hostilities "in the performance of acts of valour which would, in the opinion of the Commander-in-Chief of the Forces in the Field, have entitled them to be recommended for that distinction has they survived." This was followed by citations for all six men. It was a curious formula; the Victoria Cross was not being "awarded" but it was being "delivered" to "representatives" (i.e., next of kin). Finally, the *London Gazette* of 15 January 1907 carried the following notice:

The King has been graciously pleased to approve of the Decoration of the Victoria Cross being delivered to the representatives of the under-mentioned officers and men who fell in the performance of acts of valour, and with reference to whom it was notified in the London Gazette *that they would have been recommended to Her Late Majesty for the Victoria Cross had they survived:*

This was followed by the names of six men who had been singled out earlier than the South African War – Private Edward Spence, 42nd Regiment (described above), Ensign Everard Aloysius Lisle Phillips, 11th Regiment of Bengal Infantry (previously cited in the *London Gazette* of 21 October 1859), Lieutenants Teignmouth Melvill and Nevill Joseph Aylmer Coghill, both of the 24th Regiment (*London Gazette*, May 1879), Trooper Frank William Baxter, Bulawayo Field Force (*London Gazette*, 7 May 1897) and Lieutenant Hector Lachlan Stewart MacLean, Indian Staff Corps (*London Gazette*, 9 November 1897). Posthumous awards of the Victoria Cross were commonly gazetted thereafter, although the regulations governing the honour were not amended to specifically authorize posthumous awards until 1920.

Other awards were created. The Distinguished Conduct Medal, though dating from 1855, was as much a reward for long service as for gallantry, although it had evolved into a bravery decoration by 1862. The Distinguished Service Order (for officers) appeared in 1886, the Military Cross (for officers and senior warrant officers) in 1914 and the Military Medal (for privates and junior NCOs) in 1916. As honours other than the Victoria Cross became possible, VC standards were raised. Yet those standards were not defined – could probably *never* be defined – and each case had to be decided on its own merits. The result was that uniformity of standards could not be attained, and the standards of 1914-18 were very different from those of 1939-45.

During the First World War the British army, facing its greatest and most prolonged test in history, sometimes increased the issuance of medals to maintain morale. This also extended to "upgrading" recommendations to honours higher than originally intended, and possibly higher than merited. The Victoria Cross awarded Lieutenant (later Brigadier) F.M.W. Harvey, Lord Strathcona's Horse, reportedly began as a recommendation for a Military Cross following a routine trench raid; it was upgraded to a Distinguished Service Order at Corps level and subsequently raised to a Victoria Cross at the level of BEF Headquarters.[12] The political impact of Victoria Cross awards was evident in the air war; William A. Bishop's controversial VC (awarded without the testimony of witnesses) was undoubtedly political, but in ways that still divide historians. In 1915, when Zeppelin raids on England were causing panic out of all proportion to their bomb loads, Victoria Crosses were awarded to the first two British pilots who shot down these airships; thereafter, a Zeppelin kill became a DSO action, and by 1918 it had been downgraded to a DSC, MC or DFC affair. Pilots rescuing downed comrades from imminent capture resulted in two awards of the VC; later, similar deeds brought lesser honours.

The upgrading and downgrading of recommendations was constant. An early example of this was in the Royal Flying Corps. Captain Amyas Eden Borton, a pioneer of battlefield aerial reconnaissance, was recommended for a Victoria Cross on 8 June 1915. Lieutenant-Colonel C.J. Burke, Officer Commanding, No. 2 Wing, RFC, wrote to his superiors:

I have the honour to bring to your notice the gallant conduct of Captain A.E. Borton yesterday. When a long way from our lines he was overtaken by a hostile machine that was greatly superior to his both in climbing power and speed. Almost immediately Captain Borton was very badly wounded through the neck and jaw and the machine became out of control. He apparently pulled himself together by a tremendous effort and regained control. The situation he was then in might strike terror into the bravest. He was badly wounded, bleeding terribly without ability to stop it. The hostile machine could with impunity fire at him when it liked and he was miles from home.... Only if he was not hit again could he hope to have strength to last until he reached the British lines, or would loss of blood do what his enemy wanted? If ever there appeared a hopeless and defenceless position, this was one.

It is a marvellous thing that in his condition he could follow his course, but he doggedly stuck to it. The gallant conduct and devotion of this officer cannot be brought out in a report, but after the most careful thought and consideration, it forces itself on me that he is worthy of the highest reward and I have the honour to submit that he be rewarded with the Victoria Cross.

Shooting Down a Zeppelin by Charles Dixon depicts the destruction of Zeppelin L-70 on 5 August 1918 by Major Egbert Cadbury and Captain Robert Leckie, both of the RAF. In 1915 such a feat might have brought a VC but by 1918 it merited only a Distinguished Flying Cross for Cadbury and Leckie. (Canadian War Museum 91225)

The burned-out remains of a Zeppelin in England, 1916. (Canadian War Museum AN19900346-C76)

At some level, and for reasons unknown, Borton's VC was downgraded to a DSO, gazetted on 3 July 1915. Authorities had certainly moved quickly on making an award, even if they had disagreed as to what it should be.[13]

Conversely, the Victoria Cross awarded to Captain Lionel Wilmot Brabazon Rees (No. 32 Squadron, Royal Flying Corps, gazetted 5 August 1916) began on 2 July 1916 as a recommended DSO.

On 1st July at 6.15 a.m. Major Rees while flying a de Havilland in the vicinity of the Double Crassiers sighted what he thought to be a bombing party of our own machines returning home. He went to escort them. As he got nearer, about Annequin, he discovered that they were a party of enemy machines, numbering eight to ten. He was immediately attacked by one of the escort; this machine he fought and after a short encounter it was observed to turn and wobble down behind the enemy line. Five more enemy machines then attacked the de Havilland at long range but Major Rees closed with them, dispersing them in all directions. Major Rees seeing the leader and two others making off west gave chase and overhauled them rapidly, but just as he was coming to close quarters he was severely wounded in the thigh. The shock caused him to lose temporary control of his rudder but as soon as the numbness passed off he regained control of the machine and immediately closed again with the enemy, firing at a range of about ten yards. After using up all his ammunition he tried his pistol but unfortunately dropped it. He then returned home, landing the machine safely on his aerodrome and was then taken to hospital.

The Officer Commanding No. 22 AA [Anti-Aircraft] Battery who witnessed the fight states that the net result of this fine performance was that a single de Havilland Scout appeared to have completely broken up a raid of 8-10 hostile aircraft, of these two were seen to retire damaged, one of which so seriously that he was observed to dive over his own lines with every indication of being no longer under control.[14]

The top Royal Flying Corps officer in France, Major-General Hugh Trenchard, had a different view and on 6 July 1916 wrote to the Military Secretary for the Commander-in-Chief, stating in part:

I am of the opinion that Major Rees' action is well worthy of a higher reward and he should be granted a VC.[15]

Trenchard was pushing for two VC awards, one to Rees and the other to A.L. Gordon-Kidd (ultimately awarded a DSO). The field commander (Field Marshal Sir Douglas Haig) apparently approved, for a letter went out on 7 July 1916 from the Military Secretary, British Armies in France (Major-General William E. Peyton) to Headquarters, Royal Flying Corps:

With reference to your remarks concerning the acts of gallantry performed by Captain (Temporary Major) L.W.B. Rees, Royal Garrison Artillery and No. 32 Squadron, RFC, and 2nd Lieutenant A.L.G. Kidd, General List and RFC, the General Officer Commanding-in-Chief has decided to recommend these officers for the honour of the Victoria Cross.

Will you therefore forward corroborative evidence of the acts of gallantry in support of the recommendation.

One might assume that "corroborative evidence" was supplied for Rees but not for Gordon-Kidd. On the other hand, Gordon-Kidd's achievement of bombing and destroying an ammunition train on 1 July 1916 and attacking a heavily defended train at low level on 3 July 1916, may have been deemed slightly less deserving of a VC than Rees's aerial combats. Equally, since the principal deed of each man was on 1 July 1916 (the opening day of the Battle of the Somme), authorities may have recoiled from awarding two Victoria Crosses to pilots who had survived their bold actions (Gordon-Kidd, unlike Rees, emerged unwounded).

Anecdotes and legends about the Victoria Cross flourished then and after the war. A British officer, Commander Arthur M. Asquith, despite his naval rank, was commanding an infantry battalion in the 63rd (Royal Navy) Division in France. He recommended his regimental surgeon, William J. McCracken, for a VC but was asked to downgrade it to a Bar to McCracken's DSO. It turned out that Asquith's superiors had already recommended him for a Victoria Cross, and they were reluctant to forward two such recommendations from the same regiment. Asquith was adamant: "McCracken's name must go forward." The result was that both recommendations were reduced;

McCracken received a Bar to his DSO; Asquith was awarded a second Bar to his DSO.[16]

Awards or non-awards of Victoria Crosses did not necessarily go unchallenged. C.G. Grey, the caustic, iconoclastic editor of *Aeroplane* wondered why Victoria Crosses were not tied more directly to the military value of an act. On 26 August 1915, the Admiralty reported that Squadron Commander Arthur W. Bigsworth, Royal Naval Air Service, had destroyed a German submarine off Ostend. Although the enemy denied this loss (and ultimately were correct in their denial), Grey wrote:

> *In the event of the information proving exact, what is the adequate reward for the pilot? If one Zeppelin is worth a VC, and one submarine is worth a dozen Zeppelins as a weapon, if not as a scout, what decoration can be given?*[17]

Bigsworth was awarded a Distinguished Service Order on 13 September 1915 and a Bar to the DSO two years later.

Victoria Cross actions continued in the period between the two world wars although awards for 1919 services with the North Russian Relief Force might be considered as an extension of the First World War. Nevertheless, British campaigns in Iraq and on India's Northwest Frontier (modern Pakistan) resulted in awards of five more VCs, including the only one presented during the brief reign of Edward VIII (to the widow of Captain Godfrey Meynell). In the same period, by way of comparison, the United States bestowed four Medals of Honor for combat in Haiti and Nicaragua. That nation also awarded 18 Medals of Honor to military personnel exhibiting great personal courage in non-combat situations – awards which in the British scheme of things would probably have generated a knighthood (Charles Lindbergh might here be compared to Charles Kingsford-Smith) or a different award: Private Albert J. Smith's rescue of an American mechanic from a burning airplane in 1921 would have been comparable to Pilot Officer Sidney N. Wiltshire's rescue of his instructor from a burning airplane in 1929; Smith got a Medal of Honor; Wiltshire received a "Medal of the Military Division of the Order of the British Empire," which was later replaced by a George Cross.

The Second World War witnessed the awarding of 182 Victoria Crosses. It was a truly heroic time, with no uncertainty as to the justness of the cause. Commanders on both sides bestrode their worlds to a degree unheard of today; even today names such as Doolittle, Harris, MacArthur, Montgomery, Patton, Rommel, Rundstedt and Zhukov are more familiar than those of contemporary generals. It was the last war in which the British Empire and Commonwealth fought as one, as English soldiers defended India and Indian soldiers fought in Italy. It was a war where technology was still matched in importance by

Sergeant John Hannah, RAF, who remained in his burning Hampden bomber to fight the flames. (Canadian Forces Photo PL-982)

the human will, though it ended with the first long-range rockets, cruise missiles and the atomic bomb. The fact that since 1945 only 12 Victoria Crosses have been awarded bespeaks not a lessening of valour but technological developments that have increasingly allowed combatants to kill their enemies from afar or above, without the nastiness of hand-to-hand combat.

Early wartime experience demonstrated a need for additional decorations. When Sergeant John Hannah, an air gunner, remained in his burning Hampden bomber to fight the flames, Air Ministry authorities seemed to think his actions a little short of a VC standard, yet deserving more than a Distinguished Flying Medal. The Station Commander suggested awarding him an Empire Gallantry Medal but Air Vice-Marshal A.T. Harris, then Air Officer Commanding, No. 5 Group, came down in favour of a Victoria Cross.[18] Nevertheless, the Hannah case helped bolster the argument for creation of a gallantry decoration ranking between the VC and DFM. This issue was pressed again when a VC was proposed for Sergeant James Ward (see below, page 27); the result was the appearance in 1942 of the Conspicuous Gallantry Medal (Flying), itself equivalent to the army's Distinguished Conduct Medal (DCM) and the navy's Conspicuous Gallantry Medal (CGM).

A little-noted amendment to the Victoria Cross warrant took effect as of December 31, 1942. It permitted direct submission of recommendations from Dominion "Ministers of State" to the King. This opened the way for Victoria Crosses to be recommended *without reference to a British chain of command*. This change had originally been requested by South Africa, but it was also almost certainly inspired by the case of a failed VC recommendation on behalf of Chief Petty Officer Max Leopold Bernays of the Royal Canadian Navy (see below), which had aroused considerable dissatisfaction in Canadian circles. The amendment would also have simplified submissions from Australia, which by then had considerable forces in action in New Guinea and the Southwest Pacific, where Commanders-in-Chief were either American or Australian – but not British. Nevertheless, in that war at least, none of the Dominions exercised their new-found right of direct submission to the Crown.[19] The clause would be useful, however, when Australia recommended members who were fighting in a war that had *not* engaged Britain – the Vietnam War.

A recipient's attitude to his Victoria Cross said much about the man. Some men flaunted it. Some, their pride overwhelmed by poverty, pawned it. Private Ernest Alva "Smokey" Smith, Seaforth Highlanders of Canada, tried not to be impressed with his Victoria Cross. In 1944, when asked how it felt to be one of that famous group, de-  scribed his Victoria Cross as "a nice Christmas present to take home to Mom."[20] He spent the last ten years of his life denying that he was a hero, repeatedly saying that all the heroes were buried in Europe. A few imposters invented Victoria Crosses for themselves, usually to swindle impressionable people.[21]

The subsequent careers of survivors varied in the extreme. Alexander

Ernest Alva "Smokey" Smith with his Victoria Cross. (Canadian War Museum 19910238-824)

Roberts Dunn, the first Canadian to win the VC (as a lieutenant in the 11th Hussars in the Charge of the Light Brigade, 1854), rose to the rank of colonel but proved to be a disastrous commanding officer, having too great a taste for other men's wives. His promotions were through purchase rather than merit. Dunn's death in Ethiopia in 1868 was officially described as a hunting accident, but there were rumours of murder.[22] William Hall, the third Canadian recipient, declined an opportunity to become a middle-ranking civil servant and chose to farm for 40 years in Nova Scotia. A British sailor, Duncan G. Boyes, was awarded a Victoria Cross at the age of 17 (1865), was court-martialled and dismissed from the service at 19 and committed suicide at 22. Milton F. Gregg, awarded the VC in 1918, dedicated his life to Canadian public service as a soldier, educator, cabinet minister and diplomat. Martin Doyle became an IRA spy and a founding member of Eire's post-independence army. Bomber Command's legendary Leonard Cheshire, who established homes for handicapped persons after the Second World War, came as close to being a saint as any VC recipient could get.

The history of the Victoria Cross is replete with unexpected facts. The

Lieutenant A.R. Dunn of the 11th (Prince Albert's Own) Hussars was the first Canadian VC winner. (Library and Archives Canada C5835)

Canadian-born William Hall, serving with the Royal Navy, won a VC for heroism in the Indian Mutiny, 1857-58. (Library and Archives Canada C18743)

17

Normandy landings on 6 June 1944, perhaps the most famous date in the history of the Second World War, generated only one Victoria Cross, yet 19 years earlier (April 25, 1915) the initial landings at Gallipoli generated 12 such awards (six of them to the Royal Navy), and although that campaign is most closely associated with Australian and New Zealand troops, it was not until 19 May 1915 that an ANZAC soldier performed a deed that was deemed worthy of a VC.

The Gallipoli awards resulting from the landings of 25 April 1915 included six to a single unit, the 1st Battalion, Lancashire Fusiliers. However, the circumstances of their bestowal were peculiar. Major-General Sir Aylmer Hunter-Weston recommended two officers and four Other Ranks for the Victoria Cross. These six were approved by the General Officer Commanding (General Sir Ian Hamilton), but the process foundered in the War Office. Subsequently a ballot was held which resulted in the selection of one officer (Captain Richard R. Willis) and two other ranks (Sergeant Alfred J. Richards, Private William Keneally). That left three of the original nominees out in the cold, although Corporal John E. Grimshaw was subsequently awarded a Distinguished Conduct Medal for his heroism on 25 April 1915.

Nevertheless, Brigadier Owen Wooley-Dod, himself a Lancashire Fusilier, a member of General Hunter-Westons's staff, and one of those who had landed on the hotly contested beach on 25 April 1915, felt a grave injustice had been committed. He lobbied on behalf of the other three nominees, urging that their cases be re-examined. He succeeded. In March 1917 the *London Gazette* announced Victoria Crosses to Captain Cuthbert Bromley, Sergeant E.E. Stubbs and Sergeant Grimshaw, whose DCM was cancelled whilst the VC was substituted. By then he was the only one of the trio still alive.

Auction records track the growing monetary value of all gallantry medals, but especially Victoria Crosses. The medals of Alexander Roberts Dunn, including his Battle of Balaklava VC, were sold at auction for £155.[23] In 1897 the VC awarded to Private William Griffiths (one of the few Victoria Crosses awarded for non-combat bravery) fetched only £33 at a London sale. As late as February 1972 the medals of Colonel James Travers (Indian Mutiny) realized only £2,400. A decade later, however, the D-Day Victoria Cross awarded to Company Sergeant Major Stanley Hollis went under the hammer at £32,000. Since that date, museums and private collectors have vied for the opportunity to possess these icons. In 1983 the Royal Air Force Museum had to resort to a public appeal to raise money for the VC and associated medals that had belonged to Wing Commander Eric James Nicolson (the only member of Fighter Command to win a VC); they won with a bid for £110,000.[24] This figure has been routinely surpassed in recent years. Those associated with particularly significant actions and individuals have been the object of very aggressive bidding. At the time of writing (February 2006) the record VC sale has been that of Sergeant Norman Jackson, RAF, whose medals sold to a private collector on 30 April 2004 for £230,000 – roughly $400,000 (U.S.) or $480,000 (Canadian, 2006 values).

In view of the very high prices that Victoria Crosses command, museums with limited budgets have been fortunate to obtain as many such medals as they have. Families frequently donate Victoria Cross medal groups in return for generous tax benefits. However, there are occasions when families insist on sale by auction. Such was the case of the Nicolson VC, and the affair was even incorporated in a novel, *First Among Equals,* by Jeffrey Archer. The family had used the sale to publicize the plight of service widows and pensioners. In 1974 a wealthy Canadian, Stephen Roman, advised his agents to bid at a Sotheby's auction for the VC and associated medals awarded to Captain Edward Bellow; he paid $13,800 for the lot, which were donated to the Canadian War Museum.[25]

Corporal Fred Topham, 1st Canadian Parachute Regiment, was awarded the VC for heroism on 24 March 1945 during the crossing of the Rhine. He died in 1974, and for many years his widow had his medals on loan to the Canadian War Museum. It was understood that she would eventually bequeath them to the museum. However, on learning that they were not consistently displayed, she changed her will and instructed that the medals should be sold at auction for her beneficiaries. A committee of interested veterans groups and regimental associations negotiated with the executor of Topham's estate, and it was agreed that a private sale would be made, the funds to be raised through public subscription; the minimum price set on the medals was $260,000 (Canadian), and this could go as high as $300,000 if that sum were raised (the family had received an overseas private offer of $319,000). Schools, newspapers, corporations, individuals and municipal councils all contributed; $300,000 was raised, and on 24 January 2005 the medals were transferred to the Royal Canadian Military Institute, which in turn deposited them with the Canadian War Museum.

Since 1857 all Victoria Crosses have been struck by the same London jeweller (Hancocks and Company), supposedly using bronze from the cascabels of two Russian cannons that were captured at Sebastopol.* However, at least one VC was fluoroscoped in the Tower of London and found to be made of common brass, suggesting that a few First World War crosses were made with material from another source. A recent book presents a strong case that the metal from the original Russian guns was exhausted about 1914, and that two former Chinese cannons were thereafter stripped of their cascabels to provide material for Victoria Crosses. What is left of these ingots, whether they be Russian or Chinese bronze, is stored by 15 Regiment, Royal Logistics Centre, Donnington, which issues blocks to Hancocks at intervals. At the time of writing it is estimated that there is enough of this sacred metal left to manufacture 85 Victoria Crosses.[26]

The awarding of a Victoria Cross normally began with a recommendation from a man's immediate commanding officer. However, other figures might play a role in starting the process. It would appear that the first correspondence leading to Captain Paul Triquet's VC was a letter from Major Hershell A. Smith, "C" Squadron, 11 Canadian Armoured Regiment (himself awarded a Military Cross), who on 22 December 1943 addressed the following letter to the commanding officer, Royal 22e Regiment:

Sir:

I wish to submit the following report on the commendable work done by Captain Triquet, P., who commanded "C" Company of your Battalion, with which I worked in close contact on December 14th and 15th.

Throughout these two days, despite severe casualties this officer set an example of leadership which was of the highest calibre. During the advance, despite heavy enemy opposition and fire, and with the loss of all his officers and the greatest percentage of his Non-Commissioned Officers, he kept the Company organized as a fighting unit and pushed home the attack.

---

* The cascabels were large knobs at the rear of the cannon to which ropes were attached when man-handling the guns into position. The two cannons, minus these cascabels, are displayed outside the Officers' Mess at Woolwich.

The following day when the enemy counter-attacked he again took command of the situation and gathered the remnants of the troops, organizing them successfully in a defensive line.

At all times his cheerfulness and personal disregard of danger was apparent.[27]

Although commanding officers' recommendations were the normal means of initiating a VC, there was a peculiar method incorporated in the original Victoria Cross warrant that survives to this day. That was nomination by ballot, whereby a unit was advised that it would be entitled to one or more such awards, the individuals themselves being chosen by a ballot of those in the regiment or ship. In all, 46 Victoria Crosses have been awarded in this fashion, the last time in 1918 when four of nine awards connected with the blocking of Zeebrugge and Ostend harbours (22-23 April 1918) involved balloting by the recipient's peers and comrades.

Once an award (VC or otherwise) had been recommended, it passed through the chain of command, at any level of which it could be halted, downgraded or upgraded. In wartime, most awards were approved at the level of local commander-in-chief (such as Field Marshal Bernard Montgomery, Air Chief Marshal Arthur Harris or Admiral Andrew Cunningham). It was at this level that many VC recommendations were transformed into lesser awards that remained within the C-in-C's authority to grant. However, even a Montgomery, Harris or Cunningham could not give the final stamp of approval to a Victoria Cross. There remained two hurdles – the Victoria Cross committees organized within the War Office, Air Ministry or Admiralty, and the King himself.

The influence of the King is difficult to judge, being anecdotal in nature. Nevertheless, it is evident that George

Captain Paul Triquet, Royal 22e Regiment, with his VC. Triquet was not allowed to return to front-line service after receiving the VC – heroes were too important to risk their being killed. (Library and Archives Canada PA157376)

V and George VI, restricted in their powers as constitutional monarchs, took great personal interest in the matter of honours and awards in general, Victoria Crosses in particular.* George V effectively ended the practice of revoking Victoria Crosses from recipients subsequently convicted of a crime. George VI took a direct part in the creation of the George Cross and George Medal, was instrumental in Fighter Command seeking out a VC nominee from the Battle of Britain, and even cancelled a DCM award that had already been gazetted to Warrant Officer Peter H. Wright (3rd Battalion, Coldstream Guards) in order to upgrade the award to a Victoria Cross. He may also have requested the raising of a Victoria Cross recommendation on behalf of Captain Fogerty Fegen of HMS *Jervis Bay* (killed in action 5 November 1940; VC gazetted 22 November 1940).[28]

Virtually all awards that are the gift of the Crown may, in theory, be revoked by the Crown, and such was the case with the Victoria Cross. The original warrant provided for a VC to be cancelled, the recipient's name erased from the register and military pensions revoked in cases where the soldier or sailor had been convicted of a crime. This occurred in eight instances between 1857 and 1901, the various offenders having been convicted of desertion, assault, theft or bigamy. In 1920, however, the widow of one such unfortunate (James Collis) wrote to King George V begging that his name be restored to the official VC register. Subsequently, on 26 July 1920, the King's Private Secretary (Lord Stamfordham) wrote:

> *The King feels so strongly that no matter the crime committed by anyone on whom the VC has been conferred, the decoration should never be forfeited. Even were a VC sentenced to be hanged for murder, he should be allowed to wear the VC on the scaffold.*[29]

---

* "Honours" are generally considered to be granted in recognition for services, be they in the fields of entertainment, science or statecraft. "Awards" are normally deemed to be in recognition of specific brave deeds. In practice, the distinctions have not been so clear. The Victoria Cross has always and undeniably been an "award." The British Empire Medal, on the other hand, has been awarded for many reasons. Of 388 awarded to RCAF personnel during the Second World War, the vast majority were for "services" (aircraft maintenance, clerical work, messing efficiency, etc), but at least 31 were granted for rescues of persons from fire or drowning, while two were awarded to RCAF non-commissioned aircrew for escape and evasion after being shot down in enemy-occupied territory.

There were no forfeitures of Victoria Crosses thereafter, although the clause permitting such forfeitures has remained part of the royal warrant. Meanwhile, other honours remain open to revocation. Gallantry awards are seldom cancelled; a rare example was the 1924 announcement that "the Military Cross to Arnold Harrow-Bunn, late temporary Captain, Royal Air Force, gazetted on 10 January 1917, shall be cancelled, and that his name shall be erased from the register, in consequence of his having been convicted by the civil power."[30] A study of the Military Medal identifies five cases of forfeiture between 1923 and 1955 arising from such charges as mutiny or desertion.[31] In March 1945 a Canadian soldier, Private Cletus Murdock, First Special Service Force, was awarded an American Silver Star for valour, only to have it rescinded a year later. He had become a deserter, and American regulations forbade "award or presentation to any individual whose entire service subsequent to the time he distinguished himself has not been honourable."[32]

On the other hand, non-combat awards have been the subject of numerous forfeitures in Britain, approximately 100 since 1945, chiefly of MBE and OBE awards in both the civil and military divisions of the Order of the British Empire.[33] In recent years the most prominent such cancellation was that of the Knighthood of Sir Anthony Blunt (Keeper of the Queen's Pictures) in 1979 when his activities as a Soviet spy decades earlier were discovered. Canada has had its own system of awards since 1967 and provisions for forfeiture can be found in several warrants governing these honours. Two members of the Order of Canada have been removed from that Order, one upon conviction for fraud, the other for conviction of disseminating hateful remarks.

Such has been the prestige of the Victoria Cross that, given practicality and family consent, the recipient of a Victoria Cross is entitled to a military funeral; the last such funeral in Canada was that of E.A. "Smokey" Smith in 2005.[34] There is, however, no truth to the oft-repeated story that a VC recipient was to be saluted, regardless of rank. On the other hand, recipients of the Victoria Cross and George Cross have been automatically granted (since 1937) medals celebrating coronations and royal jubilees. In Canada this has extended to medals celebrating the 100th and 125th anniversaries of Confederation.

CHAPTER 2

THE MEASURE OF THE MEN:
VICTORIA CROSS "STANDARDS"

When there is no peril in the fight, there is no glory in the triumph.

Pierre Corneille (1606-84), *Le Cid*

A ship in harbour is safe, but that is not what ships are built for.

George "Punch" Imlach (1918-87)

The design of the Victoria Cross was so simple that even the Queen initially doubted its appearance. The inscription was equally spartan – "For Valour." The *degree* of valour required to earn the VC has been debated and discussed from the very beginning. It is an argument that has revolved around many decorations in numerous countries.

Queen Victoria herself directed that one man should *not* receive the VC because his deeds had demonstrated as much treachery as courage. Private P. McGwire, 33rd Foot, had been taken prisoner by two Russians, who relieved him of his musket and pouch, then commenced to march him back to Sebastopol. When they relaxed their vigilance, McGwire leaped upon one, seized back his musket, shot the other dead, then beat the remaining Russian to death with the butt of the weapon. He next took their uniforms and returned to British lines. The French awarded him a *Médaille Militaire*. Queen Victoria thought it "of very doubtful morality," but she also expressed practical objections fearing that to sanction such acts might "lead to the cruel and inhumane practice of never taking prisoners, but always putting to death those who may be overpowered, for fear of their rising on their captors."[35]

Fears were expressed at the outset that a decoration such as the VC might lead to soldiers rushing to perform acts that were "rash and contrary to discipline." On the other hand, there were questions as to where a soldier's duty left off and extraordinary courage took over. It has already been noted that initial lavish distributions led to concerns that it was being debased. Indeed, the prodigality of awards during the Zulu Wars may have led to greater care in recommending personnel, although the institution of the DSO in 1886 undoubtedly helped narrow the selection. Following the Battle of Colenso (15 December 1899), General Sir Redvers Buller recommended several men for the VC, their particular deed having been the retrieval of field guns under fire. However, he deemed Captain Harry N. Schofield to be merely carrying out his duties and obeying orders as an artillery officer and recommended only a DSO, which was awarded in April 1901. Many who witnessed the action believed that Schofield had gone far beyond the execution of his orders and had actually been the principal actor in saving the guns. An extraordinary public campaign on behalf of Schofield resulted in General Buller being virtually overruled; the *London Gazette* of 30 August 1901 cancelled the DSO and bestowed the Victoria Cross instead.[36]

Hints of self-promotion sometimes hung about the Victoria Cross. A letter to *The Times* in 1891 asserted that several had been awarded to people seeking it even to the point of exaggerating their exploits.[37] No specific cases were mentioned, but one is reminded how, following the South African War, a Canadian militia colonel waged a campaign on his own behalf (writing frequently to governors general and senior British officers), maintaining that he had performed not one but *two* Victoria Cross deeds. This was, of course, Sam (later Sir Sam) Hughes, who from 1911 to 1916 was Minister of Militia.[38] A humble trooper, Clement Roberts, having rescued reporter Winston Churchill from an Afrikaaner ambush in 1900, pleaded (unsuccessfully) through intermediaries for a Victoria Cross, describing it as "in itself a recommendation for life."[39] An interesting case of "VC lobbying" involved a *bona fide* hero. Lance-Corporal Albert Jacka, Australian Imperial Force, earned the Victoria Cross at Gallipoli in 1915. Subsequently commissioned, he performed heroic deeds in France in August 1916. This time he was awarded a Military Cross. He complained bitterly and publicly that he should have received a Bar to his VC, something that Australian historian W.W. Bean supported in his official war histories.[40].

M.J. Crook argues that by the time of the South African War (1899-1902) VC standards were "over-strict," yet the number of awards in that conflict totalled 78. The matter of "duty" vs. "heroism" was raised in regards to saving of comrades under fire. Writing in 1901, Lord Kitchener declared that "steps should be taken to discourage recommendations for the Victoria Cross in *civilized warfare* in cases of *mere bringing in of wounded and dismounted men*" (emphasis added by this author). In September 1902 General Sir Ian Hamilton described his reluctance to recommend Victoria Crosses for rescues of wounded men "when (if they lay quite still) they were probably safer than being rescued." Their reservations may have had some effect, for in 1908 three VC and five DCM recommendations were altered to two DSO and six DCM awards. The particular incident involved a campaign against hostile tribesmen in India; the War Office concluded that bringing in the wounded was an obligation on the Northwest Frontier. In 1914 both Sir Douglas Haig and Sir John French expressed their view that VCs should not be awarded for the rescue of wounded officers and men "unless under very exceptional circumstances."[41]

Clearly such "exceptional circumstances" were found, as several Victoria Crosses were awarded for battlefield rescues. Nevertheless, the issue of such acts remained contentious, even into the Second World War. A letter dated 3 July 1944 addressed from Headquarters, Eighth Army (Italy), to component formations put the matter starkly (emphasis added by this author):

> *A number of recommendations for Immediate Awards are being received for very gallant actions by individuals, in the face of the enemy and under fire, in rescuing their comrades from burning tanks or other vehicles.*
>
> *Whilst appreciating that such conduct undoubtedly merits some recognition the Commander-in-Chief has decided that,* unless the action has some bearing on the immediate success of the operation *or is accompanied by a further action with such bearing,* recommendations cannot be accepted for Immediate Awards, but will be recognized by Mentions-in-Despatches.[42]

Although civilian Canadian *voyageurs* had participated in the Sudan campaign of 1884 and New South Wales volunteers arrived in Africa in 1885, the

South African War was the first Imperial war which saw large-scale employment of "colonial" contingents. The largest of these (not surprisingly) were regiments drawn from Britain's African colonies (Rhodesia, Cape Colony, Natal), but there were also substantial contributions from Canada, New Zealand and the various Australian colonies which would come together as the Commonwealth of Australia only in 1901. The British army having chosen to keep it a "white man's war" by excluding Indian forces, their dependence on "colonial" units was all the greater. In 1901 Lord Roberts observed (with perhaps greater foresight than he realized) that VC awards to two nominees (Lieutenant Frederick W. Bell, Australia, and Farrier-Major William J. Hardham, New Zealand) should be supported because it was "desirable to show the Colonials that we appreciate their gallantry and their coming forward to help us. *We may require them to do so again perhaps ere long.*"[43] This foreshadowed instances in which being a Canadian would favour a VC where all other considerations were equal (see William A. Bishop, Cecil Merritt and David Hornell cases below).

At some point the British War Office files relating to VC submission from 1915 to 1918 vanished. There is some uncertainty as to how or why; the most widely accepted view is that they were discarded by an over-zealous bureaucrat clearing office space, but another holds that they fell victim to German bombing during the Second World War. The wholesale destruction of these files, complete with recommendations and official discussions, made even Crook despair of assessing how standards were expressed and applied in that conflict, and at the time he was writing *The Evolution of the Victoria Cross* the bulk of Second World War documents remained classified. In 1972 the Public Record Office was able to open numerous files to scrutiny. Even so, there is much to be desired in explaining official thinking, although one can infer the rationale of some awards (and non-awards) from a comparison of particular cases.

An interesting submission involved Sergeant James A. Ward, Royal New Zealand Air Force, second pilot of a Wellington bomber. On the night of 7/8 July 1941 his aircraft was attacked by a night fighter and a stubborn fire close to the starboard engine took hold. Ward volunteered to climb out onto the wing to attempt to smother the fire with an engine cover that was being used as a cushion. He was tied to a dinghy rope and, assisted by the navigator, struggled out, breaking hand and foot holes in the fabric. Battling the slip-stream, he briefly suppressed the flames, but ultimately failed to extinguish the blaze when the engine cover/cushion was blown away. Nevertheless, the fire's spread was checked, chiefly because most of the fabric on which it fed had burned away. Again with the navigator's aid, Ward clambered back to the fuselage and re-entered the aircraft. The pilot eventually landed in Britain.

When recommended for the Victoria Cross, Sergeant Ward's feat was weighed against that of Sergeant John Hannah, whose own VC action a year earlier had been described as a weak case. The pros and cons went rather like this:

- Hannah had fought a fire successfully; Ward had not.

- Hannah had fought a fire amid exploding ammunition and been burned in the process; Ward had faced different hazards, including the danger that, had his grip failed, the dinghy rope would likely have broken, and, if it had not broken, he might instead have been swung into the tail-plane and battered to death.

- Before his parachute was burned, Hannah had the option of baling out over land; Ward, over the North Sea, did not have that option.

- Hannah had worked unassisted; Ward, to the extent that he had been helped in and out of the Wellington, had shared the work with the navigator.

- Hannah's parachute had been destroyed while he fought the fire; Ward, although he offered to venture out with no parachute, was persuaded to wear one as he worked in the slipstream.

The Air Ministry committee weighing these arguments concluded that Ward's was a "borderline case," yet the hard fact remained that there was as yet nothing between a VC and DFM for non-commissioned aircrew; the CGM (Flying) was still a year away. His venturing out into the slipstream, struggling with the engine cover, with an uncertain sea running below, clearly merited more than a DFM. The Air Member for Personnel favoured a DFM; Air Chief Marshal Sir Charles Portal, Chief of the Air Staff, (and most other committee members) supported a VC. Nevertheless, Portal's summary foreshadowed a line that would be taken in other considerations of VC submissions:

Much as anyone admires the kind of courage displayed by Sergeant Ward on this occasion, I must say that I think the VC should more often be given to a man who displayed exceptional valour in getting himself into great danger, than to one who shows equal bravery in getting out of the kind of desperate situation which is latent in all air operations.

The first type knowingly raises the odds against himself in the pursuit of his duty, whereas in the latter type of case the move of self-preservation may sometimes dominate his actions.

Nevertheless, as Sergeant Ward volunteered from among six comrades to perform an act of the greatest bravery which saved their lives and their aircraft, I agree that he should be recommended for the Victoria Cross.[44]

The old conundrum of "duty" vs. "valour" raised its head in another field, that of aerial attacks on U-boats. Early in the Second World War enemy submarines usually dived at the sight of patrolling aircraft. By 1942, airborne radar and faster bombers had given Allied aircrews many more opportunities to achieve surprise and execute deadly attacks with an increasing array of weapons. In turn, the German navy fitted U-boats with formidable anti-aircraft defences and encouraged crews to fight on the surface. The result was numerous and dramatic duels between patrol bombers and submarines, with losses on both sides. In the autumn of 1943, Air Ministry officials had two VC recommendations before them arising from just such duels. That for Flying Officer William T.H. Jennings (No. 172 Squadron) read, in part:

On his next patrol, on 24th July 1943, this officer piloted a Wellington aircraft over the Bay of Biscay. At approximately 1715 hours a large U-boat was sighted on the surface. All its guns were manned and no attempt to submerge was made. Its crew clearly intended to fight to the finish.

Flying Officer Jennings warned his crew that he intended to attack and dived from 1,000 to 100 feet in the face of exceptionally accurate and deadly fire. The aircraft was repeatedly hit and large portions of its structure were shot away during the approach. Nevertheless, depth charges were released accurately by Flying Officer Jennings.

The disabled aircraft crashed on to the U-Boat, tearing away the quadruple mounting and the starboard 20-mm gun, and killing or wounding the gun's crew. The rear gunner was subsequently rescued from the sea but the remainder of the crew are missing.

Two depth charges which lodged in the after part of the submarine caused such damage that it could not submerge. Another aircraft then arrived and found the vessel well down by the stern and turning out of control. Oil was pouring from its tanks and a number of the crew were on deck preparing to abandon ship.

In pressing home his attack at low level, Flying Officer Jennings displayed courage and determination of the highest order, setting an example in keeping with the best traditions of the Royal Air Force.

Jennings had performed a signal act, culminating in the destruction of *U-459*, a 1,600-ton supply submarine or "Milch Cow" that delivered fuel and replacement torpedoes to U-boats at sea. The vessel had been equipped with a quadruple 20-mm gun mount near the base of the conning tower, two 20-mm guns elsewhere, a pair of machine guns on the bridge and a 37-mm gun forward of the conning tower. These had concentrated on a target that was

The formidable anti-aircraft defences of a U-boat are evident here. (Library and Archives Canada PA173333)

forced to approach in a direct line, with no evasive action, in order to execute its attack.

At the same time as the Jennings VC nomination reached Air Ministry, another remarkable submission was received. It was unusual in several respects, not least of which was that the sole witnesses were enemy – survivors of *U-468* which had been sunk off West Africa. The pilot, Flying Officer Lloyd A. Trigg, RNZAF, was a pilot in No. 200 Squadron. He had made two attacks on U-boats and had been awarded a Distinguished Flying Cross before the events that led to his being recommended for a Victoria Cross. The draft citation read, in part:

Flying Officer L.A. Trigg, RNZAF, was awarded the VC on evidence supplied by the enemy – a submarine crew. (Canadian Forces Photo PL-23728)

His next sortie took place on the 11th August 1943, when the urgency of the U-boat situation demanded that he be despatched in a Liberator aircraft on patrol, though the squadron was in process of converting to Liberators and he had not made any operational sorties on this type. After an eight hour search a surfaced U-boat was sighted.

Flying Officer Trigg immediately prepared to attack. During his approach the aircraft received many hits from anti-aircraft fire and burst into flames. Though he could have broken off the engagement and executed a forced landing, Flying Officer Trigg continued his run-in and completed the attack with such accuracy that the U-boat sank within less than half an hour.

Immediately afterwards the aircraft crashed into the sea at high speed. Seven survivors of the submarine were later rescued from the rubber dinghy which broke loose from the aircraft when the crash occurred, but the gallant crew of the aircraft are missing.

Flying Officer Trigg displayed magnificent gallantry and self-sacrifice, knowing full well the risk entailed by his decision to continue the attack in a burning aircraft.[45]

The Jennings nomination had arrived first, and the RAF Awards Committee pondered it, not only in light of similar attacks made by other aircrews, but alongside a VC action of 6 April 1941 when Flying Officer Kenneth Campbell lost his life attacking German warships in Brest harbour. Two paragraphs in the committee's deliberations demonstrate the dilemma:

The grant of a high award would enhance the morale of those engaged in anti-submarine operations, which are of the greatest importance to the war effort of the United Nations.

The gallantry shown by Jennings was, however, clearly not comparable with that of Campbell who not only ran the gauntlet of most formidable anti-aircraft defences but risked crashing into the rising ground behind the enemy battle cruiser. Like Jennings, he also crashed on his target.

Suddenly, the committee found itself weighing not "Jennings vs. Campbell" but "Jennings vs. Trigg." Official correspondence clearly indicates a predisposition to award a VC to *somebody* for the sake of morale among anti-submarine aircrews. In evaluating the two cases, Jennings's attack looked too much like dozens of other such engagements, although most did not have such dramatic finales. "An award in this case might make it difficult to refuse the VC for many other similar attacks on submarines or indeed on surface ships," wrote one officer.

The Trigg case seemed to differ in one important respect – his aircraft had been hit and set on fire even *before* he was committed to the attack on *U-468* and thus he had an option to ditch and hopefully save some or all of his crew. This option he had not exercised. The Secretary of State for Air himself urged that "we should try and stretch a point in favour of Flying Officer Trigg if we possibly can." Others concurred. Trigg was awarded a Victoria Cross on 4 November 1943. Jennings and the other members of his crew were posthumously Mentioned in Despatches on 14 January 1944.[46]

The Jennings and Trigg recommendations (and how they were decided) invite comparison with a later VC recommendation, that respecting Flight Lieutenant David Hornell, which is dealt with elsewhere (pages 122-129).

On 27 March 1943, the commanding officer of No. 427 Squadron submitted a recommendation for a Victoria Cross to Flight Sergeant Geoffrey Frank Keen, DFM, in the following terms:

> *Flight Sergeant Keen was the wireless operator in an aircraft bombing Essen on March 12th, 1943. In the target area the aircraft was hit by heavy flak, the Navigator being killed. Flight Sergeant Keen's right foot was blown off and he received cuts in both legs. Despite this, he regained his seat in the Wireless Operator's cabin from the astrodome and for over two hours worked to repair his damaged wireless set. He was not in Radio Telephone communication with the rest of the crew owing to damage to the aircraft, but when the Bomb Aimer spoke to him on at least a dozen occasions he found him still conscious working on his wireless set or giving directions for the manipulation of various secret installations. He offered to assist in navigating the aircraft and twice, somehow, reached the navigator's compartment to obtain essential navigational information.*
>
> *Flight Sergeant Keen displayed courage and determination of the very highest order whilst seriously wounded.*

On 28 March 1943 the station commander, Middleton St. George, wrote:

> *I consider this Non-Commissioned Officer's superb display of courage and devotion to duty whilst seriously wounded fully merits an award of the Victoria Cross.*

Air Vice Marshal G.E. Brooks (Air Officer Commanding, No. 6 Group) wrote on 28 March 1943:

> *This case is considered to be an outstanding example of coolness and tenacity of purpose on the part of this Non-Commissioned Officer when seriously wounded, and demanding courage of the highest Order. An award of the Victoria Cross is recommended.*

This appears to have passed muster with the Air Officer Commanding-in-Chief (Air Chief Marshal Sir Arthur Harris), who passed it quickly to Air Ministry, but on 8 April 1943 the following letter was addressed to Harris:

> *In reply to your letter of the 29th March, I am commanded by the Air Council to inform you that your recommendation for the award of the Victoria Cross to 923049 Flight Sergeant G.F. Keen, DFM has been carefully considered.*
>
> *In the Council's view this airman showed magnificent bravery and determination in remaining at his post whilst seriously wounded but his action does not amount to the* acceptance of a risk involving almost certain death, which is a necessary condition for the award of the Victoria Cross. *They consider, therefore, that the Conspicuous Gallantry Medal (Flying) is the appropriate award and assume that you will wish to confer this medal under the powers delegated to you by the King.*[47]

The CGM (Flying), described by some as "the NCO's DSO," was a prestigious award in its own right – and ultimately even more rare than the Victoria Cross. Doubtless Flight Sergeant Keen preferred to have received it (and lived) than to have died in the act of winning a VC. A similar case involved Sergeant Thomas P. Petrie, who piloted a Wellington bomber back to its base in North Africa on the night of 12/13 April 1943 after numerous flak hits which wounded all the crew and almost completely severed his left foot. He, too, was recommended for a Victoria Cross and instead awarded the CGM (Flying).[48]

The measure of VC valour being "the acceptance of a risk involving almost certain death" as a "necessary condition for the award of the Victoria Cross" is chilling. Even that led to contentious discussions as to what nominees knew or believed at the time of their deeds. The case of Sergeant John Henry Addis makes particularly painful reading. A VC was considered as early as 1942, but action was deferred pending more information. This did not become available until 1945 with the release from POW camps of other aircrew whose testimony resulted in the Air Officer Commanding, No. 3 Group, drawing up the following recommendation.

On the night of 25/26th March 1942, Sergeant Addis was the second pilot of Wellington X3652 which had been sent to bomb a target in Essen. Over the target very heavy flak opened up and the aircraft was hit in the bomb bay and set on fire. The fire filled the fuselage of the aircraft with smoke and in spite of the efforts of two of the crew to master it, the flames spread fore and aft and destroyed one of the parachutes.

When it became clear to the Captain that the aircraft could not be saved the crew prepared to bale out. Sergeant Addis adjusted a parachute on to his Captain's chest and passed the remaining one to the Wireless Operator, insisting on regarding the one which had been destroyed as his own. When their turn came to bale out, Sergeant Addis and the Wireless Operator jumped together with one parachute attached to the latter. At the jerk of the opening parachute, however, Sergeant Addis was torn from his companion who was unable to maintain a grip firm enough to prevent this, with the result that Sergeant Addis fell several thousand feet to his death. The remaining members of the crew landed safely in Germany and were taken prisoners.

Sergeant Addis courageously sacrificed an opportunity to save himself when he handed over the last parachute well knowing that the act would probably cause his death. His action, performed without the slightest hesitation, for he did not even pause to inform his Captain that one parachute was burnt, was one of supreme self-sacrifice willingly undertaken.

Whether to forward a VC recommendation for Addis to the King was kicked back and forth between the Secretary of State for Air, the Permanent Under-Secretary and the Chief of Air Staff. Much of the discussion turned on what had been in Addis's mind. A summary of the case included the following (emphasis added by this author):

The current recommendation has been reviewed by the RAF Awards Committee who are still of the opinion that, though Sergeant Addis acted with extreme gallantry and took a great risk in attempting to descend with a shared parachute, the fact that he did attempt to save his own life takes the case out of the VC category.

Even in 1942, the Chief of the Air Staff commented that if Addis had managed to attach himself to the other man's harness and descend safely in the shared parachute, no one would be considering a VC for him. The Secretary of State for Air added his final assessment on 9 August 1945 (emphasis by this author):

> *When Addis jumped clinging to the other airman, he may in fact have had no chance of saving himself* but we cannot know that he did not believe he had a good chance of getting down safely. *In other words we* cannot be certain that the airman willingly and knowingly accepted the risk of almost certain death, which is an essential condition for the award of the VC ... ...
>
> *We and the other Service Departments have always insisted on "strict proof" for the VC.* We cannot give a man the benefit of the doubt, *otherwise the prestige of the award would suffer. There are very many cases of men who may have earned a VC who inevitably go unrecognized, and the VC must in fact be regarded as a* token award given to a few in recognition of the bravery of the many.[49]

These various statements may be borne in mind when one considers a curious campaign to obtain a Victoria Cross for Major Frederick Phillip Griffin, the Black Watch (Royal Highland Regiment of Canada), who was killed on 25 July 1944 in an action now best known as the Battle of Verrières Ridge. The battalion was to attack uphill to capture Fontenay-le-Marmion, but enemy opposition was unexpectedly heavy. Barely one-sixth of the unit reached the crest of a hill, and there they encountered even more murderous fire. There is little doubt that Griffin urged his men on until it was clear that nothing could be achieved, and then directed survivors to save themselves as best they could. On 3 February 1945, it was reported that he had been posthumously Mentioned in Despatches.

On 15 February 1945, Griffin's father wrote to the Governor General in Ottawa. He considered that his son had been sent to "certain death" in what he described as "another Balaklava," cited stirring accounts published in newspapers, then declared, "It was the popular opinion (and still is) that our son would receive a VC." In Ottawa, Army Headquarters requested their overseas counterparts to look into this perceived injustice, although Lieutenant-Colonel D.G. Ross guessed at what was most likely the reason for this protest:

This may well be another case of personnel writing letters of condolence to next-of-kin indicating that the deceased was recommended for a specific award.

On 17 March 1945, Brigadier W.J. Megill, Officer Commanding, 5 Canadian Infantry Brigade, summarized the events leading to the attack. As the officer who would most likely have been in a position to recommend an award, his report was particularly relevant. It read, in part:

From the information available both then and since I was and am convinced that Major Griffin's actions were in the highest traditions of the Service. Had he lived he would undoubtedly have been recommended for the Distinguished Service Order. *As this award may not be granted posthumously he was recommended by me to be Mentioned in Despatches* which was the only possible alternative.*

Megill was being less than frank – the alternatives were to recommend Griffin for either a Mention in Despatches *or* a Victoria Cross, and he had chosen not to pursue the latter course. The Griffin family were unforgiving and relentless in a campaign lasting more than 20 years to have the case re-examined. In 1967, H.H. Griffin, older brother of Major Griffin, refused to accept a Canada Centennial Medal as a protest against what he still considered an injustice. For much of the 1960s, the elder Griffin and Brigadier Megill lived within two blocks of each other; if they ever discussed the matter, it is not evident from surviving official correspondence. The Griffin family seemed resigned to the final non-award of a VC to Major Frederick Griffin, but in 1994 the issue was revived and aired in public again, when a television documentary, *The Valour and the Horror,* recounted the Battle of Verrières

---

* The suggestion that survival might have brought a DSO has an echo in Air Ministry deliberations over Andrew Mynarski's VC recommendation; see page 94.

Ridge, blamed the disaster on Griffin's superiors, and pointedly suggest-ed that he had been denied a VC in part because officers like Lieutenant-General Guy Simonds were "covering up" their own mistakes.[50]

The fact that no Victoria Cross was recommended provides a sort of negative proof for the critics, but there was no assurance that a VC would have been approved, even if recommended. As we shall see, Field Marshal Montgomery was exacting in his vetoing or supporting VC nominations. Simply put, in the Normandy campaign, he backed nominees who were "winners" (like Major David Currie), not men who had been as much vic-tims as warriors. Experience elsewhere shows that even "winners" were not guaranteed a VC, even when dying in small victories that resembled a Hol-lywood script (see Appendix D). When it comes to movie scripts, the last wartime exploits of Lieutenant-Colonel Robert Blair "Paddy" Mayne were so spectacular that one wonders at the reasoning that led to his award being downgraded from a VC to a fourth Bar to his DSO. The recommendation for the latter appears as Appendix E; the closest one comes to a rationale for its being reduced is found in a letter written by Brigadier J.R.C Gannon (Deputy Military Secretary, Headquarters, 21 Army Group) to Colonel J.W. McLain (Deputy Military Secretary, Headquarters, First Canadian Army) dated 3 July 1945; it read, in part:

> *You will remember putting up Lieutenant-Colonel R.B. Mayne for a VC, and while I myself thought it was a magnificent act of heroism, there was* a certain flaw *in it that made me doubtful as to advising the Chief to recommend it without further advice. I therefore sent it to the Military Secretary at home who deals with the VC Committee.*
>
> *He has replied saying that he has discussed this case without actually taking it up and he is afraid that the VC Committee would not regard Mayne's case as quite up to VC standard.* It was not a single-handed act of heroism, *rescuing the wounded, as another officer was present in the jeep giving covering fire. Nevertheless, it was a magnificent performance and it is suggested that the rare distinction of a third Bar to the DSO would be the appropriate award.*
>
> *Would you please be so good as to put this letter before General [H.D.G.] Crerar before making his final recommendation.*[51]

This writer has emphasized portions; Brigadier Gannon did seem to be nitpicking. "A certain flaw" is a weak, weasel phrase, and "not a single-handed act of heroism" zeroed in on one portion of a very detailed text. In any case, many VC actions had significant supporting casts. It is also curious that he had apparently bypassed Field Marshal Montgomery ("the Chief") and solicited advice in London without actually putting the submission before the War Office VC Committee. However, subsequent claims that the VC submission had been "clearly altered" to make it into a DSO do not ring true. In the case of VC recommendations for Canadians that had been turned into DSO or DCM awards, the texts of final citations did not differ significantly from those of the original VC recommendations. Notwithstanding the curious handling by Gannon, the recommendation appears to have re-entered the stream of award recommendations, to be signed off by General Crerar about 20 July 1945 and by Montgomery at an unknown date. At some point the original submission had been altered to the extent that "VC" had been stroked out and "3rd Bar to DSO" substituted, but in whose handwriting this alteration was made is uncertain; it might even have been Crerar himself.

Clearly, defining a "VC standard" practically defies description. Brief notes in files saying that this or that recommendation was "not up to standard" do little to enlighten us. Indeed, it is evident that "VC standard" differed from service to service. In considering how the British and Commonwealth armies treated the subject, one might well consider the directions of Major-General Guy Simonds to his subordinates in October 1943:

> *In the case of the VC the act must be so outstanding as to provide an example to the Army for all time and its effect in damage to the enemy and furtherance of operations must be marked beyond question and of the first importance.*

This was hard-nosed realism that few would take to its logical conclusion, for as one official remarked in September 1942:

> *The classic VC case would be that of Samson who in immolating himself destroyed the enemy – the Philistines.*[52]

39

CHAPTER 3

NAVAL AWARDS AND
NON-AWARDS

*Parade training is the first step in inculcating an instant obedience to orders
upon which lives and the safety of the ship will almost certainly depend, and the
process has been known and practised for centuries, long before Pavlov's dog and
"conditioned reflex" became household words. A man doesn't die in battle for his
country, or democracy, or to protect his womenfolk at home. He may have come
to the scene of his death for these reasons, but when the moment arrives and the
primal urge of self-preservation would send a man diving for cover, he does his
duty and in doing so he dies.*

Hal Lawrence, *A Bloody War: One Man's Memories
of the Royal Canadian Navy, 1939-45*

The Victoria Cross that was not awarded to Chief Petty Officer Max
Leopold Bernays is of particular interest to Canadians. His deeds
were part of an action on 6 August 1942 involving HMCS *Assiniboine* and the German submarine *U-210*. Unlike most anti-submarine engagements, which usually involved one or more warships patiently tracking
a submerged U-boat until it either evaded their searches or was crushed by
depth charges, this turned into a surface battle in which *U-210* used its deck
guns to such effect that *Assiniboine* was set on fire. The U-boat was finally
sunk after being twice rammed by the destroyer and finished off with depth
charges. An account, prepared in the course of recommending an award,
described Bernays' role:

*A fire caused by enemy shells broke out on the flag deck, compelling the
telegraphmen to leave the wheelhouse, leaving Acting Chief Petty Officer*

HMCS Assiniboine vs. *U-210* by Harold Beament (1898-1984). (Canadian War Museum 10033)

Chief Petty Officer Max Leopold Bernays (left) was recommended for the VC for action on 6 August 1942 between HMCS *Assiniboine* and *U-210* but was awarded the Conspicuous Gallantry Medal. Fire (right) rages aboard *Assiniboine* during the battle with the submarine. (Canadian War Museum C.36314 & AN20000224-028)

Bernays alone. With complete disregard for his own safety, with flames and smoke obscuring his only exit, with enemy explosive shell fragments entering the wheelhouse, this comparatively young rating remained at his post for nearly forty minutes. Appreciating the crucial importance of his duties in an action, the success of which depended in a large measure on the precise steering of the ship and execution of telegraph orders, he not only carried out exactly and effectively all the helm orders but also dispatched 133 telegraph orders, necessary to accomplish the destruction of the U-Boat. The final success of the sinking of the U-Boat was largely due to the high courage and determination of Acting Chief Petty Officer Max Leopold Bernays who, in circumstances of the gravest personal danger carried out not only his own, but two other ratings' duties in exemplary fashion. His conduct throughout the action added another incident of the utmost bravery to the annals of the Royal Canadian Navy.

Rear Admiral L.W. Murray, the senior RCN officer in Halifax, had personally recommended Bernays for the Victoria Cross, and when the British Admiralty hesitated, the Canadian cabinet took the extraordinary step of issuing an Order in Council which virtually petitioned the Admiralty to forward the recommendation to the King. Canada's High Commissioner to Great Britain, Vincent Massey, also took up the issue; how vigorously we do not know. An anglophile to the hilt, he had the reputation of being more British than the British. Still the Admiralty objected, suggesting in turn a Conspicuous Gallantry Medal (one step down from a VC). The Canadian government finally agreed and Bernays was awarded a CGM on 3 December 1942.[53]

The case is interesting in that the Canadian Army and government had just extracted a questionable VC on behalf of Lieutenant-Colonel C.C. Merritt (see pages 79-80). If the Canadian government and the Canadian High Commissioner to London could not convince the Admiralty that Bernays' efforts matched a VC "standard," what then did the Admiralty deem to be a VC deed?

A closer look at the 23 Royal Navy and Commonwealth navy Victoria Crosses is revealing, for *not one was associated with standard anti-submarine actions.* An analysis of what constituted a VC action in RN eyes reveals the following (* denotes posthumous award):

- Raids into enemy harbours, St. Nazaire and Oran actions – 4 (S.H. Beattie, F.T. Peters,* R.E.D. Ryder, W.A. Savage*).

- Fleet Air Arm action – 2 (E.K. Esmonde,* R.H. Gray*)

- Surface actions with enemy warships – 5 (E.S.F. Fegen,* G.B. Roope,* B.A.W. Warburton-Lee,* R. St. Vincent Sherbrooke, T. Wilkinson*).

- Midget submarines – 4 (D. Cameron, I.E. Fraser, J.J. Magennis, B.C.G. Place)

- Submarine actions – 5 (T.W. Gould, J.W. Linton,* A.C.C. Miers, P.S.W. Roberts, M.D. Wanklyn)

- Action during air attack on land – 1 (J.F. Mantle* – it is possible that had his action occurred a few months later he would have been awarded a George Cross instead, but that honour had not yet been created when Mantle died)

- Action during air attack at sea – 1 (A.E. Sephton,* who stayed at his post on HMS *Coventry,* though wounded and losing blood, until the enemy were driven off)

- Actions during air attacks, land and sea – 1 (R.B. Stannard)

The action involving HMCS *Assiniboine* most closely resembles a surface action with an enemy warship; in that case it is worth noting that four of the five awards in that category were posthumous. A description of A.E. Sephton's VC action shows similarities to the performance of Bernays under fire – but again, Sephton's was a posthumous award. However, taking another case, we can see consistency in Bernays' award when we compare it with that of Able Seaman David C. Sherrington of HMS *Broke* on 8 November 1942. He too displayed great bravery at the wheel of a burning ship, although in this instance it was in a hostile harbour rather than on the open sea. Public announcements of Royal Navy awards were accompanied by notoriously brief citations (usually none at all); in the case of his CGM the *London Gazette* entry read:

For gallantry at the wheel of HMS Broke *when she left the harbour of Algiers under heavy fire. A shell killed all in the wheel house save him-*

self and one other; but although blinded by smoke and choked by fumes
he steered his ship with unerring skill through the gap in the boom.
Any deviation from his course would have endangered his ship and her
company.[54]

It could therefore be argued that members of the RCN were not showered with Victoria Crosses because they were in the wrong business, anti-submarine warfare, and in Bernays' case he prejudiced a possible award by inconveniently *surviving.*

Although the Bernays' case demonstrates the Royal Navy's hard line about what constituted a Victoria Cross action, further probing reveals strange inconsistencies in the Admiralty's policies, and the incongruities show an even greater tendency to restrict such awards in the cases of surface engagements.

The Norwegian campaign, lasting from April to June 1940, included some of the most heroic actions in the history of the Royal Navy. These included a bitter battle at Narvik on 10 April 1940 during which Captain Bernard A.W. Warburton-Lee was killed. His last signal, "Continue to engage the enemy," could have been drafted by Nelson. With plenty of witnesses to report on the action, Warburton-Lee was awarded a Victoria Cross on 7 June 1940, even before the campaign had closed. Other awards would have to wait for VE Day and witnesses released from POW camps to generate recommendations.

On 8 April, HMS *Glowworm* (destroyer, Lieutenant-Commander G.B. Roope in charge) pursued two German destroyers, only to encounter the cruiser *Hipper*. The enemy vessel mauled *Glowworm* with gunfire, avoided two torpedoes and pursued its tormentor into a smoke screen, where the *Glowworm* rammed *Hipper*, which survived the impact but had to withdraw briefly from the campaign. *Glowworm* herself had suffered fatal damage; wrecked and blazing, the destroyer blew up. *Hipper* rescued 40 survivors, but Roope was just being hauled aboard, exhausted, when he relaxed his grip, fell back and was drowned. The gallant captain was awarded a posthumous Victoria Cross on 10 July 1945.

It has sometimes been stated that this honour was based on an admiring account sent directly to the Admiralty, and even that Roope's award was "the sole Victoria Cross awarded on the basis of evidence from the enemy." This is manifestly untrue (see references to the VC awarded Flying Officer Lloyd A. Trigg). The fact that Roope's award was gazetted after the war clearly illustrates that it was based as much on survivors' reports as on any evidence the Germans may have provided.[55]

Yet if the Lords of the Admiralty finally processed a Victoria Cross for Lieutenant-Commander Roope, why did they not do the same for two other captains of destroyers whose actions closely resembled those of the *Glowworm*'s commander? On 8 June 1940, as Allied forces evacuated Norway, the aircraft carrier HMS *Glorious*, accompanied by two destroyers (HM Ships *Ardent* and *Acasta*) sailed independently of other convoys. In what was a clear case of mismanagement, *Glorious* flew no aircraft and was thus caught by surprise when two enemy battleships, *Scharnhorst* and *Gneisenau*, hove in view. The carrier was hit almost at once; the order to abandon ship was given at 1720 hours, and *Glorious* sank 20 minutes later. HMS *Ardent* (Lieutenant-Commander John Frederick Barker in command) was sunk about 1728 hours, leaving *Acasta* to fight alone against overwhelming odds.

Indeed, that ship could have escaped, but her captain, Commander Charles Eric Glasfurd, had other ideas. He passed a message to all positions: "You may think we are running away from the enemy; we are not; our chummy ship [*Ardent*] has sunk, the *Glorious* is sinking; the least we can do is make a show." Altering course through a smoke screen, *Acasta* fired four torpedoes, one of which hit *Scharnhorst* abreast of the after 11-inch turret. A final salvo hit *Acasta* at 1808 hours, and the crew were ordered to abandon ship. When last seen, Commander Glasfurd was taking a cigarette from his case and lighting it as he leaned from the bridge, waving encouragement to his men. In the end, only one man survived from *Acasta*'s company (Able Seaman C. Carter), and his account was subsequently accepted as the final word on what had happened.[56]

It appears that some consideration was given to Victoria Crosses for Barker and Glasfurd, but as of 16 August 1940 they were accorded only posthumous Mentions in Despatches "for gallant conduct on the occasion of the loss of HMS *Glorious*." If the Admiralty was only dimly aware of *Acasta*'s sacrifice in 1940, there were more details available by 1944. On 26 December 1943, *Scharnhorst* was sunk in a surface engagement north of Norway; from a complement of 1,968 men, 36 survivors were rescued from the icy waters. Interrogation of these produced a report somewhat at variance with that subsequently provided by Able Seaman Carter, particularly as to the sequence in which the various British vessels had been sunk, suggesting that *Ardent* had been still afloat when *Glorious* sank, but otherwise it made clear that the destroyers had been indefatigable in their efforts to defend the carrier and that they had forgone escape to attack *Scharnhorst*.

On 15 September 1944, Admiral of the Fleet Sir Charles Forbes (Commander-in-Chief, Home Fleet) addressed the Admiralty, urging that Barker and Glasfurd be considered for "a posthumous honour." Given that they had already been Mentioned in Despatches, the further "honour" could only be the Victoria Cross. Relevant parts of the interrogation report were highlighted with an "X." Subsequent correspondence reflected not only the thinking at the time but what had been in the minds of authorities in 1940. Unhappily, the signatures are not always legible, but one senior officer wrote on 11 October 1944:

> The view taken at the time [1940] was that, if it were certain that "Acasta"'s torpedo attack was made while "Glorious" was still afloat in an effort to save her, a case might be made for a V.C., but if "Glorious" had already gone down, there would be a less strong case. In view of the doubt as to the facts a Posthumous Mention was submitted.
>
> X of the "Scharnhorst" survivors' statement tends to resolve the doubt, and to show that the right submission was made, assuming that the view taken at the time was the right one. It suggests, too, that "Ardent's" part was as great as "Acasta's."

The matter was referred to the Admiralty Committee on Honours and Awards. Their deliberations were summarized by the Vice-Chief of the Naval Staff on 18 October 1944:

> I do not think there is anything in the evidence provided by the survivors of the Scharnhorst to justify the Board reversing their previous decision. The gallant conduct of the two destroyers was never in question.
>
> The only doubt was whether the torpedo attack on Scharnhorst was

made before or after Glorious' doom was certain. The new evidence (three and one-half years after the event) of the Scharnhorst survivors shows the attack was made after the Glorious sank, and therefore confirms the arguments used by the Board in reaching their previous decision.

On 31 October 1944, the decision was communicated to Admiral Forbes, who of course had first raised the issue of Victoria Crosses for Barker and Glasfurd. The letter to Forbes concluded:

My Lords much appreciate the feelings that prompted your letter, but they are reluctantly of opinion that the new evidence does not offer sufficient grounds to justify them in reversing the view taken at the time that the action of the Commanding Officers, though extremely gallant, did not quite attain to the standard demanded by the Victoria Cross. [57]

This author cannot explain the decisions of 1940 and 1944. The door having been closed on Victoria Crosses to Barker and Glasfurd, it was evidently not opened again, even a crack, when the case of Roope and the *Glowworm* came before the same committee. Perhaps its membership had changed. Perhaps there was reluctance in 1945 to approve more than one Victoria Cross for such similar naval actions and sacrifices. The evidence, however, is that *Acasta* went far beyond mere duty (which would have been satisfied once HMS *Glorious* was doomed beyond hope), attacked in the face of overwhelming odds, and in severely damaging *Scharnhorst* averted even greater losses, for had that ship (with *Gneisenau*) continued onwards after despatching *Glorious*, they would almost certainly have overtaken and overwhelmed the convoys which were evacuating the bulk of Allied forces from Narvik. For those who would argue that "politics" was involved, one can only ask, "But to whose benefit?"

The inconsistencies of decisions relating to awards was further demonstrated in the case of Lieutenant Robert Hampton Gray, RCNVR, whose Victoria Cross was notable in many respects. It was the only VC awarded to a member of the Royal Canadian Navy. It was the second of two awarded to a member of the Fleet Air Arm (the other had been a posthumous award in 1942 to Lieutenant-Commander Eugene Esmond for a suicidal attack on

German warships). The action itself that gave rise to this award occurred on 9 August 1945 – just short of the last day that the Royal Navy was in action against the Japanese. It was thus a last opportunity for the navy in general, and the Fleet Air Arm in particular, to gain a coveted Victoria Cross.

Gray, a Canadian who had been seconded to the Fleet Air Arm in 1941 and trained as a pilot, flew Corsair fighters in support of carrier-borne air strikes on the battleship *Tirpitz* in August 1944, for which he was Mentioned in Despatches. He had then accompanied HMS *Formidable* to the Pacific, where, as part of British Pacific Fleet operations, he had participated in air attacks on Japanese-held islands. For his work he had been recommended for a Distinguished Service Cross. However, as of 9 August 9 1945, this had not yet been promulgated. That day he led a strike against enemy warships in Onagawa Wan (Bay), pressing home an attack on a vessel incorrectly described as a destroyer (it was more properly classified as an ocean-going escort or frigate). He encountered intensive anti-aircraft fire that set his Corsair blazing. Nevertheless, he continued his attack, dropping a bomb that hit and sank his target before he himself plunged into the bay.

His commanding officer recommended Gray for a Victoria Cross on 12 August 1945; the *London Gazette* of 13 November 1945 announced the award. Between those dates, however, a significant number of memos were circulated that showed exactly why the award had been supported up the line. In the process, it was pointed out that the Fleet Air Arm had previously missed three opportunities to have Victoria Crosses awarded to its members. Gray, in short, was their last chance, and to get a VC some precedents had to be either set aside or explained away.

On 13 September 1945, Vice Admiral Sir Philip Vian (Flag Officer Commanding, First Aircraft Carrier Squadron, British Pacific Fleet) addressed a memo to the Commander-in-Chief, British Pacific Fleet (emphasis added by this author):

> *In recommending the award of the Victoria Cross Posthumous to the late Temporary Lieutenant R.H. Gray, DSC, RCNVR, I have in mind his brilliant fighting spirit and inspired leadership, an unforgettable example of selfless and sustained devotion to duty without regard to safety of life and limb;*

Finale by Don Connolly depicts the attack by Lieutenant Robert Hampton Gray (right) on a Japanese warship on 9 August 1945 that resulted in the sinking of the ship and the posthumous award of the Victoria Cross to Gray. (Canadian War Museum 19880046-001; Library and Archives Canada PA133296)

Secondly, that you may think as I do that a Victoria Cross is the just due of the gallant company of Naval Airmen who have from December last have fought and beat the Japanese from Palembang to Tokyo *and;*

Thirdly, that the award of this highly prized and highly regarded recognition of valour may fittingly be conferred on a native of Canada, which Dominion has played so great a part in the training of our Airmen.

Admiral Vian attached a list of Gray's exploits, from August 1944 to August 1945, as though arguing as much for a "periodic" Victoria Cross as an immediate one. It will be noted further on that the Royal Air Force had toyed with such awards, yet had supported only two (Guy Gibson and Leonard Cheshire). Whether this weighed upon the Admiralty's Honours and Awards Committee is unknown, but one thing that did concentrate their minds was a series of embarrassing precedents in which Fleet Air Arm submissions for Victoria Crosses had been rejected. A minute dated 19 October 1945 read, in part:

While the Committee appreciates that it is very difficult to separate this case from other similar cases in which the Victoria Cross has been considered, but not awarded, e.g. the cases of Lieutenant Kindersley, Lieutenant Hartley, and Lieutenant Commander Richardson … it is of opinion that the success achieved by the action which cost Lieutenant Gray his life should perhaps be allowed to weigh the scales in his favour, and it is therefore submitted that the King be asked to approve the posthumous award of the Victoria Cross to the late Temporary Lieutenant Robert Hampton Gray, Royal Canadian Volunteer Reserve [sic].[58]

Who were "Lieutenant Kindlersley, Lieutenant Hartley and Lieutenant Commander Richardson" whose deeds had merited a recommendation for a Victoria Cross, but no award?

Lieutenant (Air) Alistair Thomas James Kindersley was a pilot with No. 808 Squadron (HMS *Ark Royal*). On 25 July 1941, during a fierce action protecting ships heading for Malta, he and another pilot shot down two Italian SM.79 bombers and damaged a third. His Fairey Fulmar (a poor excuse for a fighter) was then shot down, killing Kindersley and his observer, Petty

Officer Frederick A. Barnes. The bare facts do not suggest a Victoria Cross deed, but other documents from the period might provide a rationale for the recommendation. Both men were ultimately Mentioned in Despatches.

Lieutenant (Air) John Vernon Hartley was killed in action on 8 November 1942 whilst operating with No. 822 Squadron from HMS *Furious*. Piloting an Albacore aircraft, he was leading a strike against La Senia airfield, Oran, during Operation TORCH (the Allied invasion of French North Africa). Vichy French fighters intercepted and his aircraft was set on fire. Ignoring opportunities to bale out or force-land, Hartley attempted to continue the mission but ultimately crashed in flames. Also killed were his observer (Lieutenant John Nares) and gunner (Leading Airman Gordon Dixon). Although three Albacores were lost on this mission, the other two crews survived. The attack resulted in the destruction of 47 French aircraft. The bare facts suggest why a Victoria Cross was proposed but give no idea why it was not pressed further. Hartley, Nares and Dixon were all Mentioned in Despatches..

Lieutenant-Commander Archibald Ronald Richardson, Royal New Zealand Naval Volunteer Reserve, commanded No. 1840 Squadron (HMS *Indefatigable*) from 1 March 1944 onwards, flying Grumman Hellcat fighters. The unit took part in several attacks on the German battleship *Tirpitz*, then sheltering in a Norwegian fiord. On the first two occasions Richardson dropped 500-pound bombs, destroyed two float planes, and generally attacked any secondary targets that came his way. On 24 August 1944, he led the squadron during another massed air attack on *Tirpitz* – his third strike on the behemoth, and one where he had sworn in advance to score a hit. Ship and shore anti-aircraft defences were massive down an 18-mile gauntlet. Accounts of his demise varied. One stated he was shot down while attempting to rip up a wireless aerial using his arrester hook. Another version was that he was last seen diving onto the ship from 3,000 feet, was hit by flak at about 1,600 feet and blew up. Comrades spoke of his unequalled courage and determination. As in the other cases mentioned above, Richardson was posthumously Mentioned in Despatches.[59]

The Admiralty committee which weighed the Gray submission had suggested it be given special consideration in view of the "success achieved by the action" – and indeed his attack had sunk an enemy vessel, whereas Lieutenant-Commander Richardson had not. Even so, that was not a fair comparison, for the *Tirpitz* had been an armoured monster while the *Amakusa* (Gray's target) was not. The previous Fleet Air Arm VC hero – Esmonde, February 1942 – had failed even to dent the warships he was assailing. His, indeed, had been a forlorn mission, leading a small force of obsolete torpedo bombers against warships defended by their own guns and by swarms of fighter aircraft. His courage and dedication had been a bright spot in what was otherwise a debacle. Approval of "Hammy" Gray's Victoria Cross, earned by more success and equal sacrifice, clearly owed as much to timing as to his courage, dedication and self-sacrifice.

CHAPTER 4

VICTORIA CROSSES DENIED
(ARMY)

*I expected to be sent quickly to the trenches, rescuing the wounded in
no man's land with that calm courage that warranted, even if it did not
receive, the Victoria Cross. The reality was very different; I became a night
orderly at the camp hospital.*

Lester B. Pearson (1897-1972), recalling his early military service

I t is impossible to say how many Victoria Cross recommendations have
failed to result in an award, and the reasons for known failures are difficult to ascertain. Even more difficult to account for are Victoria Crosses
never even recommended. Passions run high as people argue the case for this
or that overlooked champion – and sometimes for themselves. For years following the Crimean War, Corporal William Courtney waged a campaign in
the British press declaring that Sergeant William McWheeney (44th Foot)
should *not* have been awarded a Victoria Cross (for, among other things,
rescuing Courtney under fire at Sebastopol) and that he (Courtney) had
been the true hero. His efforts were fruitless, the weight of documentation
being against him.[60]

In 1920, Professor Alfred O'Rahilly published a book which argued that a
particular Catholic chaplain, Father William Doyle, had deserved a VC and
never been recommended because he was a Jesuit and an Irish nationalist.
Appearing as it did during the Anglo-Irish War, the accusation gained some
currency. Sixty years later, a more detached author noted that Jesuits had not
been the object of discrimination in the matter of decorations. It was also
noted that the officer in the best position to recommend a VC would have

been Father Doyle's divisional commander, Major-General W.B. Hickie, who was a southern Irish nationalist as well. Frontal attacks such as that mounted by Professor O'Rahilly are often turned back by the withering fire of facts.[61]

If a tree falls in the forest, and there is no ear present to hear it, does it make a sound? The VC deed performed with no one to witness it is akin to the tree. Similarly, the valour which is demonstrated yet inspires something less than a VC recommendation is hardly wasted or in vain; the persons best able to judge whether certain actions were "above and beyond" or merely "part of the job" are those who are present. That said, we can survey at least some of those recommendations which failed to clear all the hurdles that stood between the battlefield and the *London Gazette* announcement of a VC award.

Given the unfortunate loss of First World War records pertaining to the Victoria Cross, it is difficult to assemble recommendations that fell short of final approval. An exception to this are Australian recommendations; documents held by the Australian War Memorial in Canberra indicate that at least 73 members of the Australian Imperial Force were unsuccessfully put forward for the Victoria Cross compared to 55 who did receive that honour. Most of the unsuccessful submissions were downgraded to DSOs or DCMs; one became a posthumous Albert Medal. In almost all cases, the original texts are available, although the documentation explaining why they were revised or ignored is not.

Canadian archives yield nothing so detailed as the Australian War Memorial. By the happy circumstance of an officer whose papers included many recommendations for various awards, and which were preserved, we can identify a Canadian instance of two VC recommendations for a single action – a gas attack and trench raid opposite Vimy Ridge on 1 March 1917. The commanding officer of the 54th Battalion put forward the names of Major Frederick T. Lucas and Captain Noel L. Tooker, both of whom were killed in the raid. It is not clear whether the submissions went any further than the headquarters of 11 Canadian Infantry Brigade, but the texts survive in the papers of the Brigade Commander, then-Brigadier (later Major-General) V.W. Odlum. Given the rarity of these documents, it is worth noting why these two officers were singled out, although ultimately they were not even accorded Mentions in Despatches. That for Major Lucas read:

A dramatic rendering of a First World War VC action involving Lieutenant Robert Shankland, 43rd Battalion, Canadian Expeditionary Force) (Artist unknown, Canadian War Museum 71-5979)

In the Gas Attack against the German lines in the Berthonval Sector on March 1st, 1917, by the 54th Canadian Infantry Battalion, was in command of his Company as well as directing the assault of the Battalion. Although twice wounded he continued to lead his men forward until he was killed close to the German wire. His splendid courage and determination was a great example to the men.

The submission for Captain Tooker was somewhat longer:

In the Gas Attack against the German lines in the Berthonval Sector on March 1st, 1917, by the 54th Canadian Infantry Battalion, was in command of the left Company of the Battalion. By splendid leading and organization his Company were able to reach the German wire, place the Armament Tube in position and fire it. He was the first to lead the way through the gap thus formed but fell dead before he could get through. He showed wonderful coolness and determination throughout the operation, encouraging and leading his men to the last.

On a previous occasion he showed conspicuous bravery in bringing in wounded under heavy fire as follows:-

On the night of September 16th/17th, 1916, after a successful raid on the enemy's trenches at St. Eloi one of the officers who had been bringing out another officer was wounded and Captain Tooker and Lieutenant D.A. McQuarrie went to their assistance and in the face of heavy fire brought both officers safely back to our own lines.

Lucas's recommendation was accompanied by at least one witness statement; that for Tooker was accompanied by two, all being second- or third-generation carbon copies and one of which is impossible to decipher in its entirety.[62]

During the Second World War at least 15 Canadian soldiers were recommended for this honour, yet received either lesser awards or none at all. These were as follows:

Lieutenant Norman Alexander Ballard, 48th Highlanders of Canada, recommended for actions in the Liri Valley (Italy) on 17 May 1944. He was ultimately awarded a Distinguished Service Order.[63]

Lance-Sergeant Jean-Paul Beauvais, Fusiliers Mont Royal, killed in action during the Dieppe Raid (19 August 1942). He was ultimately Mentioned in Despatches on 9 February 1946 and awarded the French *Croix de Guerre* with Silver Star on 25 November 1946.

Private Lawrence Bowman, 48th Highlanders of Canada, killed in action on 17 May 1944; recommended for VC in conjunction with Lieutenant Ballard; details lacking and no award made.

Private Sidney John Cousins, Princess Patricia's Canadian Light Infantry, from Bagot, Manitoba, killed in action at Leonforte, Sicily, on 22 July 1943. The recommendation for a posthumous Victoria Cross was turned down at the level of Eighth Army Headquarters. A comrade who had witnessed Cousins's exploits subsequently wrote the family, stating that their son had been put up for the Commonwealth's highest honour; needless to say, the friend should not have known about the recommendation. Private Cousins' family was upset when no award was immediately forthcoming and could not have been happy when he was ultimately (and belatedly) honoured only with a Mention in Despatches.[64]

Sergeant Clarence Kenneth Crockett, the Calgary Highlanders, recommended by his commanding officer on 7 October 1944 for heroism at the Albert Canal (Belgium) on 21 September 1944. The VC recommendation was supported at all levels up to and including H.D.G. Crerar, General Officer Commanding-in-Chief, First Canadian Army, who signed off on it on 11 December 1944. It was subsequently downgraded to a Distinguished Conduct Medal by Field Marshal B.L. Montgomery, General Officer Commanding-in-Chief, 21 Army Group. The DCM was formally gazetted on 10 February 1945

Private Gordon Cecil Crozier, Stormont, Dundas and Glengarry Highlanders, recommended on 18 November 1944 for heroism at Roedenhoek, Holland, on 15 October 1944. This was approved at all levels up to and including that of General H.D.G. Crerar, General Officer Commanding-in-Chief, First Canadian Army, who passed it forward on 25 December 1944. It was subsequently downgraded by Field Marshal Montgomery without explanation to a DCM (gazetted 19 February 1945).

Lance Corporal Gerard Gagnon, Royal 22e Regiment, killed in action on 30 July 1943 in Sicily. The recommendation in this instance resulted in no award whatsoever, not even a Mention in Despatches.[65]

Captain Ian Donald Grant, 12 Canadian Armoured Regiment (Three Rivers Regiment). He appears to have been initially recommended for a Victoria Cross about 1 August 1944 for an attack on Casamaggiore (Italy) on 28 June 1944. The paper trail of this particular submission is unclear, but it was evidently downgraded somewhere at the level of Eighth Army Headquarters and emerged as a Distinguished Service Order, gazetted on 21 October 1944.

Corporal Herman Cyril Keys, South Saskatchewan Regiment. Corporal Keys was captured at Dieppe on 19 August 1942. Upon his release from captivity he was recommended for a Victoria Cross by no less a figure than Lieutenant-Colonel C.C. Merritt, VC. Nevertheless, it was downgraded to a DCM (gazetted 9 February 1946).

Private John Low, Loyal Edmonton Regiment, recommended for a VC for heroism at Regalbuto, Sicily, on 2 August 1943. It was downgraded to a DCM (gazetted 25 December 1943); the level of this decision and reasons are not clear.[66]

Acting Corporal Jack McGrath, Princess Patricia's Canadian Light Infantry, recommended for heroism in Italy, 19 December 1944; award downgraded to Distinguished Conduct Medal.[67]

Major John Wilson Powell, MC, 6 Canadian Armoured Regiment (First Hussars). He was recommended for a VC on 15 March 1945 for heroism displayed on 26 February 1945 during an attack on Cleve, Germany. The submission was approved to the level of General H.D.G. Crerar (General Officer Commanding First Canadian Army), but reduced without explanation by Field Marshal B.L. Montgomery to a DSO (gazetted 7 July 1945).

Lieutenant William David Louis Roach, Princess Patricia's Canadian Light Infantry, recommended for the same action as gave rise to a submission on behalf of Acting Corporal McGrath; awarded a DSO.[68]

Captain and Acting Major David Munce Rodgers, Queen's Own Cameron Highlanders of Canada, recommended for heroism south of Calcar, Germany, on the night of 25/26 February 1945 but reduced without explanation by Field Marshal B.L. Montgomery to a DSO (gazetted 7 July 1945).

Captain George Donald Skerrett, Royal Hamilton Light Infantry, another casualty during the Dieppe Raid of 19 August 1942. His commanding officer, Lieutenant-Colonel R.R. Labatt, wrote from captivity recommending a posthumous VC for Skerrett, but the submission was diverted through various British and Canadian channels in Britain, which delayed any consideration of the VC submission on its merits. Meanwhile, a posthumous Mention in Despatches was gazetted (30 October 1943), which effectively cut short any further examination of the VC recommendation.[69]

Captain Jack Birnie Smith, Royal Canadian Regiment, recommended for a posthumous VC following an assault on German positions near Rimini. Mentioned in Despatches; see Appendix D.[70]

Private and Acting Corporal Norman Eugene Tuttle, Highland Light Infantry of Canada. Recommended on 3 November 1944 for heroism on 1 November during the Battle of the Scheldt, and particularly for an attack on a German position so heavily fortified that it was called "Little Tobruk." The VC submission was supported up to and including Headquarters, First Canadian Army; General H.D.G. Crerar signed off on it on 3 January 1945. Nevertheless, Field Marshal B.L. Montgomery subsequently stroked out "VC" on the document and wrote, "DCM. A very good one."

Lieutenant William George Rogers Wedd, Royal Regiment of Canada, killed in action at Dieppe, 19 August 1942. His was one of several VC recommendations submitted by returning POWs at the end of the war; he was ultimately Mentioned in Despatches on February 1946.[71]

Corporal Francis Roy Weitzel, Highland Light Infantry of Canada, killed in action at Buron, Normandy, on 8 July 1944. In spite of his exploits, his commanding officer drafted only a cursory recommendation, which may explain why the submission appears never to have progressed beyond his divisional commander and he was awarded only a Mention in Despatches.[72]

It was not only Canadians whose VC recommendations were reduced to lesser awards, and many were turned down at levels much lower level than

Army Group Headquarters. In the case of a British officer, Captain John Jackson Pollock (Royal Electrical and Mechanical Engineers, serving in the 79th Armoured Division), the recommendation was downgraded very soon after the process began. His heroism was demonstrated in Holland in the closing stages of the war. The original recommendation, drafted about 18 April 1945, read as follows.

At approximately 1100 hours on the 13th April 1945, the "build-up" for the bridgehead forced over the River Ijssel was in full progress, when a most severe shell and mortar concentration covered the Buffalo approach to the river.* Two Buffaloes were hit while in the water and were swept down to a demolished bridge at MR 779765.** This bridge had been demolished by the enemy blowing extensive charges, thereby causing a large number of broken girders protruding in the water. This resulted in a great "step up" of the speed of the current, through the water now having to flow through confined spaces. Captain Pollock was some two hundred yards from the river but, observing the Buffaloes out of control, raced to the bridge to render assistance. To reach the bridge meant running the gauntlet of the intense shell and mortar fire concentration, but quite oblivious of his own safety, he managed to get to the bridge. Staff Sergeant [A.] Thom, who arrived at the bridge to assist Captain Pollock, was sent to obtain rope in order to evacuate crews of the Buffaloes. On return, he worked on the girders of the bridge.

The bridge was now under complete enemy observation and the mortaring was now "stepped up." Showing amazing courage, Captain Pollock placed planks of wood to the nearest Buffalo, now grounded, but some twenty feet away from the bridge, and rescued the four members of the crew. The crew commander of the Buffalo, Corporal [R.E.] Jones, who had himself been subjected to much mortaring and shelling prior to his evacuation, volunteered to assist Captain Pollock in rescuing the other Buffalo's crew. This second Buffalo was now being swept about helplessly owing to the strength of the current, estimated at six knots.

* The Buffalo was an amphibious vehicle.
** A map reference.

Standing on a post of the demolished bridge, but in complete view of the enemy, Captain Pollock threw a rope to the Buffalo which was made fast and himself made the other end secure by tying it to the bridge. By this time the second Buffalo crew of four were rescued, but as the last man evacuated his craft, the Buffalo immediately sank. This last man was still in the water, and having been twice completely submerged, reached the bridge but, in attempting to clamber ashore, grabbed Captain Pollock's legs, throwing him into the water. The strength of the current nearly swept them both under the bridge, but Captain Pollock managed to hold fast to a projecting portion and haul the man ashore. Whilst this rescue was taking place, a Naval Launch, completely out of control, crashed into a part of the bridge, but too far out for the crew to reach the bridge. Once again, Captain Pollock threw a rope to the craft and took off the crew of five. During the whole of this outstanding gallant action, intense and accurate mortar fire had been directed at the scene of the rescues, but Captain Pollock, through his devotion to duty, saved the lives of eight Buffalo personnel and five Naval Ratings.

Lieutenant-Colonel S.I. Howard-Jones, commanding officer of the 11th Battalion, Royal Tank Regiment, had drafted the submission. He forwarded it with supporting statements of three witnesses – Staff Sergeant Thom (who had assisted Pollock), Corporal Jones (one of the rescued Buffalo crewmen) and Leading Seaman Dugald Stead (one of the naval personnel rescued). It next went to the Officer Commanding, 30 Armoured Brigade, Brigadier N.W. Duncan. It was at this level that the VC recommendation was downgraded to a DSO and on 28 April 1945 was sent to Headquarters, First Canadian Army, the controlling formation. Brigadier Duncan did not explain his decision.[73]

Another example of a "failed" VC recommendation involving a British officer is that of Lieutenant Kenneth James Pillar, 50th Royal Tank Regiment, whose tank was set on fire in Italy by a German tank (30 November 1943). Having escaped from his burning tank, Pillar returned to it to rescue his trapped and wounded driver while the Germans continued to lay down machine gun fire. Pillar was killed, recommended for a VC and accorded a Mention in Despatches.[74]

A further instance of a British "failed" VC was that recommended for Lieutenant Michael D.K. Dauncey, whose heroism at Arnhem extended over six days (20-25 September 1944), during which he defended a hopeless position, repeatedly counter-attacked when it was overrun, was three times wounded and finally captured. He escaped from a prison hospital in December and made it back to British lines. Dauncey was awarded a DSO – and that only on 27 September 1945.[75].

The amount of effort and documentation going into a VC recommendation varied greatly. Some submissions appear to have been accompanied by minimal supporting evidence and may well have been downgraded on that basis alone. On the other hand, some failed VC nominations were supported by substantial witness statements. From the list of Canadians just given, the instances of Crockett, Crozier, Gagnon, Low, Powell and Tuttle are noteworthy for attention given to substantiating the recommendations.

Lance Corporal Gagnon's case is striking, given that no recognition whatsoever was accorded to him. His commanding officer, Lieutenant-Colonel J.P.E. Bernatchez, recommended him as follows:

For valour and conspicuous bravery in the presence of the enemy. On 30 July 1943 at Hill 204 near Catennova [sic] when his company was heavily engaged by enemy artillery and machine gun fire. After his section had taken up a covering position for the rest of his platoon, Lance Corporal Gagnon spied an enemy anti-aircraft gun which was firing on our troops who were trying to clear the main road and causing heavy casualties on the Engineers doing this work. He continued to advance on this enemy post and destroyed it by throwing a grenade, killing the crew and putting the gun out of action.

After this had been accomplished, in spite of the fact that an enemy section was advancing to protect it, he made for the main enemy gun position which was a 105-mm gun and which was now coming under our own artillery fire but was still firing on the road clearing party. With complete disregard for his own personal safety and knowing full well that the Bren which up to now had been giving him covering fire to his left flank was no longer in action, he nevertheless kept crawling up to the enemy position under the covering fire of only one rifle. He got up to grenade range and by throwing grenades and firing at the gun crew, killed part of them and routed the rest. It was then that one German came out of his position with a white flag. Lance Corporal Gagnon sat up [to] cover this man with his rifle and was killed by the last occupant of the position who after killing him fled, leaving the position clear of the enemy.

By his outstanding gallantry and devotion to duty, two enemy guns were captured and silenced and one heavy machine gun was forced to withdraw. His action allowed his company to get on and stay on its objective, which up to now had been pinned down by machine gun fire and prevented many casualties both in his company and to the engineer party and number of vehicles and personnel working on the main road.

This statement was signed by three witnesses to the events described. Nevertheless, the wording of the submission was rough and Lieutenant-Colonel Bernatchez was induced to draft another version or sign one that had been redrawn for him. It differed substantially from the original:

Lance Corporal Gagnon, a section leader of 17 Platoon, "D" Company, Royal 22e Regiment, received orders to protect the right flank of the Company attack on Hill 204, Catenanuova, 30 July 1943 and to destroy the enemy posts known to exist there. Hill 204 is a rocky, rugged, towering feature dominating the surrounding countryside, and its open approaches, devoid of cover, were swept by German mortar, artillery, rifle and machine gun fire.

The platoon rapidly advanced, but soon came under fire from a convertible anti-aircraft gun, 105-mm gun and a machine gun post, all mutually supporting, and the advance lost momentum.

Lance Corporal Gagnon, showing initiative and gallantry, accompanied by Sergeant Drapeau, immediately charged the anti-aircraft gun some 150 yards away, and despite the lack of cover and heavy fire safely reached it and killed the entire crew with grenades.

This soldier, assisted by Sergeant Drapeau, endeavoured to traverse the anti-aircraft gun without success, and then to the amazement of the platoon watching him, he started for the 105-mm gun, carrying out what could only be termed a sacrificial act.

Exhibiting complete devotion to duty and utter disregard for his own life, Lance Corporal Gagnon, now covered only by the fire of Sergeant Drapeau, crawled 150 yards, hugging the bare rock, to within grenade range and then with accuracy and skill he threw his grenades.

The Germans manning the machine gun post, apparently astounded by this gallant soldier's advance against tremendous odds, now were seen to evacuate their position and flee across the height.

One of the only two remaining occupants of the 105-mm gun position now came out carrying a white flag. Lance Corporal Gagnon rose up to cover him with his rifle but the remaining German shot Lance Corporal Gagnon dead and then fled leaving the post unoccupied.

By the valour, initiative and devotion to duty of Lance Corporal Gagnon, two enemy guns and a machine gun were captured and his conspicuous bravery is mainly responsible for the successful advance of "D" Company to its objective.

The three witnesses to Lance Corporal Gagnon's exploits were Captain B. Guimond (Officer Commanding, "D" Company), Lieutenant André Langlais (Platoon Commander, 17 Platoon) and Sergeant Louis René Drapeau (Platoon Sergeant, 17 Platoon). Although repetitious, their statements demonstrate the degree of proof advanced and the conviction of these men that Gagnon deserved the highest honour. The reader should remember that English was the second language of these soldiers:

I am commander of "D" Company Royal 22e Regiment. On the 30 July 1943, when moving up to attack Hill 204 near Catenanuova, I gave to 17 Platoon the task of protecting the right flank of the company and of destroying the enemy position which was known to exist there. Lance Corporal Gagnon, G., who was leading the first section of the No. 17 Platoon advanced himself with his Platoon Sergeant, Sergeant Drapeau to assault an enemy anti-aircraft gun which they had spotted some 30 yards away from them. This they did by dashing into the position and killed the gun crew with grenades. They then tried to turn the gun towards an enemy 105-mm gun position. This had been for some time and was still then firing on the road being used by our transport and causing casualties to our sappers, our advancing infantry, and our transport.

When assaulting the anti-aircraft gun position Lance Corporal Gagnon and Sergeant Drapeau were fired upon by an enemy machine gun situated on their left flank as well as by the occupants of the 105-mm gun position. Nevertheless they kept advancing, dashing from one enemy truck to another until they came into grenade range of the position. There they threw their grenades which caused casualties to the enemy. At that time our artillery was firing on the enemy position and their platoon commander recalled the small party but before the artillery fire had stopped, on his own initiative, Lance Corporal Gagnon dashed again towards the enemy position and there covered by only the fire of one rifle and under fire from the enemy's weapons and of our own guns he crept forward to grenade range again and threw grenades into the position, thus preventing the enemy from organizing any sort of retreat.

At that point one of the only two remaining occupants of the position came out showing a white flag. Lance Corporal Gagnon sat up to cover him and was shot dead by the last occupant who ran away leaving the position unoccupied.

The great courage and determination of Lance Corporal Gagnon allowed our sappers to work freely and saved a great number of casualties and the initiative which he showed caused the enemy to retire in complete disorder and with the loss of the greatest number of their men.

Captain B. Guimond.

I am Platoon Commander of 17 Platoon and Lance Corporal Gagnon was one of my section commanders.

On 30 July 1943 at about 1000 hours my platoon was taking part in an attack on Hill 204 near Catenanuova, over very difficult country. Lance Corporal Gagnon with Sergeant Drapeau advanced under covering of his section on an enemy anti-aircraft gun and assaulted it with grenades and put the crew out of action. This had been firing on the main road and holding up both transport and troops who were trying to get along the road. He tried with Sergeant Drapeau to turn the gun on an enemy 105-mm gun which was a hundred yards south of them but was unable to do so. This gun was still firing and causing considerable damage to transport and troops on the road. Gagnon decided to stalk this gun and with only the covering fire of Sergeant Drapeau he proceeded towards it. When they got within grenade range, before Sergeant Drapeau could stop him, he assaulted by himself the 105-mm gun with a grenade killing all but two of the crew. Whilst this was going on he was being fired on from an enemy position which were trying to prevent him from reaching the gun. One of the survivors put up the white flag and he got up to motion him forward. As he did this, the other occupant of the gun pit killed him.

While assaulting this position our own artillery were firing on the gun itself. Throughout this operation over difficult terrain, this Non-Commissioned Officer displayed great courage, valour and initiative and at the cost of his life silenced two enemy gun positions and caused the enemy who were trying to prevent him to attain his objective to retire.

Lieutenant André Langlais

On the 30 July 1943 I was Sergeant of No. 17 Platoon while my company was moving to attack Hill 204; my platoon was protecting their right flank and I was with the leading section.

After spotting an enemy anti-aircraft gun position I went forward with Lance Corporal Gagnon who was our leading section commander at the time to assault the enemy position. We then threw grenades in the enemy gun position and waited for the explosion. As soon as it did explode we dashed into the enemy gun position destroying what was left of the crew. We then tried to turn the anti-aircraft gun on to the 105-mm gun position which we had spotted some 150 yards south of our position but we did not succeed to do so. We were then being fired at from our left flank and also from the main gun position.

We started to make for the 105-mm gun position. We managed to get up to grenade range of the position and then threw our grenades. Since artillery fire was being brought down on the position by our own guns our Platoon commander recalled us.

On his own initiative Lance Corporal Gagnon under heavy fire from enemy weapons and our own guns started again for the 105-mm gun position being covered by the fire of only one rifle. He went up to approximately 30 yards of the 105-mm gun position. He then threw grenades and *one of the last occupant came out with a white flag; as he was getting up to cover him he was killed by the last occupant who ran away leaving the position unoccupied.*

Sergeant Louis René Drapeau*

The subsequent travels of the recommendation and its supporting evidence are unknown, and as noted earlier, no recognition was forthcoming, not even a posthumous Mention in Despatches. This is all the more puzzling in that a recommendation for a Distinguished Conduct Medal for Sergeant Drapeau was initiated at the same time. It progressed relatively slowly through the chain of command, being signed off by General B.L. Montgomery (General Officer Commanding, Eighth Army) on 1 October 1943 and finally approved by General H.R. Alexander (General Officer Commanding-in-Chief, 15 Army Group) on 15 October 1943. Although classified as an "immediate" award, it was not gazetted until 25 December 1943 – almost *five months* after the actions which had given rise to its submission.[76]

There is every possibility that the recommendation for Gagnon was simply lost and nobody bothered to retrieve it. If this appears outlandish, one need only think of what happened in the case of Private Sydney John Cousins, who was killed only eight days previous to Gagnon. He, too, had been recommended for a Victoria Cross, but it had been turned down without explanation, and for over a year Canadian authorities took no action to raise even a Mention in Despatches. However, in September 1944 his father wrote to National Defence Headquarters, inquiring about an award to his son. Through informal channels (likely battalion comrades), the elder Cousins had learned of the VC recommendation. Authorities overseas went on a hunt for the original submission, found it, and initiated proceedings for a Mention in Despatches, which was gazetted in May 1945. Authorities had acted on the basis of "better late than never," but without a squeaky wheel (the father) even that honour might never have been granted. Gagnon's parents made no

---

* Drapeau had a very distinguished career. As a company sergeant-major he was awarded a Bar to the DCM on 30 September 1944 for gallantry displayed the previous May; he was the only Canadian NCO awarded a Bar to DCM in the Second World War. Later commissioned, he served in the Korean War and was awarded an American Air Medal for work as an observer in unarmed T-6 aircraft.

inquiries about an award to their son until 1946, and they had no information comparable to that which Mr. Cousins possessed about a recommendation. The different outcomes of these two submissions – both failed Victoria Cross submissions, but one accorded a Mention in Despatches – demonstrate one example of family pressures forcing official action.

In Tuttle's case, he was originally recommended for a VC as follows:

On the 1st November 1944, Corporal Norman Eugene Tuttle was acting in command of 12 Platoon, "B" Company, Highland Light Infantry of Canada. As a result of casualties the Platoon was at that time 23 men strong.

The battle of the Lower Scheldt Estuary was nearing its close and the enemy had been forced into a pocket in the area of Heyst, Knocke-sur-Mer and "Little Tobruk", the German fortress along the Scheldt east of Knocke-sur-Mer. Ninth Canadian Infantry Brigade was ordered to clear this pocket.

The Highland Light Infantry of Canada was given the task of clearing up the east end of Knocke-sur-Mer and the "Little Tobruk" fortress area which would allow the remainder of the brigade to advance west to take out the balance of the enemy pocket.

"B" Company was given the task of attacking "Little Tobruk", the rapid capture of which was essential to the success of the battalion battle and the subsequent completion of the battalion task.

"Little Tobruk" was a self-contained fortress. It consisted of mutually supporting concrete and earth work positions situated on the high sand dunes just inland from the sea, and supplemented by normal infantry dug-in positions. The perimeter of the fortress was protected, from the landward side, by a belt of heavy concertina wire 30 feet in depth, and 100 yards of flat open ground, heavily mined.

"B" Company advance was held up when 12 Platoon, in the lead, came under intense enemy machine gun fire from the fortress. The only approach was across the minefield and the wire, directly through the enemy fire.

Corporal Norman Eugene Tuttle, seized the initiative. He sited the Brens of his platoon to provide covering fire and, with only this support and smoke from the 2 inch mortar, he crawled forward through the enemy fire. Using his bayonet to prod for mines he picked a path through the minefield to the barbed wire. The enemy machine guns continued firing through the smoke, the bullets landing throughout the wired area around Corporal Tuttle.

Completely ignoring the enemy fire, Corporal Tuttle worked for twenty minutes cutting his way through the wire. He then called to his platoon to follow him through the gap. His men, inspired by his act, rushed through behind him and charged the enemy position. Corporal Tuttle, in the lead, threw two 36 grenades into the first pillboxes killing 5 Germans and wounding 12. He then led his platoon through the maze of wire, entrenchments, earthworks and pillboxes to force the surrender of a Lieutenant-Colonel, seven other officers and approximately 250 other ranks. The outstanding skill with which he commanded the platoon during this action contributed materially to the ultimate success of the battalion and the Brigade operation.

Corporal Tuttle's complete disregard for his own safety and courageous leadership were an inspiration to his comrades and will remain for all time and outstanding example of the high tradition of valour of the Canadian Army.

The original VC recommendation was accompanied by an affidavit dated 6 November 1944 and signed by Major K.C. King, Officer Commanding "B" Company, Royal Hamilton Light Infantry:

On the 1st of November 1944, during an attack on "Little Tobruk", a German fortress east of Knocke-sur-Mer, Corporal N.E. Tuttle was acting as Platoon Commander of No. 12 Platoon in my Company.

No. 12 Platoon was leading and were forced to ground under heavy enemy fire. Corporal Tuttle took the situation into his own hands. He placed his Bren guns in position and ordered smoke from the 2-inch mortar. Corporal Tuttle under cover of this fire then crawled forward to the minefield. He reached his way through the enemy mines using the "prodding" method, until he came to 30 feet of barbed wire. All this time he was under enemy machine gun fire, the bullets could be seen landing all about him.

For 25 minutes under this intense fire he cut his way through the barbed wire before the task was finished.

His Platoon, inspired by this act, charged through the gap behind him. Corporal Tuttle threw grenades into the first pill box killing five Germans and wounding twelve.

Pushing ahead he and his Platoon then forced the surrender of an Oberst Lieutenant, seven other officers and 250 German soldiers.

Another document submitted was dated 27 November 1944 and signed by Private A. Berrington:

I was the platoon runner of No. 12 Platoon, "A" Company, The Highland Light Infantry of Canada, on 1 November 1944. "D" Company and "B" Company were the two leading companies in the attack against the German strong point we knew as "Little Tobruk". We came under extremely heavy fire from pill box positions on high ground. The situation seemed hopeless because the pill box positions were surrounded by thick belts of concertina wire. Our officer and Sergeant had been knocked out and Corporal Tuttle was in charge of the platoon. He asked us to give him covering fire. He crawled out through the anti-personnel minefields to the wire. He worked for 20 minutes cutting the wire and the bullets were flying all round him. Then he shouted, "Are you with me men", and we followed him through the gap and charged the first pill box, killing or injuring the Germans who held it. Then we went on through the maze of slit trenches and concrete emplacements.

Yet a third affidavit was submitted on 27 November 1944, this one signed by Private A.C. Dick:

On 1 November 1944, Corporal Tuttle, N.E. was acting as our Platoon Commander. We were attacking over dykes and polders towards a series of enemy strong points. When our artillery stopped firing we came under heavy fire from the enemy strongpoints. Our platoon was forward and we were forced to lie in the ditch along the dykes because it was impossible to go any further in the face of such heavy machine gun fire. Cor-

poral Tuttle ordered the Bren gunners to give him covering fire and told the 2-inch mortar men to smoke out the enemy position. Corporal Tuttle then crawled out through the anti-personnel minefield to the thick belt of barbed wire which surrounded the German position. He worked for a long time with lead flying around him. Then I heard him shout, "Are you with me men". We all rushed out through the gap he made until we reached the dead ground about 15 yards from the first pill box. Corporal Tuttle then crawled forward and threw a couple of No. 36 grenades in through a slit into the German pill box. He threw another one into a second slit and then we went in to clear out the place. I saw five Germans lying there dead and about twelve others were wounded. We then went forward through the network of trenches and concrete pill boxes.

Without Corporal Tuttle leading the way we would never have been able to take the enemy strong points without a lot of additional support.

To the litany of unsuccessful VC recommendations involving Canadians we may add one more, this one from the Korean War. On 21 October 1951, Lieutenant-Colonel Robert A. Keane, commanding officer of the Royal Canadian Regiment, submitted a lengthy submission describing the valour of Corporal Ernest William Poole, Royal Canadian Army Medical Corps:

On 3 October 1951 the 2nd Battalion, the Royal Canadian Regiment was moving forward against enemy opposition as part of a general attack launched by our own forces. "B" Company was ordered forward from the Naechon feature, an intermediate objective, to the final object on the right flank of the Battalion, the feature Nabu'Ri.

At 1745 hours Number 6 Platoon came under very heavy and accurate enemy small arms and mortar fire from the left flank and intense machine gun fire from the right flank. Within a few minutes, a dozen casualties had been suffered by the Platoon, some of them critical. Because of the steep slopes and thick underbrush it was not possible to determine precisely the nature and location of all the casualties, and there was a real danger that some of them would be lost to the enemy where they fell.

L.800192 Corporal Poole, E.W., RCAMC was the Non-Commissioned Officer in charge of stretcher bearers with "B" Company during this operation; his actions in dealing with the casualties suffered gave evidence of courage of the highest order under enemy fire and contributed very markedly to the ultimate success of the operation.

Corporal Poole proceeded forward through intense enemy mortar and shell fire to render first aid and arrange for the evacuation of the wounded. He was warned that he could be killed but he insisted, "I have a job to do and I am going to do it." He searched meticulously the whole area and did not stop until satisfied that all casualties had been accounted for. Enemy artillery and mortars were harassing the area, and enemy snipers and machine gunners made any movement hazardous but nothing could deter him in his search for the wounded. Two of the casualties were again hit while he was tending them but he continued with unruffled calm to render aid.

While still under fire Corporal Poole improvised stretchers from rifles and branches of trees; he bound the casualties securely by using thick vines. He moved from man to man with complete disregard for his own safety; his steady hand and quiet courage brought relief to all the wounded.

Number 5 Platoon was ordered to pass through Number 6 Platoon in order to maintain the momentum of the attack. They too came under heavy fire and suffered serious casualties. Corporal Poole was on hand at once and urged the Platoon Commander "Go on, I will see that your men get good care."

When the wounded had been prepared for evacuation, Corporal Poole led his party of bearers back some 3,000 yards in the dark to the Regimental Aid Post. The route was subjected to continuous shell fire, enemy patrols had infiltrated along both sides, the area was heavily mined, and even the natural hazards were enough to deter any but the most brave. But Corporal Poole led his party with confidence and all the casualties were borne safely to the Regimental Aid Post. Undoubtedly his leadership and the persistence with which he carried out his duties against any odds was vital in saving the lives of one Officer and three Other Ranks and in preventing two of the wounded from falling into the hands of the enemy.

Throughout the day of 3 October, all that night and the next day, Corporal Poole continued his task of attending the needs of the wounded. Whenever first aid was required, he was present to administer it. He was utterly tireless in his work. During the operation one thought only dominated his action: *That the duty was to tend his wounded comrades. No obstacle, no hazard, no personal danger, was allowed to stand in his way; his selfless devotion to his work was in the highest traditions of Military Service.*

Corporal Poole's conscientious determination to carry out his duties, his complete disregard for his own well being, his exemplary conduct under the most adverse conditions and his outstanding leadership resulted not only in saving the lives of five men and making possible the evacuation and treatment of many others but, even more, inspired his comrades to maintain the fight and contributed largely to the successful attainment of the objective.

This recommendation was accompanied by three supporting statements. The battalion's Medical Officer, Captain H.C. Stevenson, RCAMC, had not personally witnessed Poole at work, but he testified to the professional skills that had been exhibited ("I found they [the casualties] had been exceptionally well tended. Splints, stretchers and tourniquets had been improvised in a remarkably skilful manner under extremely difficult circumstances...."). He also commented on Poole's impact overall ("I have never known a man with more courage, initiative, disregard of personal safety, with such sense of duty and such high standard of morale and personality. Corporal Poole's work has been highly praised by his Company Commander on several occasions.") Lieutenant E.H. Devlin had seen Corporal Poole up close and was impressed ("There was intense fire all around him, yet he dodged his way from one man to the next, with complete disregard for his own safety.... His confident manner and his coolness under fire gave great encouragement to all my platoon.") Private H.J. Roach, shouting to Poole to keep his head down, that he was going to be killed, heard the reply, "I can't help it, I have a job to do and I'm going to do it."[77]

The line between Victoria Cross bravery and something just short of that remains blurred, shifting, arbitrary and uncertain. Nor is this situation unique to the VC, for many lesser awards have been upgraded and downgraded. In the case of the recommendation on behalf of Corporal Poole, the award of a Victoria Cross was supported by Brigadier J.M. Rockingham, Officer Commanding, 25 Canadian Infantry Brigade, who signed the form on 20 November 1951. It then went to Major-General Sir James Cassels, General

Officer Commanding, 1 Commonwealth Division, who, without apparent explanation, substituted a Distinguished Conduct Medal and signed off the form on 23 January 1952. The final word was that of Lieutenant-General William Bridgeford, Commander-in-Chief, British Commonwealth Forces Korea, who confirmed a DCM on 9 February 1952.

Was this a VC action? Or was it an instance of a skilled medical orderly doing a job for which he had been trained? Captain Stevenson's statement stressed Poole's professionalism, but Colonel Keane's submission indicated that by his presence and care of the wounded, Poole had encouraged junior officers to press their attack, leaving the casualties to his care ("Go on, I will see that your men get good care"). Only four Victoria Crosses were awarded in the Korean War (two posthumously), all to British soldiers (three officers, one private) and all for close-quarters combat. The information for comparison is meagre, but one is reminded of Montgomery's notation on Tuttle's VC form – "DCM, a very good one."

Australian, British, Canadians, Indians, New Zealanders, South Africans – all would agree that there were never enough Victoria Crosses to go around. If there had been enough, the honour would not have been as famous, valued or respected as it is today.

CHAPTER 5

THE CURIOUS TALE OF DIEPPE
VICTORIA CROSSES

Nothing except a battle lost can be half so melancholy as a battle won.

Arthur Wellesley, Duke of Wellington, following the Battle of Waterloo (1815)

The Dieppe Raid of 19 August 1942 is both famous and controversial. Historians debate whether it was even necessary – whether any lessons were learned that could not have been gained from previous experiences (such as Gallipoli) or from realistic exercises.

Three Victoria Crosses were awarded for events connected with Dieppe. The one to Major Patrick Anthony Porteous (Royal Marines) was straightforward enough: as part of the commando force operating on the flank, he was three times wounded, engaged in furious hand-to-hand combat, dashed across open ground under fire to take command of a detachment that had lost its officers and led a successful bayonet charge on a German position. One might think the two Canadian VC recipients would have equally uncomplicated stories. Nevertheless, the circumstances surrounding each were remarkable.

The business of bestowing decorations began on 21 August 1942, with talks between junior officers at Canadian Military Headquarters, London, and the War Office. The matter was further discussed with Combined Operations Headquarters and with the GOC First Canadian Corps. By 26 August 1942, the general policy had been laid down. First Canadian Corps instructed the General Officer Commanding, 2 Canadian Division (Major General J.H. Roberts) to submit recommendations for 100 immediate awards in respect of Dieppe operations. It was suggested that 40 should go to officers and 60 to other ranks. First Canadian Corps also requested that approximately 150

75

A German photograph of the beach at Dieppe after the disastrous raid of 1942. Almost 6,000 soldiers landed, 4,912 of them Canadians, of whom 907 were killed and 1,946 taken prisoner. (Library and Archives Canada)

Mentions in Despatches be submitted with similar officer/other rank proportions. MiDs could cover posthumous awards, but with respect to awards of medals only posthumous VC recommendations could be entertained. However, VC recommendations would not be counted among the 100 specified. The letter went on to state, "As regards Prisoners of War, recommendations may be included but action will not be taken until after the war."[78]

As commander of the operation, Roberts was responsible for awards to British personnel as well as Canadians engaged. On 8 September 1942, he despatched his recommendations to First Canadian Corps. The honours as finally published in the *London Gazette* differed from some of his initial suggestions. He had recommended seven rather than eight DSOs (the eighth, to Roberts himself, would be added by higher authorities); he submitted 25 names for Military Crosses (only 16 were gazetted) while the number of DCMs recommended was 14 (12 gazetted). Roberts requested 44 Military Medal awards; the number granted was 45. His suggested 100 Mentions in Despatches were reduced in the *London Gazette* to 91.

Roberts also forwarded citations for Nos. 3 and 4 Royal Marine Commando – seven gallantry awards for officers, 16 gallantry awards for Other Ranks, two MiDs for officers, seven MiDs for Other Ranks. This seemed to annoy him, for he wrote:

You will note that they [the Royal Marine Commandos recommendations] are far in excess of what should be their numerical allotment for awards. Canadian forces embarked were 4,912, whereas all three Commandos comprised some 800 all ranks. On a purely numerical basis, the allotment for all Commandos should be some 13 awards and 20 mentions in despatches. I have made no comments to COHQ [Combined Operations Headquarters] concerning this.

The matter of awards for prisoners of war presented a problem. When Roberts sent forward his recommendations, they included two for Victoria Crosses (Porteous and Lieutenant-Colonel C.C. Merritt, South Saskatchewan Regiment). That for Merritt (accompanied by four witness statements) read as follows:

For matchless gallantry and inspiring leadership whilst commanding his battalion during the Dieppe raid, 19 August 1942.

From the point of landing, his unit's advance had to be made across a bridge in Pourville which was swept by very heavy machine-gun, mortar and artillery fire and the first parties were mostly destroyed and the bridge thickly covered with their bodies. A daring lead was required; waving his helmet, Lieutenant-Colonel Merritt rushed forward shouting "Come on over ! There's nothing to worry about here."

He thus personally led the survivors of at least four parties in turn across the bridge. Quickly organizing these, he led them forward and when held up by enemy pill-boxes he again headed rushes which succeeded in clearing them. In one case he himself destroyed the occupants of the post by throwing grenades into it. After several of his runners became casualties, he himself kept contact with his different positions.

Although twice wounded, he continued to direct the unit's operations with great vigour and determination and while organizing the withdrawal he stalked a sniper with a Bren gun and silenced him. He then coolly gave orders for the departure and announced his intention to hold off and "get even with" the enemy. When last seen he was collecting Bren and Tommy guns and preparing a defensive position which successfully covered the withdrawal from the beach. In this he is believed to have lost his life.

MEN of VALOR
They fight for you

"When last seen he was collecting Bren and Tommy Guns and preparing a defensive position which successfully covered the withdrawal from the beach." — *Excerpt from citation awarding Victoria Cross to Lt.-Col. Merritt, South Saskatchewan Regt., Dieppe, Aug. 19, 1942*

The exploits of Lieutenant Colonel C.C. Merritt at Dieppe, in which he was believed initially to have been killed, earned him a Victoria Cross and formed the basis of this well known recruiting poster. (Canadian War Museum 71-258 & Library and Archives Canada PA501232)

To this Commanding Officer's personal daring the success of his unit's
operations and the safe re-embarkation of a large portion of it were chiefly
due.

By mid-September it had been confirmed that Merritt was alive as a POW.
The intended award of a VC became contentious. British policy was that
officers and men who were taken prisoner should be considered eligible for
awards only after they either escaped captivity, died or until the conclusion
of hostilities. This would lead to several wartime awards to soldiers taken
prisoner at Dieppe who managed to escape, plus 90 more awards to Dieppe
Raid participants after the war, but if applied strictly in 1942 there would
have been no VC for Merritt at that time.

The British policy was based on recommendations from 1922 drafted by
a body known as the Monro Committee, which had laid down that submissions for awards concerning personnel captured in normal operations
should only be considered when they escaped or at the close of hostilities *unless special circumstances were involved.* As it turned out, the British
themselves admitted at least one precedent of an award to a British officer
captured in the course of his heroic exploits – Major Trevor Allan Gordon
Pritchard, a paratroop leader who landed in Italy in February 1941 to sabo-
tage viaducts. Although taken prisoner, he was awarded a DSO as a special
case. One might think that the nature of Pritchard's mission made capture
virtually inevitable, and hence a decoration more defensible, but an escape
plan had been laid down in conjunction with the operation so his capture
had been no more inevitable than Merritt's.*

Canadian authorities argued that Merritt's was a "special case." The line of
argument used is not recorded in detail, but on 20 September, the Adjutant
General, Major-General H.F.G. Letson, cabled Major-General P.J. Montague
(Senior Combatant Officer, Canadian Military Headquarters, London) that
an award to Merritt would have a good effect on army morale; two days later,
Montague replied that a precedent (singular, not plural) existed, though he
gave no name.[79] One can guess that another consideration would be that
matters would appear unseemly if a VC went to one of 800 British Comman-

---

* A memo that also mentioned "a VC was awarded a naval officer captured in Crete" was erroneous; it was probably intended to describe the case of Sergeant Hinton.

dos with no comparable award to any of the nearly 5,000 Canadian soldiers involved. Merritt's VC was duly gazetted with the other Dieppe awards on 2 October 1942. Apart from correcting the statement about his having lost his life, the citation differed little from that which Roberts had first proposed.

The objections raised to Merritt's award while he was still a POW invite comparison with other cases. As of the autumn of 1942 there were already three VC recipients in enemy POW camps. Lance Corporal Harry Nicholls had been wounded and captured in France on 21 May 1940 but was believed to have been killed; the citation to his Victoria Cross (gazetted 30 July 1940) made that statement. Captain Eric Charles Twelves Wilson (wounded and captured in British Somaliland, 15 August 1940) was also believed to be dead when his Victoria Cross was gazetted (14 October 1940); the citation described him as being killed "fighting to the end." Sergeant John Daniel Hinton, a New Zealander (captured in Crete, 29 April 1941) was known to be alive in captivity and was admitted as such in the citation to his Victoria Cross (gazetted 17 October 1941). On the other hand, Lieutenant-Colonel Augustus Charles Newman had performed heroic deeds at St. Nazaire (27/28 March 1942) comparable to those of Merritt and had become a prisoner of war; it was not until 19 June 1945 that his Victoria Cross was gazetted. Similarly, the Bar to the Victoria Cross awarded to Captain Charles Hazlitt Upham (another New Zealander) was gazetted on 26 September 1945, more than three years after his heroism and capture in North Africa (14-15 July 1942).

Subsequent to Merritt's case being accepted as "special," Major Herbert Wallace Le Patourel was awarded a "posthumous" Victoria Cross on 9 March 1943 for heroism in North Africa; a week later the London Gazette corrected itself, reporting that he was a POW. Squadron Leader Leonard Henry Trent (Royal New Zealand Air Force) performed his most famous deed on 3 May 1943 and was recommended for the VC on 15 May 15, but it was not gazetted until 1 March 1946. Two Victoria Crosses were awarded to Royal Navy officers known to be POWs, Lieutenant Donald Cameron and Lieutenant Basil Charles Godfrey Place, who laid mines under Tirpitz using midget submarines and were immediately captured (22 September 1943); their Victoria Crosses were gazetted on 22 February 1944; the nature of their operation – virtually guaranteed to be a one-way trip – distinguishes their case from Merritt and even Pritchard. Looking ahead one more war, we may note that Lieutenant-

Honorary Captain John Foote, VC, the chaplain who took gun in hand. (Canadian War Museum ZK1075)

Colonel James P. Carne was captured in his VC action of 22/23 April 1951, and his award was gazetted only on 27 October 1953, three months after the Korean War had ended.

If Merritt's VC was wrestled from the War Office and from King George VI himself, the case of Honorary Captain John Foote was one of bizarre circumstances. As early as 10 October 1942 Major-General Roberts had handled a recommendation for a Military Cross for Foote. The original text read as follows (highlighted material run through with a pencil, as it was feared the actions described would compromise his position as both a chaplain and a prisoner of war):

> *Honorary Captain Foote accompanied his unit, Royal Hamilton Light Infantry, into action at Dieppe, 19 August 1942, and landed with the Medical Officer, Captain D.W. Clare, Royal Canadian Army Medical Corps. He worked under very heavy fire, moving back and forth across the beach, assisting to treat and carry in wounded, loading casualties into boats, and administering morphine to serious cases. He constantly exposed himself to carry on his work, showed no sign of fear or self-regard, and was a great and heartening example to all ranks.* He later seized a Bren gun, although wounded in the left arm, and climbed a small knoll from where he laid down fire to cover the final withdrawal of the unit. *He consistently refused to leave those wounded whom it was impossible to evacuate. He is now reported a prisoner of war.*

The suggested Military Cross for Foote was based on accounts provided by a lance corporal, a corporal and a sergeant. None of the returning commissioned officers had witnessed his heroics, and since the chaplain was now a POW, the matter of an award was deferred. Nevertheless, Major-General Roberts was troubled by statements made concerning Foote. On 4 November 1942 he wrote to Headquarters, 1 Canadian Corps, advising that the documents collected to date be placed on Foote's personal file. In conclusion, Roberts wrote:

> *May it be noted that Canadian Military Headquarters have requested that all reference to Captain Foote's gallant action in employing a Bren gun be deleted from the original recommendation. This was indicated as being liable to cause political complications in the case of a Chaplain, who is normally not supposed to bear arms at any time. This was agreed to by this Division.*

The matter of an award for Foote was revived in 1945 when the Dieppe POWs were liberated. Their numbers included at least one more witness to the chaplain's heroism, Captain David W. Clare, Royal Canadian Army Medical Corps, who had been helped by Foote as they handled casualties on the beach. Clare himself would be awarded a Military Cross in February 1946. However, in the early summer of 1945 Canadian military authorities were swinging between an MC and an MBE (Member, Order of the British Empire) for Foote. In the hierarchy of gallantry awards, these were at least two rungs below that of a Victoria Cross.

Precisely when the talk turned to a VC is unclear, but a Canadian Army file records a peculiar series of events. Foote's heroism was reported back to Canada almost immediately via a broadcast by Leonard Brockington. The Presbytery of Stratford wrote on 17 May 1945 to Dr. J.W. MacNamara, secretary of the Chaplaincy Committee in Toronto, urging that Foote "should receive the highest award for this valour". On 1 June 1945, MacNamara wrote to Honorary Brigadier C.G. Hepburn, the Principal Chaplain (Protestant) of the Canadian Army. He enclosed the Stratford letter and went on to declare, "Our Committee on Chaplaincy Service fully endorses what is said in the letter regarding the devoted and heroic services performed by Captain Foote, and feel that he is entitled to some honorary recognition. We are referring the matter to you for your consideration, as you would know best what steps could be taken in the matter." This in turn was referred within Department of National Defence to a Major G.E.F. Sweet on 8 June 1945. The file does not further trace action and when a VC recommendation was drafted, and by whom, remains unknown.[80] But then, the Lord does move in mysterious ways.

CHAPTER 6

AIR FORCE VICTORIA CROSSES, GRANTED AND DENIED

The race is not to the swift, nor battle to the strong.

Ecclesiastes, Chapter 9, verse 11.

For many are called, but few are chosen.

Matthew, Chapter 22, verse 14.

On the night of 21/22 June 1943, a Halifax bomber of No. 408 Squadron went missing. Early in 1944, Pilot Officer G.F. Pridham, the bomb aimer, was repatriated from a POW camp. He reported that on his last mission his aircraft had been hit by flak which killed two crewmen outright and mortally wounded a third. Pridham himself was gravely injured, with one leg almost torn off. With fire sweeping the cockpit, fanned by winds howling through the shattered perspex, Sergeant Clifford C. Reichert (the pilot), stayed at the controls, keeping the bomber level to allow survivors, including Pridham, to bale out. In so doing he missed his own chance to escape; the Halifax exploded. Pridham subsequently wrote to Reichert's family, describing his pilot as "the bravest man I ever knew." On the basis of this evidence, Royal Canadian Air Force authorities recommended some recognition for Reichert (who had been posthumously commissioned); on 1 January 1945 it was announced that he had been Mentioned in Despatches.

Documents found in the Public Record Office in London include a recommendation from No. 422 Squadron that Flight Lieutenant Paul Treneman Sargent be awarded the Victoria Cross. The facts behind this were stated clearly. In October 1943, piloting a Sunderland flying boat, he attacked an enemy submarine in the North Atlantic in the face of withering anti-aircraft fire. Only three of his depth charges dropped; Sargent turned and made another run. By now the flak was brutal; two crewmen were killed; the navigator suffered wounds that proved fatal; the controls were damaged and the aircraft was almost unmanageable. Sargent held his course, dropped two depth charges, which damaged (but did not sink) his quarry, then headed for a convoy. He force-landed in heavy seas, and though the Sunderland sank quickly, the rest of Sargent's crew escaped and were rescued; Sargent went down with the aircraft. He had previously completed 34 sorties, involving 457 hours flying and, in the words of the recommendation, "had invariably displayed great courage, skill and devotion to duty." This recommendation was supported as far as Coastal Command Headquarters. Nevertheless, Flight Lieutenant Sargent was not awarded a Victoria Cross; instead he was Mentioned in Despatches.

On 10 January 1944, Wing Commander A.N. Martin, commanding officer of No. 424 Squadron, submitted a recommendation that Sergeant Vernon Frederick McHarg be awarded a Victoria Cross. Martin was relying on evidence supplied by crewmen then held prisoner by the enemy. Nevertheless, he was able to write a stirring account. Piloting a Wellington aircraft on the night of 27 January 1943, McHarg had remained at the controls of his burning aircraft, giving up precious seconds as his crew baled out of the doomed bomber, which crashed in flames before he could escape. The recommendation concluded by declaring, "Sergeant McHarg's deliberate sacrifice of his own life to save those of his crew is an outstanding act of bravery and devotion."

To this the station commander added his own comments:

Sergeant McHarg deliberately and with full knowledge of the consequences of his act gave his life to enable other members of his crew to live. No greater contribution could be made to the Empire or the Service than that exhibited in this fearless example of self-sacrifice.

Some of his crew, now prisoners of war, have most justly said, "We can surely be proud of him". It is earnestly considered that this most valorous deed should be recognized by the award of the highest order of gallantry and in consequence strongly recommend the posthumous award of the Victoria Cross.[81]

Notwithstanding the recommendation, backed by the station commander's support, Sergeant McHarg was granted no posthumous recognition whatsoever.

It should be noted that it was service policy that people should not be told they had been recommended for a decoration until the award had been finally approved at the highest levels; otherwise, it might be embarrassing for all concerned if a "gong" was not approved. This extended even to the families of deceased personnel; they were *not* to be told that their loved one had been recommended for a Victoria Cross unless that honour was formally approved and gazetted. Thus, although Pilot Officer Pridham could write to the family of Sergeant Reichert, describing the latter as "the bravest man I ever knew," neither he nor Reichert's parents would ever be aware of the VC recommendation.

Victoria Cross awards (or lack thereof) rankled RCAF authorities. On 10 March 1944, a section known simply as P.1d in RCAF Overseas Headquarters gave the matter special attention. Copies of all air force VC citations hitherto awarded were studied and compared to recommendations previously submitted on behalf of RCAF aircrew. The diary of P.1d does not indicate the conclusions drawn, but on 28 July 1944, the document noted the RCAF's first VC award (to Flight Lieutenant David Hornell) and commented:

> *When it first became known that this recommendation was on its way to Air Ministry, P.1d kept in close touch with the department concerned at Air Ministry. Close contact was kept with the members of the U.K. Honours in War Committee, and every effort was made to facilitate the passage of this much coveted award through the rigorous channels of investigation necessary before this highest ranking decoration could be approved by His Majesty The King.*[82]

The Second World War correspondence in Britain shows officials agonizing over who should receive a Victoria Cross and what might be substituted should a VC be vetoed. The problem was compounded by the fact that *posthumous awards* could be made with only three honours – the Victoria Cross, George Cross and Mention in Despatches. In the hierarchy of gallantry awards, these were the two highest and the very lowest. A gallant man who survived his brave feat could be rewarded with many types of decorations, but one who died in the course of his courageous act could be given a VC, GC or MiD – but nothing in between. Thus, in the three cases cited earlier – McHarg, Sargent and Reichert – it had to be a VC, an MiD or nothing.

British authorities from the outset were uneasy about awards to fighter pilots – or more particularly, about Victoria Crosses awarded merely for piling up large numbers of "kills" – and whereas at least eight First World War Victoria Crosses (one third of the air VCs of that conflict) went to high-scoring fighter pilots (Ball, Bishop, Barker, Hawker, Jerrard, McCudden, Mannock and Beauchamp-Proctor), only two Commonwealth fighter pilots were awarded the Victoria Cross during the Second World War, and neither was a "high scorer" like James E. "Johnny" Johnson (38 victories), Adolf G. Malan (30) or George F. Beurling (30). There is more than a hint that Flight Lieutenant Eric James Nicolson's VC was motivated as much by political concerns as his brave act (remaining in a burning Hurricane long enough to shoot down an enemy airplane, thereby sustaining terrible burns himself). The necessity of recommending a VC for a Fighter Command pilot was raised as early as 29 August 1940, but when such a submission was made it was by upgrading a DFC recommendation for Nicolson (dated 26 October 1940 and referring to an incident on 16 August) to a Victoria Cross (the change being made two days later by Air Vice-Marshal Sir Keith Park). Although one official commented on 6 November that Nicolson's case was "less strong" than that of four previous aerial VCs (all to bomber crewmen), the same sceptic conceded the strength of political arguments favouring Fighter Command. The submission to the King was drafted on 7 November and the award itself was gazetted on 15 November 1940.[83] The other fighter VC, to Lieutenant Robert Hampton Gray, has already been noted as having been bestowed to honour the Fleet Air Arm at the moment of victory.[84]

But what was most often stated in the Air Ministry correspondence (and widely communicated to senior officers in the field) is that a Victoria Cross should be awarded for *getting into trouble* and not for *getting out of trouble*, enunciated ever since the Sergeant Ward case in 1941. In other words, desperate acts of self-preservation should not count as meriting the Victoria Cross. Desperate acts to execute a mission would qualify – from the suicidal attack on the Maastricht bridges in May 1940 on through Guy Gibson's famous dams raid. Desperate acts to save others would qualify (Andy Mynarski's

Victoria Cross action is the finest possible example), but furious self-preservation alone was not enough. William Barker's fight against odds of October 1918 would not have been a VC action by Second World War standards.[85]

Apart from David Hornell and Andrew Mynarski (who did receive the Victoria Cross), at least eight RCAF men were recommended for the award, either by peers or superiors, yet did not receive it (there may have been more). They were as follows:

Flight Lieutenant John Alan Anderson, whose VC recommendation was downgraded to a Distinguished Service Order, awarded in February 1945 for services with No. 419 Squadron (see Appendix F).

Flying Officer Harold Freeman, killed in action 24 May 1944. A Typhoon pilot with No. 198 Squadron, shot down and killed attacking German radar units near Cherbourg.

Pilot Officer Harvey Edgar Jones, killed in action 6 June 1944. A Dakota pilot with No. 233 Squadron, shot down as he delivered paratroopers to the Caen area in the early hours of D-Day.

Flight Sergeant Vernon Frederick McHarg, killed in action 26 January 1943. A pilot with No. 424 Squadron.

Flight Lieutenant William Eugene McLean, killed in action 3 February 1945. A bomber pilot with No. 514 Squadron.

Pilot Officer Clifford Clarence Reichert, killed in action 23 June 1943. A pilot with No. 408 Squadron.

Flight Lieutenant Paul Treneman Sargent, killed in action 17 October 1943. A Sunderland pilot with No. 422 Squadron.

Flight Lieutenant James Andrew Watson, killed in action 27 April 1944. A bomber pilot with No. 622 Squadron.

Why did the Mynarski and Hornell recommendations succeed while these eight did not? It is significant that six of the eight – Jones, Sargent, McHarg, McLean, Watson and Reichert – involved pilots staying at their posts while others were saved. As early as September 1940, Pilot Officer Kenneth H. Higson of No. 10 Squadron sacrificed himself by remaining at the controls of a

Flying Officers Harold Freeman and C. Abbot (right) with squadron mascots. Freeman was another RCAF pilot recommended for the VC and accorded a Mention in Despatches. (Canadian Forces Photo PL-26471)

Flight Lieutenant Harvey Edgar Jones was also recommended for the VC and recognized with a Mention in Despatches. (Canadian Forces Photo PL-19653)

Whitley bomber while his crewmates baled out over Italy; the bomber crashed and exploded. When he was recommended for a Victoria Cross, Air Commodore Allan Coningham, Air Officer Commanding, No. 4 Group, quibbled over missing facts that could never really be found. At what height was the Whitley flying when a crash became inevitable? Did Higson know what altitude would be the point at which his own escape would be impossible?[86]

In fact, this sort of action happened with such frequency in Bomber Command that awarding a Victoria Cross in every instance would have devalued the award; "uncommon valour" was actually so common that it could not be properly rewarded. Moreover, it was stated more than once that pilots had a duty to remain at their posts for as long as possible; it smacked a bit of the adage that "the captain should go down with the ship," which was literally so with Flight Lieutenant Sargent, who went down with his Sunderland.

This rule was bent slightly in the case of a posthumous VC award to Squadron Leader Ian Willoughby Bazalgette, a Canadian who had enlisted directly in the RAF. He, too, had remained with his burning Lancaster in an attempt to save comrades. He actually rode the bomber down to a crash-landing in France because two injured crewmen could not bale out, but the aircraft exploded just as he touched down. Nevertheless, events preceding this had marked Bazalgette out for a VC rather than a Mention in Despatches; with his aircraft already heavily damaged by flak, he had nevertheless pressed on to a target to execute the duties of master bomber, remaining over the target as his own plight worsened.[87]

Flying Officer Paul Treneman Sargent "went down with the ship" (his Sunderland flying boat) and was recommended for the VC, but received a Mention in Despatches instead. (Canadian Forces Photo PL-36259)

It should be noted, however, that in one instance Air Ministry apparently forgot its "captain must go down with the ship" policy. A Victoria Cross awarded to Pilot Officer Leslie T. Manser (*London Gazette*, 23 October 1942) was for deeds almost identical to those that had been performed by Jones, McHarg, McLean, Reichert, Sargent and Watson, as well as others in Bomber Command. The only significant difference was that Manser declined to wear a parachute which he felt would hinder his efforts to control the aircraft (which extended over 30 minutes) and refused a parachute at the last minute to give the last crew member a better chance to bale out. These actions may partially explain the apparent anomaly, but two additional factors might also have been in play:

1. The Air Ministry committee ruled on the Manser case at a time before the rigorous sense of pilot responsibility to the last had hardened into doctrine.

2. The Air Ministry decision coincided with a realization that, as of September 1942, there had been 25 Victoria Cross awards to the army and only nine to the Royal Air Force.[88]

The preceding has some bearing on another case, that of Warrant Officer John Horan, discussed elsewhere in another context (see pages 171-172). Although not recommended for a VC (he was Mentioned in Despatches), the possibility of raising such a submission years after the Second World War invites a question. If VCs were denied to pilots who died at their posts because, put bluntly, that was in their job description, could not the same rationale be applied to an air gunner (like Horan) who died at his guns doing what he had been trained to do?

The Victoria Cross warrant specified that it should be awarded for outstanding acts of valour rather than sustained gallantry over a long term. As early as October 1942 consideration was being given to VC awards for just such "long-haul" performances. Although the Royal Air Force had adopted a policy of *not* recommending high-scoring fighter pilots (whose job it was to destroy enemy aircraft), the examples of Ball, Beauchamp-Proctor, Mannock and Mc-Cudden were put forward as examples of VC recipients whose careers had been marked by months of small victories rather than brief, violent and titanic exploits. The first proposal for such a VC appears to have been put forward in December 1942. It involved Wing Commander Reginald Sawrey-Cookson, DSO, DFC, whose name became a byword in his group for constancy under fire. He was killed in action 6 April 1942, by which time he had flown 270 operational hours in Bomber Command. The lapse in time between his death and the submission may have prejudiced its success, and the uncertainty persisted as to the propriety of what would amount to a "periodic VC." [89]

In fact, only two such VCs were ever awarded – to Wing Commander Guy Gibson and to Group Captain Leonard Cheshire, the latter only after protracted discussions at Air Ministry Honours and Awards Committee level. Cheshire was a very brave man who had won three DSOs and a DFC by 1944; he had flown four tours totalling 100 sorties (536 operational hours) in the most dangerous of all RAF commands; there was almost nothing more to give him other than a Victoria Cross.

Gibson is generally thought to have been awarded his VC for the famous dams raid on 16/17 May 1943, but Air Ministry correspondence reveals the extent of his service (four tours, 173 sorties) as factors. Indeed, the correspondence related to his Bar to the DSO (gazetted 2 April 1943) reveals a predisposition by one important officer to award him a VC at the earliest possible moment. The recommendation for this second DSO had been drafted on 12 March 1943 by the Officer Commanding, Station Syerston; this had gone to the Air Officer Commanding, No. 5 Group, Air Vice-Marshal Sir Ralph Cochrane, who added his remarks on 17 March 1943:

Wing Commander Gibson has now handed over command of No. 106 Squadron after an outstandingly successful tour as squadron commander. In view, however, of the recent award of the Distinguished Service Order I recommend that he should now be considered for the award of a Second Bar to his Distinguished Flying Cross rather than a Bar to the Distinguished Service Order.

Air Chief Marshal Sir Arthur Harris disagreed. In his own hand, on 20 March 1943, he wrote:

Any captain who completes 172 sorties in outstanding manner is worth two DSOs if not a VC – Bar to DSO approved.[90]

If Harris had a predisposition to award Gibson a VC, the dams raid provided the finishing touch. In the immediate aftermath of the attack there was a rush to distribute honours, but on the issue of Gibson there was no doubt whatsoever. "A record of prolonged and heroic endeavour and a *comble* which is really outstanding," wrote one officer. The general consensus was that Gibson was earning his VC from the moment that, having dropped his own weapon, he proceeded to accompany following aircraft in their attacks, drawing flak onto himself.[91]

Nevertheless, Air Ministry shrank from rewarding distinguished bomber pilots with a "long-haul" Victoria Cross. From April to August 1943, "Bomber" Harris supported efforts to have a VC awarded to Squadron Leader Joseph R.G. Ralston, who when first recommended had completed 83 sorties. He failed and finally settled for a Bar to Ralston's DSO.[92] Group Captain J.B. Tait, recommended for a Victoria Cross, was granted a third Bar to his DSO, in part because authorities claimed that Tait's exploits (including the final sinking of the *Tirpitz*) had been blown out of proportion by the press, and because they were loath to treat the Cheshire case as a precedent to be followed. Similarly, a VC recommendation for Group Captain P.C. Pickard (DSO and two Bars, DFC, three tours, 105 sorties, killed while leading the famous low-level raid on Amiens prison on 18 February 1944) was turned down on two grounds. Quoting Air Ministry minutes, these were:

1. He had already been sufficiently decorated in relation to other officers with comparable records of service.

2. Press reports of his last sortie exaggerated its importance.[93]

Given the reluctance of officials to award "long haul" VCs, it was almost inevitable that J.A. Anderson's VC nomination would be downgraded to a DSO. Like Pickard and Tait, the recommendation had been for a series of brave acts rather than for a single death-defying gamble. Compared to

Cheshire's four tours, and the three tours completed by Gibson and Tait, Anderson had completed only one tour. In fact, given the reluctance with which Air Ministry approved a VC for Cheshire and his four tours, it was unlikely that Anderson's recommendation would succeed, given that he flown only 22 sorties. Air Marshal Robert Saundby, the Deputy Commander-in-Chief of Bomber Command, wrote on 17 December 1944:

> *I do not think that this is up to V.C. standard. It mostly consists of bringing back aircraft on a number of occasions which had been damaged by flak. No doubt very gallant efforts, and it is rather surprising that F/L Anderson was not recommended for a DFC at some time earlier in his operational career, since the incidents quoted extend from July 28th 1944 to October 14th, 1944.*
>
> *I agree that a DSO would be appropriate.*[94]

The case of Flying Officer Freeman generated considerable correspondence within Air Ministry. Leading a formation of eight Typhoons to attack a radar station prior to D Day, his aircraft had been hit by flak; the tail was almost completely shot away. He nevertheless pressed on to his target, dived to very low level and fired his rockets with deadly effect. As he attempted to pull up, the wingtip of the following aircraft touched Freeman's fuselage; both aircraft crashed in flames. His VC nomination failed on several grounds; he was conducting a mission of a type carried out before and by many others, "part of the general offensive rather than as a forlorn hope entailing exceptional risk"; many others were taking the same risks as Freeman; it was not clear that the flak hit had damaged his aircraft beyond all hope of return. Freeman's VC might still have succeeded but for the fact that officers in 2nd Tactical Air Force disagreed; Air Marshal Arthur Coningham did not consider Freeman's bravery up to VC standards while Coningham's immediate superior, Air Chief Marshal Trafford Leigh-Mallory, supported the VC recommendation.[95]

But perhaps the most interesting correspondence is associated with David Hornell's Victoria Cross, a recommendation that succeeded. On 4 July 1944 the Air Officer Commanding, Coastal Command, Air Chief Marshal Sholto Douglas, forwarded the Hornell nomination to Air Ministry. His arguments in support of the nomination were blatantly political:

Only one Victoria Cross has been awarded to Coastal Command in the course of the war. That award was made more than two years ago to the captain of a torpedo aircraft, who carried out a very gallant torpedo attack against a battle cruiser in Brest Harbour. I would point out that no award of the Victoria Cross has been made to any officer or airman engaged in anti-U-boat duties.

I feel that, apart from the outstanding heroism displayed by this officer, some recognition of the gallantry displayed by the crews of the anti-U-Boat squadrons in Coastal Command is well deserved.

The fact that this officer is a member of the Royal Canadian Air Force, serving in a Canadian squadron, if anything strengthens the recommendation, in that it would be some small recognition of the very great part played by Dominion squadrons and Dominion air crew personnel in Coastal Command's successful war against the U-boat.[96]

Air Ministry did not agree entirely with Air Chief Marshal Douglas; Flying Officer L.A. Trigg's 1943 posthumous Victoria Cross was pointedly mentioned as a VC awarded for anti-submarine work. However, he had flown under West African Air Forces control rather than that of Coastal Command. Within Air Ministry the Hornell case was considered "borderline"; three factors appear to have swung opinion towards a VC: the fact that he was flying a cumbersome, underpowered Canso amphibian; his skill in making a crash-landing on the water without injury to his crew; his sustained leadership in the 21 hours that followed when the survivors endured exposure to the North Atlantic and depressing incidents, including a failed life-boat drop. It is interesting to note, however, that Air Ministry, having decided to support a Victoria Cross for anti-submarine work, proceeded to support *two* (Hornell and Flying Officer John A. Cruickshank, a Catalina pilot in No. 210 Squadron).

Andrew Mynarski's Victoria Cross was apolitical, yet the Air Ministry discussions concerning it reveal divisions and differences of opinion. It is worth remembering that in this instance the Canadians were not pushing for any specific award. Surviving crewmen had written to RCAF Headquarters asking if there could be some recognition for "Andy", and RCAF authorities considered it only in general terms; when RCAF Overseas Headquarters contacted Air Ministry in February 1946, it was merely to request that the circumstances of Mynarski's death be investigated "with a view to the possibility of a posthumous award to P/O Mynarski." It would appear that Air Marshal Norman Bottomley, Air Officer Commanding Bomber Command, recommended a VC for Mynarski, in a document dated 30 August 1946.

Yet once the recommendation had been submitted, officials within Air Ministry debated whether his actions had been up to VC standards. There was no doubt that had he survived, he would have received a Distinguished Service Order, but dying did not automatically upgrade his deeds to those befitting a Victoria Cross. The circumstances were similar to those of a VC to Flight Sergeant George Thompson, RAF, who had gone through fire twice to save comrades; Mynarski, it was suggested, might not qualify as he had attempted to rescue only one man. The Chief of the Air Staff disagreed. In a strong minute, dated 10 September 1946, he wrote:

> *In my view the* quality *of the action in the two cases was identical, the* quantity *was different because P/O Mynarski only had one member of the crew to try and rescue, Flight Sergeant Thompson had two. I suggest that the award of the VC should be given on grounds of quality and* not *of quantity.*

Virtually all officers agreed that Mynarski had deliberately sacrificed himself in his attempt to save a comrade, and the recommendation was duly agreed upon.[97]

It is not surprising to find cases of sustained campaigns mounted to secure a Victoria Cross for a person whose sponsors considered deserving. One example is that of Flight Lieutenant James Andrew Watson of Hamilton, Ontario. He enlisted in the RCAF on 22 September 1941, graduated as a pilot in October 1942 and was promptly despatched overseas. Extensive operational training followed, and on 11 September 1943 he was posted to No. 622 Squadron, flying Stirling bombers but soon to convert to Lancasters.

Even in the course of operational training, Watson soon made a deep impression on others, including a British navigator with the improbable name of Surrender Berry. In an affidavit sworn on 22 June 1946 Berry recalled an incident three years earlier (10 June 1943) when Watson has successfully landed a Wellington following an engine fire at No. 12 Operational Training

Unit. The Canadian pilot had not only executed a fine landing in hazardous circumstances but had also taken pains to avoid injuries to his crew had the landing been less than perfect. Berry also recalled an incident at No. 1667 Heavy Conversion Unit in August 1943 when, under the direction of an instructor, he landed a Stirling that had developed control problems.[98]

Once they went on operations with No. 622 Squadron, Berry witnessed further exploits involving Watson, up to the end of early January 1944 when Berry was diagnosed with tuberculosis and sent to a sanatorium. These included a minelaying sortie in the Bay of Biscay on 18 September 1943, when they almost ran into a flak barrage from a ship; the bomber sheared away just in time. On another sortie (27 September 1943) while flying at 14,000 feet en route to Hanover, the Stirling encountered a He.111 bomber whose crew was probably as surprised to meet the British bomber as were Watson and crew startled to meet the Heinkel. The gunners opened fire, driving off the He.111, which was subsequently claimed as "probably destroyed."

When Watson was not flying, some members of his crew were occasionally "borrowed" by other captains. On 2 October 1943 Surrender Berry and flight engineer Roy Clive Eames were detailed to fly with another captain during minelaying operations in the Frisian Islands. Watson remained on duty until the aircraft had returned safely with "his" boys. Both men were moved and impressed by Watson's concern for their safety.

On the night of 26/27 April 1944, Watson took off in Lancaster ND781 (code letter "R"), briefed to attack Friedrichshafen. At about 0130 hours, while en route to the target, and flying at 17,000 feet a little south of Strasbourg, they were attacked by a night fighter. This was driven off, but further attacks continued, evidently by a second fighter, and the bomber sustained increasing damage. The rear gunner, Flight Sergeant Murdock Daniel MacKinnon (RCAF), subsequently reported that his turret was knocked out; 30 seconds later the starboard wing and starboard inner engine were set on fire. Watson maintained control but efforts to fight the fire were unsuccessful and he ordered the crew to abandon the aircraft.

The first account of what had happened came in August 1944 when F/O William Ransom, navigator of the doomed aircraft, wrote from POW camp:

On the night of 27th/28th April 1944 our aircraft was attacked northwest of Colmar and set on fire. The captain gave the order to abandon aircraft. The civilian authorities at Colmar told me that the body of F/L Watson was found in the wreckage of the aircraft. I did not identify the body, but they said he was going to be buried in a village near Colmar. Would you please bring to the notice of my Commanding Officer the fact that it was due to F/L Watson remaining at the controls until the crew had left that their lives were saved. As the last member left it was obviously too low for F/L Watson to have left the aircraft.

The above was communicated (without comment) to his father, Major R.S. Watson, MC, on 21 September 1944. On 26 September 1944 the father wrote to RCAF Headquarters. In passing he stated:

A book has been written by one of his friends and dedicated to my son. The book covers the story of Jim and his crew and entitled "For Those Who Wait and Wait." It has been passed by the censor and has received permission from the Royal Air Force authorities in England, and is now in the hands of the publishers. *

Meanwhile, Ransom made another statement from POW camp, 15 November 1944; it read, in part:

Our aircraft was attacked north of (censored) and went out of control. F/L Watson gave the order to abandon aircraft. F/L Watson was uninjured in the attack. I was third to leave the aircraft and saw F/L Watson still trying to control the aircraft while the rest of the crew abandoned it.

Also on 15 November 1944, P/O R. Wilson made a similar statement:

Our aircraft was attacked west of (censored) and was set on fire. F/L Watson gave the order to abandon. I was last but one to leave the aircraft and saw F/L Watson at the controls. He was uninjured at that time. The aircraft crashed near (censored).

---

* The book, eventually published in Dublin, was actually titled *For Those Who Wait: A Story for Bomber Crew Next-of-Kin.*

Flight Lieutenant Surrender Berry, whose book, though still unpublished, was known to Watson's father and dedicated to Watson himself, had returned to operations with No. 622 Squadron in July 1944. He soon learned the bare bones of the story, including the survival of most of the crew as POWs and that Watson had "sacrificed his own chances of survival in order to ensure the safety of the crew" – something that did not surprise him, given his earlier assessment of Watson's character. He described his role in the campaign that followed:

I approached Wing Commander Swales about this matter when I returned to the squadron in July 1944; my point was in view of F/O Ransom's letter. He informed me that he would like to see justice and honour done to one so gallant but the full facts could not be made known until the war was over and the testimony of each crew member pieced together.

Berry could do little so long as the principal witnesses were still POWs, but once hostilities had ceased he met as many as he could and requested affidavits describing what had happened. These were supplied by Flying Officer Ransom (navigator), Pilot Officer W.H. Russell (wireless operator), Warrant Officer MacKinnon (the RCAF rear gunner), Flight Sergeant R.J. Hayes (the mid-upper gunner, commissioned while in captivity) and Flight Sergeant Roy Eames (flight engineer). Their stories fitted neatly together into a narrative of confusion on the part of the crew, calm determination of the part of Watson. All agreed that their pilot, by voice and example, had steadied them as they prepared to bale out. He was, at the same time, maintaining a minimum of control through intense physical efforts, keeping the control column pressed tightly on his chest. Amid this chaos, two of the crew (Eames and Hayes) reported that the rear gunner was still in his turret. Indeed, MacKinnon had no contact with the rest of the aircraft and crew, but he did eventually bale out. However, nobody, including Watson, knew that. Eames, in part of his deposition, wrote:

At this time, the rear gunner was out of communication with the rest of the crew, but I heard bursts of machine gun fire from his turret. I saw that the rear of the aircraft was badly damaged and I thought that the rear gunner must have been injured

Throughout the combat, Flight Lieutenant Watson repeatedly asked for news of the rear gunner and assured us that he would look after him; I think his exact words were, "Whatever happens, he'll be O.K."

I told the skipper that his turret was still moving, but that was the only indication we had that he was alive. The damage caused by the second attack had damaged the call light communication.

The flight engineer described his subsequent bale-out, capture, and meeting several members of the crew. The last he encountered was MacKinnon, and it was a surprise:

I learned that I was to be taken to Stalag Luft VI, and on the day before my departure, I met the rear gunner, MacKinnon. Seeing him gave me a severe shock as I had convinced myself that he had been killed. We still could not have any conversation and left within a few hours of seeing him for Stalag Luft VI in East Prussia. Later I met here the rear gunner, the bombardier and the mid-upper gunner, and at last we were able to discuss the matter. Of course this was done in all security and I learned from the mid-upper gunner that F/L Watson had been killed in the crash. Hayes had learned this information at Colmar where he had been shown F/L Watson's ring and identity bracelet. The rear gunner confirmed that he had baled out unbeknown to pilot and crew. I realised at once the significance of the Captain's words when enquiring of the rear gunner during the combat, when we all had the impression that he was injured.

The words, "He'll be O.K." and with horror I realised that F/L Watson would not leave that aircraft while there was the slightest doubt that a member of the crew remained in the aircraft and as a last resort would attempt a crash landing to save that member of his crew.

It is quite clear that F/L Watson sacrificed his life knowingly and willingly to ensure the safety of his crew. His most courageous act, his great and noble sacrifice in the face of the enemy was beyond the highest ideals of his duty and merits the highest possible award for gallantry and for valour in the face of the enemy.

I recommend him for the Victoria Cross.

Hayes, the mid-upper gunner, told a similar story of confusion. At the point of baling out, he plugged into the intercom system opposite the rear exit, informed Watson that he was leaving and told him the rear gunner was still in his turret.

I would let him [the rear gunner] know we were getting out. The captain's last words to me were, "Yes, O.K., but hurry, we're at 4,500 feet. If he's (referring to the rear gunner) not hit he might make it. So long, Ron, good luck."

I opened the bulkhead door leading to the rear turret and saw the rear gunner turn his head towards me. I patted my parachute to indicate that we were baling out and as he turned away I assumed that he understood and would bale out.

I estimate the height of the aircraft at about 4,000 feet when I baled out. F/L Watson had the aircraft under perfect control, it was still losing height in a sinking fashion and the flames had enveloped the fuselage alongside the burning wing.

Hayes evaded capture for a day but was eventually taken prisoner. Like Eames, in his deposition he described how he eventually pieced together what had happened, including his role in the drama:

I was taken away by two Luftwaffe Intelligence officers to Colmar gaol where they interrogated me. After the usual questions I was asked if I would help them in a matter of identification. An officer emptied the contents of an envelope on a table. The contents of that envelope were the personal belongings of F/L Watson. They consisted of his identification bracelet, a ring. I remember he told me that his father had given it to him.

The Germans said they had taken the articles from a dead pilot, a Flight Lieutenant, who was found dead in the pilot's seat of a Lancaster. I said nothing to them for fear that it might be the beginning of a long interrogation and I also knew that the identity bracelet was sufficient.

At Colmar in a cell I thought about it and formed the opinion that the pilot, F/L Watson, had died in an attempt to save the rear gunner. He had attempted to execute a crash landing. At Colmar I saw Russell, Ransom and Eames, three members of the crew. We did not speak to each other thinking of the German methods of hidden microphones and after our removal to Dulag Luft the usual routine of the German Gestapo methods followed. I and Eames were taken to Stalag Luft VI. Ransom and Russell, being officers, were separated from us and we had not the opportunity of talking to them in secret. On our way to Stalag Luft VI I learned from Eames, the Engineer, that he had seen MacKinnon the rear gunner arrive the day before and had received quite a shock because we both thought that he too had been killed. My mind wandered back to my conversation with the pilot before I baled out. I realised the pilot thought him to be wounded and I realized from his conversation that his crash landing was a most deliberate attempt to save the life of the rear gunner.

When MacKinnon arrived later at the same camp, he told me that he had baled out without being able to inform the captain; his intercom and call light were both unserviceable.

I knew then that due to my report to the captain before baling out I had unwittingly left him the impression that Flight Sergeant MacKinnon was still in his turret and the captain had attempted a forced landing in terrible conditions in an attempt to save the life of the rear gunner.

Throughout every operation I flew with Watson, I recognised in him an inspiring standard of leadership and a man who possessed the most heroic qualities of courage. His quiet manner, his ability to avoid panic at the most terrifying moments saved us in many previous actions. There were many combats and actions in previous operations I flew with him, and although in these we had always emerged as the victors, I knew it would not have been possible without the leadership of our captain.

F/L Watson was a most conscientious captain and his sense of responsibility towards his crew was almost overwhelming. The responsibility of a bomber pilot in the event of an emergency was for the safety of his crew. His duty, however, did not go to the point of having to die for his crew in the circumstances I have outlined. His magnificent display of valour in the most adverse circumstances is unsurpassable. His devotion to duty is unsurpassable. He gave his life and he could not do more than make his most glorious attempt to save the life of the rear gunner. Knowing Watson as my captain for several months, I know it would be unthinkable to him *that he should bale out believing that a member of the crew remained in the aircraft, although he would have been fully justified in so doing and saving his own life.*

For his devotion beyond the line of duty, for his valour against the enemy, I recommend that F/L J.A. Watson of the RCAF be awarded the Victoria Cross.

Evidently, Watson's father was informed in general terms about these affidavits, for he wrote Air Force Headquarters (Ottawa) again on 6 September 1945. He recapitulated some of Ransom's earlier correspondence, then added:

I have also been advised by each of the members of my son's crew that they all made a report recommending him for a decoration. Would it be possible to have a copy of these reports for purpose of record?

This inquiry was passed to RCAF Overseas Headquarters and Air Ministry. Their reply is not on file, but on 9 November 1945 a letter was sent from RCAF Overseas Headquarters to AFHQ, quoting Air Ministry as follows:

I am directed to inform you that no such recommendation has been received by this Department. In any case, such information is strictly confidential and would not, in any circumstances be divulged.

Although Surrender Berry was industrious in pushing the case for a VC to Watson, and almost certainly was instrumental in rounding up the various affidavits, it appears that the process stalled within Bomber Command itself. No citation was ever drafted and the appropriate Air Ministry committee never considered the case. It is doubtful that a submission would have succeeded, for as has already been noted, self-sacrifice by pilots was actually so frequent that awards of a VC in such circumstances would have diluted the value of the honour. Flight Lieutenant Watson was eventually awarded a Mention in Despatches on 21 February 1947.

Flight Lieutenant Watson's family would have sympathized with that of Flying Officer Charles Edward "Pat" Porter. Even before his death, Porter was noted for courage. His commanding officer, Wing Commander M.M.

Fleming, described him as being "inclined to be too dashing as a pilot and should temper this attitude with more caution and judgement." On the night of 27 March 1943, Porter was piloting Halifax DT634 of No. 419 Squadron, part of a bomber force raiding Berlin. It did not return. Telegrams were despatched almost immediately to next-of-kin, advising them that their sons were missing. Better news soon followed; all but one of the crew had survived and been taken prisoner. The exception was Porter.

Word of his fate got back to Canada quickly. On 2 April, Flying Officer G.E. Sweanor wrote to his parents:

Look where they've got me now ! We were brought down March 27th on the return leg from Berlin. We were hit by flak and then a night fighter. The kite started to burn. Both escape hatches were jammed , so we had to chop our way out. Pat could have got out himself, but wrestled with the controls while we tried to hack our way out. I was the last one out. Pat was too late and burned with the machine. I am all right; the rest of the crew are slightly wounded. We are all here together and are moving today to a permanent camp.

Pat is buried on the outskirts of Hamburg. I wish you would write his mother at Manson Creek, B.C. and let her know how he saved our lives.

Sweanor wrote his parents again on 16 May, telling much the same story in greater detail.

I lost one of the finest pals I ever had when Pat was killed. I was bomb aimer and second pilot in the crew and the last one to see Pat alive. We were hit by a night fighter on the return leg from Berlin. The aircraft immediately started to burn. Both escape hatches were jammed shut by cannon fire so we had to chop our way out with an axe. Meanwhile Pat was doing a superb job at the controls. Most of us had been hit by pieces of cannon shell. When we finally managed to chop an exit I went back to Pat telling him to follow me out. By this time our four engines had cut and we were losing height rapidly. My chute barely jerked open when I hit the ground. When I was captured the next night I was told Pat had crashed with the machine. It had crashed a short distance from me but I was hoping against hope that Pat had got out. His death was quick and the way he would have wanted it – to go in with his ship. His magnificent handling of the controls when we were blazing furiously saved our lives at the cost of his own.

The Sweanor family did more than write to Porter's parents; they also contacted Air Force Headquarters in Ottawa, pointing out the pilot's heroism. Correspondence between AFHQ and RCAF Overseas Headquarters (London) discussed the possibilities of bestowing a posthumous award on Porter. Wing Commander Fleming himself wrote on the matter, observing:

I am of the opinion that F/O Porter's actions in saving the lives of his crew at the cost of his own, warrants official recognition.

During the period which he spent with this squadron he was a tremendous asset. His cheerful manner and fine offensive spirit coupled with his everlasting desire to attack the enemy held the admiration of the entire unit.

However I have discussed the subject of an award with the Station Commander and we find that we have only hearsay evidence emanating from a POW camp, and as the only two awards which can be made under the circumstances must be supported by evidence of a more definite character, vide BC/323190/P Para 4 and the Air Force List July 1943 section 2851, therefore it is felt that a recommendation from this quarter unsupported by higher authority could not be considered.

The officer commanding the base (and Fleming's superior) evidently did not believe an award could be supported, given the lack of further evidence. Further discussion in Britain may have taken place, but the final document on Porter's case was a letter dated 15 April 1944 from RCAF Overseas Headquarters to RCAF Headquarters in Ottawa. It read in part:

No effort has been spared on the part of this Headquarters to collect any evidence which would enable a recommendation for a suitable award to be made posthumously. Attached hereto, copies of correspondence dealing with the investigation.

A scrutiny of the letter from the squadron will reveal that the CO does not consider the evidence sufficient to substantiate consideration of either of the two awards which could be made under the circumstance.

Recommendations must, in all cases, originate with the CO concerned and Air Ministry as well as this Headquarters are not in a position to "prod" Commanding Officers in this respect. Such cases as the one in question have always been a problem to Air Ministry. It is very unfortunate that the authorities could not see "eye to eye" with Air Ministry when proposals were made to put lesser awards than the Victoria Cross in the "posthumous awards" class.

On 1 January 1945, Flying Officer Porter was posthumously Mentioned in Despatches. Again, given that bomber pilots seemed to have "self-sacrifice" written into the job description, it is improbable that any higher award could have been obtained.

Lest anyone imagine that RCAF personnel were the only aircrew unsuccessfully recommended for Victoria Crosses, the example of Warrant Officer Frank Vernon Watkins, Royal New Zealand Air Force, bears recounting. A pilot in No. 156 Squadron, he was killed in action of the night of 20/21 December 1942. The manner of his death reached England soon afterwards, in letters from surviving crewmen who had been taken prisoner. On 20 February 1943, his commanding officer submitted a recommendation for the Victoria Cross:

In reference to the consequence of a bombing raid on Duisburg on the night of 20/21 December 1942, a letter forwarded by Squadron Leader John Carter, DFC, now a prisoner of war at Stalag Luft III in Germany, is attached. In support of the opinion given by Squadron Leader Carter, the following recommendation is made:-

Firstly, it should be appreciated that Squadron Leader Carter himself is an extremely experienced operational navigator, who has on many occasions returned from operations in crippled aircraft, and that the forced parachute descent he made on the occasion referred to is the third he has made during active service in this war. His cool judgement and opinion of the behaviour of his captain on this occasion can therefore be vouched for without any doubt.

Warrant Officer Watkins joined this squadron on 1st December 1942 as a specially selected crew for pathfinder duties from No. 1 Group, where he had proved himself as an above the average captain. During his service with this squadron he displayed the highest sense of responsibility and absolute devotion to duty.

This final record of his unquestionable and unequalled courage in the face of death is considered worthy of the highest award that can be made by His Majesty the King.

Finally, it should be noted that from the evidence of this letter that Warrant Officer Watkins displayed the highest qualities as a captain of aircraft. Firstly, he ordered those members of the crew who could be of no further assistance to him to bale out, and then waited until the last moment before he ordered the navigator to bale out, when in his own mind he considered that he would be forced to make a crash landing. It would appear that at no time did the question of his own safety enter Warrant Officer Watkins' mind.

Group Captain H.J. Kirkpatrick, Officer Commanding Station Wyton, added his comments the same day.

I heartily endorse the Squadron Commander's recommendation that the highest award be granted Warrant Officer Watkins.

It is clear that he went to his death in an attempt to land knowing full well the heavy odds against his doing so in a badly damaged aircraft, in enemy territory, and at night, but hoping that the Bombardier might after all be alive, and that he might possibly effect a landing and thereby save his comrade's life. This act of unselfish sacrifice, cool devotion to duty and astonishing courage, in my opinion deserves the highest recognition by the award of the Victoria Cross.[99]

The matter of an award was weighed at the time and again upon the cessation of hostilities. Ultimately, Watkins was accorded a posthumous Mention in Despatches (*London Gazette*, 13 June 1946). The initial reasoning in 1943 had been that an award should be delayed pending further evidence. However, in light of other failed VC nominations involving pilots going down with their aircraft, we can see that the Watkins nomination was bound to fail. There had been just too many men like him to give a VC to all.

CHAPTER 7

NOT IN THE FACE
OF THE ENEMY

Courage is fear holding on a minute longer.

General George S. Patton (1885-1945)

I n August 1858 the warrant of the Victoria Cross was amended to allow awards in "cases of conspicuous courage and bravery displayed under circumstances of danger but not before the enemy." The change
had been brought about as a result of publicity surrounding a fire aboard
a troopship, the *Sarah Sands,* in November 1857 which had been marked by
great heroism on the part of soldiers aboard the vessel. The War Office, having allowed this amendment to the warrant, almost instantly regretted the
change and did its best *not* to publicize it. Nevertheless, six Victoria Crosses
were awarded for valour notwithstanding the absence of an enemy. One of
these went to Private Timothy O'Hea for fighting a fire in an ammunition
railway car near Danville, Quebec, in 1866 – the only Victoria Cross action
ever performed on Canadian soil. Another non-combat VC also had a Canadian connection – that to Assistant Surgeon Campbell Mellis Douglas, 24th
Regiment, who had been born in Canada, joined the British army, and in
1867 was instrumental (with four others) in rescuing stranded soldiers from
Little Andaman Island (Bay of Bengal) in spite of storm-lashed seas. Douglas subsequently returned to Canada and served in the Northwest Rebellion
campaign of 1885, but ultimately settled in Britain.[100]

Amendments in 1881 to the Victoria Cross warrant eliminated the clause
that had allowed the "absence of the enemy" awards. Nevertheless, M.J. Crook
points out that a few First World War VC awards were made "where the pres-

ence of the enemy was virtually irrelevant." These involved cases of soldiers who threw themselves on *British* grenades or mortar bombs that had been dropped or fallen short – situations which, in the Second World War, might have brought a George Cross rather than a Victoria Cross.[101] The irony is that grenade accidents *in France* might bring a Victoria Cross; grenade accidents *in Britain* might result in award of an Albert Medal.[102] This anomaly was to be found in other decorations, the Distinguished Flying Cross and Air Force Cross (both created in 1918). Aircrew engaged in anti-submarine flying from *French* bases occasionally were rewarded with a Distinguished Flying Cross; their Britain-based counterparts on the other side of the English Channel received Air Force Crosses.

For a time the "non-combat" Victoria Cross co-existed with another award, comparable in all but prestige. This was the Albert Medal, created in March 1866. Initially it was to be awarded to those who had engaged in life-saving at sea, whether successful or not, where the recipients had "endangered their own lives." In 1877 the terms of reference were extended to include acts of bravery on land. The Albert Medal existed in two classes, but the standard of bravery was extremely high for both. The essential feature of the Albert Medal was its *life-saving* aspect; another type of brave act (such as disarming an armed robber) would lie outside the terms of this award. Both service and civilian personnel were eligible to receive the Albert Medal. An example of a service Albert Medal (Second Class) was that of Able Seaman John Barber, whose deed was described in the *London Gazette* of 20 December 1889:

Assistant Surgeon Campbell Mellis Douglas was Canadian born but in British service when he was awarded the VC for bravery when *not* under fire at Little Andaman Island, Bay of Bengal, 1867. (Canadian War Museum C.33776)

*Her Majesty's Ship "Lily" was wrecked off Armour Point, Forteau Bay,
coast of Labrador on the 16th May, 1889, and seven of her crew were
drowned. After her boats had capsized, and although it was known that
two of the crew had drowned near the same spot in attempting to effect
communication with the shore, John Barber, A.B., volunteered to swim
with a line through the surf, which he successfully accomplished, enabling
a four-inch hawser to be hauled ashore, whereby communication was
established and the rest of the crew saved.*

*The service was one of great risk and gallantry, the bottom being rocky,
and their being at the time a dense fog with an ebb tide and a considerable swell.*[103]

Just as the earliest Albert Medals existed alongside the "non-combat"
Victoria Cross, from 1940 to 1971 they co-existed with the George Cross. A
total of 568 Albert Medals (both classes and many of them posthumous)
were awarded in its 105-year history, of which 269 were to civilians. In the
568 total, 28 went to Canadians (including pre-Confederation Newfound-
landers) or persons performing their deeds in Canada or Newfoundland.
The Halifax Explosion of 6 December 1917 resulted in no fewer than six Albert Medals being awarded, four of them posthumously. The line between
the Albert Medal and the George Cross was fine enough that when Flying
Officer Roderick Borden Gray was being considered for a posthumous award
in 1944, the initial proposal was for an Albert Medal, although a George
Cross was eventually bestowed.[104]

While the Albert Medal might appear to have been a straightforward
award with no combat connotations, at least two were awarded in circumstances that demonstrate the occasional artificiality of distinctions between
military and civilian valour. The official announcement was exceptionally
vivid:

Whitehall, June 13, 1910
*The King has been pleased to approve of the Albert Medal of the First
Class being conferred upon Mr. Charles Wagner, and the Albert Medal of
the Second Class being conferred upon Mr. Alexander James Stewart, both
of Pietermaritzburg, for gallantry in saving life, as detailed below:-*

On the 15th November, 1899, near Chieveley Station, in Natal, an armoured train which had been sent out on patrol was intercepted by the Boers and three carriages were thrown off the line. These vehicles lay between the train and the rest of the track over which it must travel on its homeward journey, and until they were removed the train, its engine and its escort – about 150 men – were exposed to a severe converging fire of rifles and artillery from the surrounding hills.

The sole means by which the line could be cleared was the engine, which moving too and fro butted at the wreckage until after about 50 minutes' work it was heaved and pushed off the track. The part played by the driver of the engine, Charles Wagner, and by the fireman, Alexander James Stewart, was therefore indispensable to the rescue of the wounded with whom the engine and its tender became crowded. The working of the engine itself was a difficult matter, because at each collision with the wreckage at which it was butting it might easily have been derailed.

The danger was exceptional. The heavy fire of shells and bullets inflicted many casualties, and more than a quarter of all in the train were killed or wounded. The shells repeatedly struck the engine and at any moment might have exploded the boiler. The driver, a civilian, under no military code, was wounded severely in the scalp by a shell splinter almost immediately. Although in great pain he did not fail during the whole of this affair to manage his engine skilfully, and by clearing the line saved from death and wounds a proportion at least of the 50 or 60 persons who effected their escape upon the engine and its tender.

Both the driver and his fireman are still in the service of the Natal Government Railways.[105]

This award, more than ten years after the events described, was one of the few instances where we can track political influence – and who is to say that politics are automatically corrupt? The account drew heavily on the eyewitness testimony of a newspaper reporter who was present at the ambush, helped organized the defence and, but for his civilian status, might well have been recommended for (though not necessarily awarded) the Victoria Cross. As a cabinet minister in 1909, he was instrumental in pushing the Wagner and Stewart awards to the fore. The reporter's name was Winston Churchill.[106]

The Albert Medal aside, another medal for extreme bravery existed between 1907 and 1971: the Edward Medal. It was established to recognize courage in mining accidents and extended in 1909 to cover industrial accidents. Like the Albert Medal, it was in two classes; its terms of reference were similar – that it should be awarded to persons who endangered their lives while saving others. In practice, the degree of risk and probability of death was not so high as with the Albert Medal, and 584 such awards were made in both grades (five of them for incidents in Canada).[107]

One further gallantry medal with very high standards existed between 1922 and 1940. The Order of the British Empire had been created (in numerous grades) in 1917, including a British Empire Medal (BEM) which was awarded chiefly for services more akin to clerkship than to hazardous occupations. Nevertheless, in 1922 a Medal of the Order, for Gallantry, was created. Better known as the Empire Gallantry Medal (EGM), it was open to both civilian and military personnel and ultimately 130 such awards were made (64 to civilians, 62 to military and 4 honorary issues to Europeans).

The standards of the EGM were not clearly defined in its warrant, but in practice it was bestowed in cases of considerable peril. Thus, two brothers (Edward and James Letch) received it posthumously for attempting to rescue a Royal Air Force pilot from a burning airplane on 4 September 1938. In 1940 all living recipients of EGMs, Albert Medals and Edward Medals were invited to exchange them for George Crosses. This conversion affected only one Canadian, Aircraftman First Class Ernest Ralph Clyde Frost of Trois Rivières, who had enlisted directly in the Royal Air Force in 1938 as an aircraft mechanic. On 12 March 1940, with another mechanic, he entered a crashed and burning aircraft to rescue anyone who might have survived, notwithstanding the risk of exploding fuel tanks. The two men dragged out the pilot (the sole occupant) shortly before the tanks blew up and the aircraft was consumed by fire. Unfortunately, the pilot died in spite of their efforts. The EGM to Frost was announced on 5 July 1940. Like Frost, most persons invited to exchange EGMs for George Crosses agreed quickly to a conversion, but a New Zealander, Michael S. Keough (whose Albert Medal dated from 1916), waited until 1972 to make the exchange.

When war came directly to Great Britain in 1940, King George VI and Prime Minister Winston Churchill recognized that the distinction between civilian and soldier had been blurred even more. To properly reward those engaged in battling fires, rescuing people from wrecked buildings and disarming unexploded bombs, the George Cross and George Medal were created on 24 September 1940. Both were open to civilian as well as military personnel, but only the George Cross could be awarded posthumously, and it quickly became established as the second-highest gallantry award in the Empire and Commonwealth. It was to be awarded for "acts of the greatest heroism or of the most conspicuous courage in circumstances of extreme danger" (the warrant for the George Medal specified only "acts of great bravery").

Doubtless there were many cases where authorities agonized over whether a George Cross or George Medal should be granted. One must compare original recommendations with final awards to see which were altered, up or down, and the submissions are difficult to trace. Nevertheless, we know that the George Medal awarded to Flight Lieutenant George Clayton Abel, RCAF, began as a recommendation for a George Cross. He returned to a burning aircraft on 27 November 1943 to rescue the trapped rear gunner. It is not clear where the submission was downgraded from a GC to a GM, although the reasons may have been lack of due diligence in gathering eyewitness accounts.[108] Such was not the case with Captain

Flight Lieutenant George Clayton Abel was recommended for a George Cross and awarded a George Medal instead for his rescue of a comrade from a burning aircraft. (Canadian War Museum C-36192)

Herbert William Mulherin. His superiors went to considerable pains to gather evidence to substantiate a George Cross, yet a George Medal only was approved. Mulherin's deed was so horrendous that only the original recommendation can do it justice:

On 16 October 1944 at 1605 hours a Spitfire bomber crashed with a full load immediately after taking off from Rimini aerodrome. Captain Herbert William Mulherin, Princess Patricia's Canadian Light Infantry, with his driver K.52216 Private Frederick Charles Smalley, Royal Canadian Army Service Corps, were driving along a highway bordering the aerodrome at the moment of the crash. Captain Mulherin and his driver immediately ran to the scene of the crash where they found the aircraft on fire and the pilot, Lieutenant W.J. Anthony, 1 South African Air Force Squadron, 7 Wing, Desert Air Force, slumped unconscious in the cockpit. Without hesitation and although he had seen the bomb under the aircraft before it crashed and knew the danger of its exploding in the heat of the flames, this officer endeavoured to extricate the unconscious pilot. He found him to be jammed in the cockpit by his parachute harness which he managed to undo. By this time the heat of the flames was almost unbearable and the aircraft ammunition was exploding. Without thought for his own safety Captain Mulherin persisted in his efforts to free the air-

Captain Herbert William Mulherin was recommended for a George Cross after his rescue of a South African pilot from a burning Spitfire but was awarded a George medal instead. (Canadian War Museum C-47224)

man. He found that one foot of the pilot was jammed in the controls and now the clothing around the pilot's leg was on fire. This army officer then reaching into the cockpit had his right hand and his face badly burned by a gust of petrol flame, but by a superhuman effort managed to pull the unconscious pilot free. He then beat out the pilot's burning clothes and he and his driver carried him to safety, still unconscious, whence he was evacuated to a medical installation. By his prompt action and resolute courage in the face of extreme danger Captain Mulherin saved the life of the pilot as the aeroplane was totally destroyed by fire. This deed is worthy of the highest praise and admiration by the Canadian Army in Italy.[109]

Even while retaining the British system of gallantry awards, Canada gained increasing control over recommendations, assessments and conclusions respecting awards, particularly when Canadians were not operating under a British command structure (as when they were performing their deeds in Canada or later within a NORAD context). By 1947 the line of communication was from Canadian authorities to the Governor General and then to the King, without reference to British officers or committees.* In the case of some honours, notably the Air Force Cross and British Empire Medal, Canadian authorities imposed even more stringent standards for awards than were found either in Britain or elsewhere in the Commonwealth. In the case of awards made for gallantry alone, it is gratifying to find cases where Canadian committees were as rigorous in applying standards as similar bodies in the United Kingdom may have been. The example of an award to Lieutenant Douglas A. Muncaster demonstrates this approach.

In the spring of 1955, Royal Canadian Navy officers recommended Muncaster for a George Cross. On 9 March 1955 he had been co-pilot of a helicopter involved in rescuing the pilot of a downed Sea Fury fighter. The recommendation read, in part:

The helicopter could not land owing to the density of the trees and undergrowth. The pilot, therefore, hovered about fifty yards from the aircraft, where the woods were more sparse, while Lieutenant Muncaster jumped to the ground from a height of about eight feet. As Lieutenant Muncaster ran towards the wreckage, one of the fuel tanks exploded. On nearing the forward section of the aircraft, from sound inside the cockpit, he realized that the pilot was alive. The perspex canopy of the cockpit was resting on the ground and the pilot was pinned inside. Being unable to open the canopy or break the perspex with his hands or feet, Lieutenant Muncaster found a rock and smashed a hole in it. By this time the flames had reached the cockpit and there was imminent danger of the remaining fuel tanks exploding. The pilot was able to push his head and shoulders through the

---

* During the Korean War, however, awards to members of 25 Canadian Infantry Brigade were filtered through the General Officer Commanding, 1 Commonwealth Division and the Commander-in-Chief, British Commonwealth Forces Korea. RCAF and RCN awards in the same conflict went directly from Canadian ministers to the King (later Queen).

hole made in the canopy by Lieutenant Muncaster who, after considerable pulling, extricated Sub-Lieutenant Searle from the flaming cockpit and assisted him from the immediate vicinity of the aircraft. The remaining fuel tanks exploded a few minutes later.

On 12 May 1955 the Inter-Service Awards Committee of the Department of National Defence (a tri-service body) weighed the submission and concluded that a George Cross was "too high an award for recognition of the deed outlines in the attached citation." Nevertheless, the members ruled that his acts were "worthy of high recognition" and substituted a George Medal.[110]

A more emotionally charged submission in 1963 involved Warrant Officer Walter R. Leja, Royal Canadian Engineers, who was assigned to assist Montreal police in disposing of bombs planted by the Front de Liberation du Québec (FLQ). On 17 May, five such bombs exploded in mail boxes and Leja went into action. Two more were discovered and neutralized, but a third device exploded as he was working on it, critically injuring him. The General Officer Commanding, Quebec Command, recommended him for the George Cross but the Inter-Service Awards Committee finally concluded that the George Medal was appropriate. The members' rationale for this discussion

is not known.[111] Canadian authorities appear to have applied an extremely harsh standard for a George Cross, if one compares this instance with three cases of British personnel disarming IRA bombs: Police Constable Roger P. Good (1978), Warrant Officer Barry Johnson (1989) and Major Stephen G. Styles (October 1971). That to Consta-

Warrant Officer Walter Leja was critically injured while disarming an FLQ bomb in Montreal in 1963. He was recommended for a George Cross and awarded a George Medal. (Canadian War Museum C.44721)

ble Good was a posthumous award, but Warrant Officer Johnson suffered injuries comparable to those sustained by Leja, while Major Styles emerged unscathed from numerous assignments, including a nine-hour session to dismantle a bomb of previous unknown design.[112]

There were some wartime cases where the precise award to be bestowed could be debated – and was. On 16 February 1942, HM Submarine *Thrasher*, having sunk a freighter near Crete, came under fierce air and naval attack which lasted more than three hours. When *Thrasher* finally surfaced, her tormentors were gone but two unexploded 100-pound bombs were lodged in the hull. Petty Officer Thomas William Gould and Lieutenant Peter Scawen Watkinson Roberts volunteered to dispose of these missiles.

The first bomb was easily pried loose, wrapped in a potato sack, and dropped overboard, where it detonated a safe distance away. The second bomb was wedged in far more tightly between the outer and inner hulls, which compelled them to work in a very confined space. Had the submarine been forced to dive again during the extraction, the two men would have been drowned. It took them 40 minutes to get it out, and as they gingerly manhandled it to the deck they could hear a ticking noise coming from the bomb. It was finally dropped over the side in the same manner as the first.

Admiral Sir Andrew Cunningham (Commander-in-Chief Mediterranean) recommended Gould and Roberts for the Victoria Cross. Authorities in London argued that no enemy had been present, and hence a George Cross was more appropriate. Cunningham, however, would not budge, declaring that the two bombs and the proximity of an enemy coastline were enemy enough. Their Victoria Crosses were gazetted on 9 June 1942.[113]

The artificiality of the line between "combat" and "non-combat" was never so evident as in August 1942 when the tanker *Ohio* reached Malta after running a hellish gauntlet of bombs and submarine attacks that had sunk 9 of the 14 ships in the convoy, as well as taking the carrier HMS *Eagle*. As a tanker, the *Ohio* was both the most vital and the most vulnerable vessel, a fact that the enemy fully appreciated. In four days the ship was struck once by a torpedo; two sticks of bombs exploding nearby lifted her out of the water, a bomb exploded in the boiler room and a Stuka dive bomber crashed on her deck. The *Ohio* was twice abandoned and twice reboarded. When she reached Malta on the 15th she was literally being carried by two destroyers that had been lashed to the vessel. On behalf of the entire crew, Captain Dudley William Mason (Merchant Navy) was awarded the George Cross with the following citation:

> *During the passage to Malta of an important convoy Captain Mason's ship suffered most violent onslaught. She was a focus of attack throughout and was torpedoed early one night. Although gravely damaged, her engines were kept going and the Master made a magnificent passage by hand-steering and without a compass. The ship's gunners helped to bring down one of the attacking aircraft. The vessel was hit again before morning, but though she did not sink, her engine room was wrecked. She was then towed. The unwieldy condition of the vessel and persistent enemy attacks made progress slow, and it was uncertain whether she would remain afloat. All next day progress somehow continued and the ship reached Malta after a further night at sea.*
>
> *The violence of the enemy could not deter the Master from his purpose. Throughout he showed skill and courage of the highest order and it was due to his determination that, in spite of the most persistent enemy opposition, the vessel, with her valuable cargo, eventually reached Malta and was safely berthed.*

This was gallantry "not in the face of the enemy"? The pat answer that, as a civilian master, Captain Mason was not entitled to a military award such as the VC does not fully ring true. The Victoria Cross warrants have always allowed the bestowal of crosses on civilians *operating under military direction,* and in its history it has been so awarded five times (to a civil servant operating as a courier and spy in 1857, another civil servant evacuating refugees in 1857, a third civil servant rescuing a wounded soldier in 1857, a civilian volunteer in 1858, and a clergyman saving a soldier from drowning in 1879). All the same, a George Cross is nothing at which to turn up one's nose.

The line between "combat" and "non-combat" gallantry was equally arbitrary in the cases of awards to personnel operating in clandestine warfare, where capture by the enemy meant almost certain death – and a horrible one at that. Consider the following cases:

Assistant Section Officer Noor Inayat-Khan (Women's Auxiliary Air Force, seconded to Special Operations Executive or SOE). Despite her East Asian appearance, she was flown into France on 16 June 1943 to serve as a radio operator. When the Gestapo began making mass arrests in her area, she was offered the opportunity to return to England, but she declined. She was finally betrayed by a French national and was taken prisoner on 13 November 1943 with her assistant and her wireless set. The Germans hoped that she could be used to send false messages back to London, but she refused; indeed, she was considered a particularly uncooperative and dangerous prisoner. Even in captivity, word of her fortitude had reached Britain, where recommendations were circulated for a George Medal or an MBE, neither of which were awarded. While these decorations were being discussed, Noor Inayat-Khan endured months of torture and interrogation, unimaginable to those in London. She arrived at Dachau on 12 September 1944 and was shot the next day and cremated.

Major Hugh Paul Seagrim (Indian Army, attached to Special Operations Executive or SOE). Major Seagrim was the leader of a party that included two other British and one Karen officer, operating in the Karen Hills (Burma), from February 1943 to February 1944. Towards the end of 1943 their presence became known to the Japanese, who started a widespread campaign of arrests and torture to discover their whereabouts. In February 1944 the other two British officers were ambushed and killed, but Major Seagrim and the Karen officer escaped. The Japanese arrested 270 Karens, torturing and killing many, but the Karens continued to assist and shelter Major Seagrim. However, the enemy succeeded in getting a message to him saying that if he gave himself up, they would cease their reprisals. To prevent civilian suffering, he surrendered himself on 15 March 1944 although he was well aware of the horrors of Japanese captivity. He was taken to Rangoon and, with eight others, was sentenced to death. Major Seagrim pleaded that only he should die, as the others had only obeyed his orders, but such was the devotion he had inspired that they all expressed their willingness to die with him and they were executed on 22 September 1944.[114]

These two examples, drawn from many George Cross cases, demonstrate the artificiality of distinctions between combat and non-combat duties. The prisoner, whether man of woman, is not buoyed by any adrenalin rush such as that which bolsters a man in combat; the prisoner has little hope that his or her body will ever be found; scant expectation that any survivor will ever know of their ordeals. The person at the mercy of his or her captors does not even have the hope of a speedy end to prolonged and lonely suffering. When one looks for Canadians who were placed in such dire peril as the cases above, one finds Captain Frank Herbert Dedrich Pickersgill. On 15 September 1945, Major-General Sir Colin Gubbins recommended him for an award:

This officer was parachuted into France on 15th June 1943 as organizer of a circuit in the Ardennes. He was arrested by the Gestapo three days after his arrival and spent more than a year in Fresnes prison where he was tortured and ill-treated. He showed great courage and self-sacrifice in refusing to divulge under torture the names of his accomplices. He made a gallant effort to escape from gaol but, in addition to breaking his arm by jumping from a window, he was wounded and recaptured.

Having been deported to Germany in August 1944 he was hanged the following month at Buchenwald concentration camp.

For his great gallantry and endurance it is recommended that this officer be Mentioned in Despatches (posthumous).

Captain Pickersgill was accordingly Mentioned in Despatches. Lest we forget.[115]

A George Cross action during the 2003 Iraq War illustrates the peculiarity of awards even to this day. It concerned Trooper Christopher Finney, and the *London Gazette* of 30 October 2003 told his stirring tale:

On 28th March 2003 D Squadron Household Cavalry Regiment were probing forward along the Shatt-al-Arab waterway, north of Basra, some thirty kilometres ahead of the main force of 16 Air Assault Brigade. In exposed desert, their mission was to find and interdict the numerically vastly superior, and better equipped, Iraqi 6th Armoured Division.

Trooper Finney, a young armoured vehicle driver with less than a year's service, was driving the leading Scimitar vehicle of his troop, which had been at the forefront of action against enemy armour for several hours. In the early afternoon the two leading vehicles paused beside a levee to allow the troop leader to assess fully the situation in front. Without warning they were then engaged by a pair of Coalition Forces ground attack aircraft. Both vehicles were hit and caught fire and ammunition began exploding inside the turrets. Finney managed to get out of his driving position and was on the way towards cover when he noticed that his vehicle's gunner was trapped in the turret. He then climbed on to the fiercely burning vehicle, at the same time placing himself at risk from enemy fire, as well as fire from the aircraft, should they return. Despite the smoke and flames and exploding ammunition he managed to haul out the injured gunner, get him off the vehicle, and move him to a safer position not far away, where he bandaged his wounds.

The troop officer, in the other Scimitar, had been wounded and there were no senior ranks to take control. Despite his relative inexperience, the shock of the attack and the all-too-obvious risk to himself, Finney recognized the need to inform his headquarters of the situation. He therefore broke cover, returned to his vehicle, which was still burning, and calmly and concisely sent a lucid situation report by radio. He then returned to the injured gunner and began helping him towards a Spartan vehicle of the Royal Engineers which had moved to assist.

At this point Finney noticed that both the aircraft were lining up for a second attack. Notwithstanding the impending danger he continued to help his injured comrade towards the safety of the Spartan vehicle. Both aircraft fired their cannon and Finney was wounded in the lower back and legs and the gunner in the head. Despite his wounds, Finney succeeded in getting the gunner to the waiting Spartan. Then, seeing that the driver of the second Scimitar was still in the burning vehicle, Finney determined to rescue him as well. Despite his wounds and the continuing danger from exploding ammunition he valiantly attempted to climb up onto the vehicle but was beaten back by the combination of heat, smoke and exploding ammunition. He collapsed exhausted a short distance from the vehicle and was recovered by the crew of the Royal Engineers Spartan.

During these attacks and their horrifying aftermath, Finney displayed clear-headed courage and devotion to his comrades which was out of all *proportion to his age and experience. Acting with complete disregard for his own safety even when wounded, his bravery was of the highest order throughout.*

It may be noted that although the aircraft were "Coalition" machines, and thus "friendly" rather than "enemy," they made two very determined attacks during the incident and might be considered as hostile as any Iraqi fighter. Indeed, being "friendly" it would have been unwise even to attempt defence against their strafing. In the strictest legal sense, this was indeed a George Cross rather than a Victoria Cross action – but the contradictions and ironies of the case will not escape the reader.

As with the Victoria Cross, questions of "duty" vs. "valour" bedevil decisions as to who should be decorated and what will be the appropriate award. These extend even to current events. In January 2006 a coroner's inquest in London hailed Andy Bradsell (Victoria, British Columbia) and Christopher McDonald (Northern Ireland) as heroes. The men were security contractors in Iraq who, in March 2004, put their vehicle between a car carrying an electrical engineer under their protection and a swarm of insurgents. The engineer escaped while Bradsell and McDonald died in a hail of machine gun and rocket fire. "They protected the other vehicle and its passenger. They died in their efforts in the most heroic manner," wrote the coroner, which might point to an eventual George Cross. Yet the same official also noted, "They did precisely what they were trained to do in an impossible situation." Were they, then, brave mercenaries or heroic citizens? Somewhere, someday, it is likely that a committee will have to decide.[116]

CHAPTER 8

GALLANTRY WITH
A SUPPORTING CAST

Yet the best pilots have needs of mariners, besides sails, anchor and other tackle.

Ben Jonson (1573-1637)

A good tank is useless unless the team inside it is well trained, and the men in that team have stout hearts and enthusiasm for the fight.

Field Marshal Bernard Law Montgomery, *Some Notes on the Conduct of War and the Infantry Division in Battle* (pamphlet distributed within 21 Army Group, October 1944).

W hen Warrant Officer Andrew Mynarski went to save the rear gunner in his burning Lancaster bomber, there was no one to witness his courage except the gunner himself.* It was by sheer luck that Flying Officer George "Pat" Brophy survived and ironic misfortune that Mynarski acted in a way that brought about his own demise. It was also the most simple drama possible – one man trying to rescue another, with nobody around to watch. If both men had perished, there would have been no one to tell the tale. Brophy would have been just another charred body in a burned-out bomber, and Mynarski simply a Canadian wrapped in flames as he parachuted into French hands, to die minutes later in the agony reserved for burned men.[117]

---

* Elsewhere this writer has referred to Mynarski as "Pilot Officer," the rank that appears most commonly in writings and records, and on his tombstone. Nevertheless, he was wearing Warrant Officer badges on the night of 11/12 June 1944 (they would later help to identify him). His last act in the Lancaster was to stand at attention, his flying clothes on fire, say "Good night, sir," and salute before baling out. The gunner he had tried to rescue was an officer. Mynarski was commissioned in September 1944, the rank being retroactive to 10 June 1944.

Many brave men have perished like that – alone or with only dead comrades about, in exploding aircraft, burning tanks, flooding engine rooms – and their stories are forever lost. Most Victoria Cross actions (and comparable George Cross deeds) have been events with several (even many) others present – enemies, friends, strangers, witnesses and participants, some clearly entitled to awards of their own. When we draw back from such episodes, we can view the principal actor in the context of others playing out their roles.

The politics (or at least pressures) which lay behind Flight Lieutenant David Hornell's Victoria Cross have already been mentioned. Equally interesting is the array of individuals who were involved in the action that led to the rescue of his crew, the only persons who could testify as to just what happened.

No. 162 (Bomber Reconnaissance) Squadron had been despatched from Canada to Iceland in December 1943. It thus passed from the operational control of Canada's home-based Eastern Air Command to RAF Coastal Command. It was also placed in a position to hunt U-boats as they transited between Iceland and Scotland, inbound to and outbound from Norway. The unit scored its first success on 17 April 1944 when Flying Officer Tom Cooke and crew sank *U-342* southwest of Iceland. Several weeks of relative quiet followed, but early in June the Canadian crews, based at both Reykjavik (Iceland) and Wick (Scotland), had a run of encounters, with losses on both sides. It began on 3 June, when Flight Lieutenant Robert E. McBride and crew surprised and destroyed *U-477*. On the 11th, Flying Officer Lawrence S. Sherman and crew sank *U-980*, but only after a gun battle. Two days later, Wing Commander Cecil G.W. Chapman surprised and depth-charged *U-715*, inflicting fatal damage. As he swooped over again to photograph the sinking submarine, a German gunner in his turn fired a devastating burst of fire. The aircraft ditched and sank; Chapman and crew took to their dinghies but three men died before rescue. That same day (the 13th), Flying Officer Sherman's Canso failed to return; it had been shot down while attacking a U-boat and only one crewman survived.

When David Hornell and his crew took off from Wick on 24 June 1944, they knew of the fight that Chapman had faced and that Sherman was missing. At 1900 hours, cruising below a 1,500-foot cloud layer and in position 62° 00' north, 00° 30' west, Flight Sergeant Israel J. Bodnoff (one of the wireless operators/air gunners) sighted the wake of a submarine from the port gun blister. It was five miles away. Hornell banked and began running in for the attack. Unfortunately, he was approaching from the U-boat's stern, which the German commander was able to present to the Canso throughout the action, exposing Hornell to the heaviest of the anti-aircraft armament, against which he had scant recourse other than machine gun fire and limited manoeuvring of shallow dips and swoops.

The flak started when the Canso was 3,800 feet away and seemed to intensify during the attack. The aircraft returned fire from its nose guns, commencing at 3,500 feet, but one machine gun jammed. Then the enemy's shells began to register. Both wings were hit at 2,200 feet with large holes appearing. At 1,400 feet the crew noticed that the starboard engine was pouring oil and a fire had begun in that wing. Hornell and his co-pilot, Flying Officer Bernard C. Denomy, were fighting to control their machine, which was vibrating furiously. Denomy applied full boost to the port engine and shut down the starboard one. Meanwhile, Hornell continued to press home the attack.

Four 250-pound Torpex depth charges dropped away, spaced 90 feet apart and fused to explode 25 feet below the surface. In the blur of events it was difficult for anyone to assess their impact. The straddle appeared good, with one depth charge exploding close to port side of the hull, throwing the bows out of the water. Hornell and his crew were too busy now to observe these results, which in fact spelled the end of *U-1225*.

As the attack was in progress, Flight Sergeant Sidney R. Cole was sending out sighting reports. The flak strikes threw him out of his seat and stunned him. His place was taken by Flying Officer Graham Campbell, who scrambled back from the nose turret and now commenced to transmit SOS signals. None of these messages were ever received; the U-boat's fire had knocked out the radio.

Up in the cockpit, the pilots were still fighting to control the Canso. Having bombed from a height of 50 feet, they managed to coax the aircraft back to 250 feet, staggering on the edge of a stall. The blaze in the starboard wing could not be extinguished, however, and finally the engine on that side fell completely out of its mounting. There was nothing to do but ditch. Hornell and Denomy brought the aircraft into the wind and executed a stalled landing. They hit the sea, bounced 150 feet, hit the water again and bounced 50 feet, then settled into a heavy swell. Incredibly, no one had been hurt either in the fight or the landing.

The Canso sank to wing level in eight minutes and finally disappeared after 20, leaving a huge column of black smoke. In those minutes the crew evacuated as best they could. Denomy tried to crawl down the starboard side of the aircraft by grasping the ASV (radar) aerials, but was turned back by flames. He then followed Hornell down the port side. All crewmen reached the side blisters. Sergeant Fernand St. Laurent launched a dinghy on the starboard side, jumped after it, and floated away. As he tried to inflate it, the dinghy turned upside down, trapping him under it. Eventually he righted it but was unable to climb into it because of his soaked clothing.

Sergeant Donald S. Scott had meanwhile launched the port dinghy and successfully inflated it. Hornell, Denomy and Flying Officer Sidney E. Matheson jumped from the Canso and swam about 30 feet to the dinghy, which already had Scott and Bodnoff aboard. That left only two men unaccounted for – Campbell and Cole. They were still in the aircraft, unaware that the starboard dinghy had been launched and frantically looking for it amid choking smoke that filled the fuselage. In spite of the smoke and confusion, they retrieved some fresh water and rations before Scott paddled up in his dinghy to fetch them. The two radio operators climbed in and they began to pull away. Cole then jumped overboard, intent on retrieving a dinghy radio that was still in the aircraft. He was grabbed by his comrades who hauled him back into the dinghy. They were anxious to get away from the Canso lest the fuel tanks explode.

Six men could crowd into the dinghy, while one man hung on outside. After discarding excess clothing (notably boots), four men (Hornell, Denomy, Bodnoff, Matheson) took to the water and propelled the craft by kicking, aiming to reach St. Laurent and the other dinghy. It took 15 minutes to link up, but as they manoeuvred to divide their numbers between the two craft, St. Laurent's exploded like a pricked balloon. It was now a fight for survival – eight men and one dinghy in chilly North Atlantic waters. They were assured that radio messages had gone out; the fact that none of those messages had been received was mercifully hidden from them.

To make more space they threw the food away, leaving only the water tins and a baling bag. Hornell's trousers, tied at the cuffs, served as another baling bag. Denomy's flying helmet served the same purpose. The men took turns in the dinghy and the sea, allowances being made for the condition of some. Morale was good, especially when a Catalina flying boat appeared overhead near to midnight (about five hours after they had been shot down). Campbell fired three distress signals and the "Cat" homed onto them. It was from No. 333 Squadron, a Norwegian outfit, captained by Lieutenant Carl Frederik Krafft. This "guardian angel" and most of his crew were graduates of Canadian flying training schools, including "Little Norway" in Toronto. A week earlier, they had sunk *U-423* only a few miles away and in circumstances resembling Hornell's attack. For the next few hours the downed Canadians were to be inextricably linked to several gallant Norwegian fliers.[13]

Krafft flew low over the dinghy, flashed several messages to its occupants, then took up station nearby on orders from base. The Canso crew were cheered immensely by the circling aircraft; help was surely on the way. Nevertheless, the sea, already too heavy to permit the Catalina to alight, was getting worse, with 50-foot waves in a 46-knot wind. Staying aboard the dinghy was becoming harder. The waves were also slowing the rescue launch that had been despatched to their aid. To keep awake and maintain morale, the men whistled, sang, and played at riding a bronco as the swell threatened to swamp the dinghy. All were tiring; only Denomy was capable of sustained bailing.

As the Catalina swept around, the Norwegians saw evidence of *U-1225*'s destruction – a growing oil patch and some 35 or 40 Germans, alive and dead, in the water. The Canadians saw some proof as well. About 0300 hours on the 25th a

Flight Officer Bernard C. Denomy and Flight Lieutenant David Hornell. (Canadian Forces Photo PL-30823)

Lieutenant Carl Krafft and his crew. Krafft's Catalina circled the downed Canadians for as long as his fuel supply permitted. Back row, left to right: Wireless Operator/Air Gunner Magnus Fritswold, Air Gunner Eivind Vetvik, Flight Engineer Tor Johannessen, 2nd Pilot Karl K. Gilje. Front: Wireless Operator/Air Gunner Arne L. Bjerkseth, Navigator Jac. Johansen, Captain Carl F. Krafft, 1st Wireless Operator Knut Svendsen, Air Gunner Rolf Hauge. (Aktive Krigsdeltakeres Forening)

body in a yellow life jacket floated by. Soon afterwards they observed a large piece of planking with bolts. They could derive only the grimmest satisfaction from these sights as their own plight was worsening.

At 0840 hours on the 25th, nearly 14 hours after their attack, the dinghy overturned in a swell. All emergency supplies were lost. With diminishing strength they managed to right it, then pushed Denomy into the craft. He in turn dragged the others aboard. All save Scott were now inside the dinghy. St. Laurent died two hours later; his body was let go and Scott was hauled aboard.

Overhead, a different drama was being played out. Lieutenant Krafft had been keeping the dinghy in sight, reporting its gradual westward drift. He was concerned that neither a launch nor a lifeboat-dropping Warwick had appeared. A Warwick had been despatched, but it had suffered radio navigation problems and had flown the wrong track. At 0635 hours, Krafft radioed base, asking if a launch was on the way. He was informed that one would arrive in half an hour. Indeed, High Speed Launch 2507 had been sent out from Baltasound (Shetland Islands) soon after midnight, as soon as Krafft had reported the dinghy, but the launch crew were having problems of their own. One of their engines had broken down, greatly reducing their speed, while their own wireless signals were not always being received at base. Thus, the ETA that Station Wick had passed to the Catalina was hopelessly unrealistic.

When the launch did not arrive, Krafft became more concerned, fearing that contact with the downed Canadians might be lost. He resorted to a stratagem of his own. He wrapped his dinghy radio in a life preserver and about 0900 hours it was dropped. It fell 150 feet from them, but the weary survivors did not notice it.

No. 281 Squadron's Warwicks were especially busy that day, as the disappearance of a Fleet Air Arm Firefly had also required their attention. They were also plagued with unusual difficulties – whether avoidable or not is unknown. Two aircraft failed to locate the Hornell dinghy owing to bad visibility, radio problems and radar failures. About 1030 hours a third Warwick made contact with Krafft's Catalina. Flying Officer John A.J. Murray (RCAF) was at the controls. Ten minutes later he had the dinghy in sight.

Once again, ill-luck or poor execution spoiled the day. Murray dropped his airborne lifeboat, but it landed uselessly downwind of the survivors. Efforts to paddle the dinghy towards it failed; the lifeboat drifted away too quickly. Hornell wanted to swim for it, but his comrades would not allow such an act. The Warwick crew passed on two fixes to the launch, now estimated some 20 miles distant, before setting course for base. About this time, low on fuel, Krafft also headed for home. As they departed, the

Flight Lieutenant J.A. Murray, whose lifeboat drop to the Hornell crew missed the mark. (Canadian Forces Photo PL-34394)

Norwegians checked the oil patch seen earlier; it had grown, and there were no longer any German survivors. With the Catalina gone there was nobody in contact with Hornell's crew.

For those in the dinghy, the failed lifeboat drop had been a crushing blow. They were dimly aware that there was now no "guardian angel" over them, and the non-appearance of a launch was baffling. It was as though they had been abandoned. The men deteriorated, sometimes to revive. About 1415 hours Scott died; his body was committed to the sea. Hornell had gone blind; only Denomy, Cole and Bodnoff were in fair condition.

Meanwhile, HSL 2507 was searching for the dinghy. A Liberator was presumed to be over it, but the launch crew could not see it, nor could they raise it on the radio. At 1341 hours a Sunderland of No. 330 Squadron, piloted by Sub-Lieutenant Ole Georg Evenson, Royal Norwegian Air Force, flew over the launch and asked if the survivors had been picked up. When a negative reply was given, the Norwegian crew took up the search. At 1445 hours they were over the dinghy, dropped a smoke float and signalled the launch. Evenson's crew, like that of Krafft before him, included several graduates of "Little Norway" in Canada.*

About 30 minutes later, working through the swell, the launch crew spotted the dinghy only 500 feet away and approached. At that time the three fittest survivors were trying to revive the three failing ones. A thrown line was caught by Flight Sergeant Cole, who pulled the dinghy alongside HSL 2507, climbed aboard, and helped Bodnoff, Matheson, Campbell and Hornell over, assisted by the indomitable Denomy, who helped from the dinghy side and climbed onto the launch by his own efforts. The ordeal, 21 hours in the water, was over, but it was too late for Hornell, who died in the launch in spite of four hours of applied artificial respiration. He was 34 years old.[118]

Flight Lieutenant David Hornell was posthumously awarded the Victoria Cross for heroism in the attack and leadership coupled with endurance thereafter. Flying Officer Denomy received a richly deserved DSO. Campbell and Matheson were awarded Distinguished Flying Crosses, while Bodnoff

---

* This crew comprised Evensen plus Quartermasters Johannes Daae Riisnes, Gunnar Johan Vold, Preben Larsen, Nils Severin Barclay Gusfre, Haakron Haalan, Trygve Aasland, John Holswick, Finn Waldemar Haakonsen and Roald Markussen. Of these, Evensen, Riisnes, Vold and Haakonsen had taken part of their training in Canada.

Hornell and crew. Front: Sergeant Fernand St. Laurent (died, MiD), Sergeant Donald S. Scott (died, MiD), Flying Officer Graham Campbell (DFC), Flight Sergeant Israel Bodnoff (DFM). Back: Flying Officer F.W. Lawrence (not in crew 25 June 1944), Flying Officer Sidney E.I. Matheson (DFC), Flight Lieutenant David Hornell (died, VC), Squadron Leader F. Poag (not in crew 25 June 1944). Not shown: Flying Officer Bernard C. Denomy (DSO), Flight Sergeant Sidney R. Cole (DFM). (Canadian Forces Photo PL-25014)

The final rescue of David Hornell's crew. (Canadian Forces Photo PL-25505)

and Cole received Distinguished Flying Medals. Sergeants Scott and St. Laurent were accorded posthumous Mentions in Despatches. Lieutenant Krafft, the Norwegian "guardian angel," was reportedly awarded a Distinguished Flying Cross for his actions on 17 June and 24-25 June.[119] Flying Officer William Wakelin Garratt, skipper of HSL 2507, was made a Member, Order of the British Empire. Although Flying Officer Murray's lifeboat drop had been a failure, his subsequent career in Air/Sea rescue work was distinguished enough to result eventually in his being Mentioned in Despatches and awarded an Air Force Cross.

The George Cross action involving Air Commodore Arthur Dwight Ross similarly demonstrates the complexities of such dramas; it also shows the care that was often taken to weigh a deed performed by many against possible awards that could be given only to a few.

The drama began at Station Tholthorpe, Yorkshire, about 0200 hours, 28 June 1944. RCAF bombers were coming home after raiding flying-bomb sites in the Pas de Calais area. Air Commodore Ross, Commanding No. 62 Base, was on hand to meet crews and follow their interrogation by intelligence officers. Several score of ground crew were on hand as well, ready for emergencies and the routine early servicing of aircraft.

But all was not well. Halifax MZ683 (QB-A) of No. 425 Squadron (Sergeant M.J.P. Lavoie, pilot), attempting to land, crashed into another "Hallie", LW380, which was parked in the dispersal area, fully loaded with bombs. Lavoie's bomber broke into three parts and started to burn furiously. Air Commodore Ross headed for the crash site, and a score of others converged on the same spot. Two of those were Flight Sergeant Joseph R.M. St. Germain, a bomb aimer who had just returned from a sortie, and Corporal Maurice Marquet, who was in charge of the night ground crew. A crash tender was also coming; its crew included Leading Aircraftmen Melvin M. McKenzie and Reuben R. Wolfe.

Ross and Marquet extricated the pilot, who had sustained severe injuries. At that moment ten 500-pound bombs in the second aircraft, about 80 yards away, exploded. They were hurled to the ground. When the hail of debris had subsided, cries were heard from the rear turret of the crashed aircraft. Despite potential further explosions from bombs and petrol tanks, Ross and Marquet returned to the blazing wreckage. They struggled vainly to swing the turret to release the rear gunner, Sergeant C.G. Rochon. Although the port tail plane was blazing furiously, Ross hacked at the perspex with an axe and then handed the axe through the turret to the rear gunner who enlarged the aperture. Taking the axe again Ross, assisted now by Flight Sergeant St. Germain as well as by Corporal Marquet, finally broke the perspex steel frame supports and extricated the rear gunner.

Another 500-pound bomb exploded, which threw the three rescuers to the ground. St. Germain quickly rose and threw himself upon a victim to shield him from flying debris. Air Commodore Ross's arm was practically severed between the wrist and elbow by the second explosion. He calmly walked to the ambulance and an emergency amputation was performed on arrival at station sick quarters. Meanwhile, Corporal Marquet had inspected the surroundings and, seeing petrol running down towards two nearby aircraft, directed their removal from the vicinity by tractor. LACs McKenzie and Wolfe rendered valuable assistance in trying to bring the fire under control and they also helped to extricate the trapped rear gunner, both being seriously injured by flying debris. Air Commodore Ross had provided heroic leadership in an action which resulted in the saving of the lives of the pilot and rear gunner. He had been ably assisted by Flight Sergeant St. Germain and Corporal Marquet, who both displayed courage of a high order. Valuable service was also rendered by LACs McKenzie and Wolfe in circumstances of great danger. All eight crewmen from QB-A (seven RCAF plus the RAF flight engineer) had escaped with their lives and only two had sustained serious injuries.

The crash that night at Tholthorpe is best remembered for the fact that Air Commodore Ross was awarded a George Cross for his courage, while St. Germain* and Marquet received George Medals; LACs McKenzie and Wolfe received British Empire Medals. Nevertheless, there was considerable official correspondence before these awards were conferred.

The initial recommendation for decorations had suggested *two* George Crosses (Ross and Marquet). Air Ministry officials would have been loath to award two George Crosses for a single incident and quickly decided that Marquet should receive a George Medal. Nevertheless, a GC for Ross still seemed doubtful. A memo within Air Ministry on 21 August 1944 noted:

---

* St. Germain was later awarded a DFC for gallantry during air operations.

Left to right: Corporal Maurice Marquet, GM (Meadow Lake, Sask.), Pilot Officer Joseph René Marcel St. Germain, GM (Montreal), Air Commodore A.D. Ross, GC, Leading Aircraftman Melvin Muir McKenzie, BEM (Tehkummah, Ont.), photographed outside Buckingham Palace after their investiture. (Canadian Forces Photo PL-33981)

Air Commodore Ross … did not do much more than Corporal Marquet, but he took the lead in the rescue efforts and his heroic action inciden- tally caused him the loss of his right arm. We may have some difficulty in getting the George Cross for him, but on the whole I think we should be justified in putting his name forward to the Central Committee.

An undated minute from Air Ministry to Sir Robert Knox commented on doubts raised with respect to the Air Commodore, but reached back to an earlier (Royal Navy) case that substantiated a GC for Ross.

We do not contest the War Office view that Air Commodore Ross shared the same risks as, and did no more than, Corporal Marquet. Nor does it seem to us to be necessary to do so, for it is well established that the George Cross has a certain leadership content (see, for instances, cases (1), (2) and (3) in G.C.M, 199, where the George Cross was given to an officer engaged in clearing Messina Harbour and the George Medal to two ratings who assisted him.

There is the further point that the action of Air Commodore Ross was entirely voluntary. By virtue of his rank, he could have directed operations from a safe distance, but he chose to take a leading part in the rescue activities and there is no doubt that he set a magnificent example to all concerned. We should, therefore, like him to receive the George Cross and not the George Medal as proposed by the War Office.

The prior case cited (G.C.M. 199) referred to the George Cross awarded to Lieutenant John Bridge, GM, and awards to Temporary Petty Officer Richard Morris Woods and Able Seaman Thomas Patrick Peters. The *London Gazette* of 20 June 1944 had reported award of the George Cross to Bridge ("for great gallantry and devotion to duty") and George Medals for Woods and Peters ("for gallantry and devotion to duty"). Bridge had previously received a George Medal (27 December 1940), Commendation (27 June 1941) and Bar to George Medal (28 October 1941). When considering the awards of June 1944, the selection committee for the George Cross, the George Medal and the British Empire Medal had before it the following submission:

Lieutenant Bridge is recommended for most conspicuous and prolonged bravery and contempt of death in clearing Messina Harbour of depth charges. Despite the fact that the whole of the previous bomb disposal party had been killed or wounded by six depth charges fired by an unknown mechanism, Lieutenant Bridge proceeded with the greatest of enthusiasm, combined with skill and ingenuity, to dispose of a similar group. After a total of 28 dives on this group they were rendered safe, and the mechanisms, which were of a previously unknown type, recovered and stripped. In addition, Lieutenant Bridge rendered safe or discredited a further 207 depth charges, above or below water, with all types of firing mechanisms. As a result of the efforts of this officer and his party Messina Harbour was declared open the day after the assault on Italy, which proved to be of the utmost value during the follow-up. The recommending Officer stated that it had never been his fortune to be associated with such cool and sustained bravery as Lieutenant Bridge displayed during the ten days of this operation. Petty Officer Woods tended Lieutenant Bridge as Diver's Attendant during the clearance of Messina Harbour. By the nature of his work it

was impossible to place him under cover and any accident to Lieutenant
Bridge would inevitably have involved Woods. His cheerful acceptance of
long hours of danger and hard work were an encouragement to all around
him. Able Seaman Peters was associated with Lieutenant Bridge through-
out the clearance of Messina Harbour and in fact stripped the unknown
mechanism under Lieutenant Bridge's orders. He always volunteered for
any post of danger and his conduct is the more praiseworthy in that the
Officer under whom he had been working for some months was killed in
the earlier disaster.[120]

The night's events at Tholthorpe and the parts played by the principals
were all vividly described in the *London Gazette* which announced their honours. Yet the official story is incomplete; examination of station records reveals that several other people were involved, and their part has never been
fully recognized.

There was also a recommendation submitted for Squadron Leader
Kenneth H. Running, the Medical Officer at Tholthorpe. It was a long statement, which paid tribute to his general organizing abilities and to his athletic
prowess, but its essential character was expressed as follows:

On the night of 27/28 June 1944, an aircraft on a three-engine landing
crashed into another aircraft at dispersal and both aircraft immediately
burst into flames. Squadron Leader Running, who was on duty at the
control tower, immediately proceeded to the scene with his staff. Squadron
Leader Running entered the burning aircraft and with assistance removed
the pilot who was seriously injured. Squadron Leader Running contin-
ued the rescue and as the last occupant was being removed the Squadron
Leader and his staff were thrown to the ground by the explosion of ten
5-cwt bombs from the aircraft in dispersal. Despite this, Squadron Leader
Running continued with his rescue and first aid, being subjected to a fur-
ther explosion a few minutes later. When all personnel were safely re-
moved the Squadron Leader proceeded to Station Sick Quarters and car-
ried out an emergency amputation on one of the injured. Other seriously
injured men were given treatment and removed to the Military Hospital
in York. During all of this work, Squadron Leader Running displayed the

greatest coolness and efficiency and he was unquestionably responsible for saving lives of all personnel.[121]

For his role in the affair, Running received a Mention in Despatches (he had been recommended for an OBE). Because MiD announcements were rarely accompanied by citations, there was no public statement linking his award to the events at Tholthorpe. Indeed, at the time of his MiD (January 1, 1945), Running had moved on to No. 83 Group; even he may not have connected his honour with the crash six months earlier.

On 3 February 1945 the Base Commander at Tholthorpe recommended an award for LAC Edgar Toussaint Foidart. On the night of the crash he had driven an ambulance to the immediate vicinity of the fire and un-hesitatingly gave assistance in the rescuing of the crew from the aircraft. Foidart was duly Mentioned in Despatches.[122]

Squadron Leader K.H. Running (Carleton Place, Ontario), shown as part of the coronation contingent in 1953. (Canadian Forces Photo PL-56910)

LAC Frederick W. Jardine drove the crash tender that night. As flames consumed the two bombers, he drove the vehicle close to the fire and worked until he was knocked unconscious by an explosion. On 3 February 1945, Jardine was recommended for an award, in terms almost identical to those describing Foidart's role but none was forthcoming. It would appear that MiDs were rationed and by ill luck the brave airman received no formal recognition.

But that was not the end of awards for the Tholthorpe incident. In the wake of the fire and explosions there were numerous bombs, including unstable delayed-action types, that posed a threat. Scrambling around in darkness, armament personnel had to find these bombs, manhandle them onto trolleys, gingerly move them to safe areas, set demolition charges, then destroy them. One bomb proved very troublesome; the demolition charge misfired and personnel had to lay another charge while fearing the bomb might detonate at any second. It was very risky business indeed, and four more recommendations were forthcoming – an MBE for Flying Officer A.D.

Squadron Leader A.N. Roth, after being Mentioned in Despatches following the Tholthorpe incident, distinguished himself again early in 1945 when he was involved in the removal of a large, very live delayed-action bomb from the middle of a bomb dump and its subsequent destruction. On that occasion he received an MBE. He is shown here at the investiture in Ottawa with his wife and daughter, Patricia, age seven. (Canadian Forces Photo PL-38695)

Baillie, a BEM for Flight Sergeant L.A. LaFleche, and MiDs for Sergeant J.G.E. Robichaud and Squadron Leader A.N. Roth – but in the end these were reduced to four MiDs for the armament personnel.[123]

Courage often was accompanied by teamwork, and the emphasis subsequently placed on "big ticket" awards frequently obscures associated heroics by men and women who have been accorded other honours, in part because there were not enough of the more prominent ones to go round. At least in the dramas just described, the "supporting cast" received some recognition. Such was not always the case.

Sergeant Rawden H. Middleton, Royal Australian Air Force, performed heroically on the night of 28/29 November 1942, first by persisting in an attack on Turin when his fuel situation made a safe return to base unlikely, continuing the attack after being severely wounded, and then foregoing a bale-out and captivity in favour of an arduous homeward flight. Knowing he could never land the bomber, he instructed the crew to parachute to safety before he ditched at sea. Five men left the aircraft and survived; Sergeants John W. Mackie (air gunner) and James E. Jeffrey (flight engineer) opted to remain with Middleton in the hope of assisting him after he ditched. All three were lost. Middleton received a posthumous VC, having both gotten his aircraft and crew *into* and *out of* danger; Mackie and Jeffrey were granted no official recognition, although the Albert Medal was suggested for both men.[124]

CHAPTER 9

"GETTING MY BUDDY" – AERIAL RESCUES UNDER FIRE

If you're ever in a jam – here I am;
If you're ever in a mess – S.O.S.

Cole Porter (1891-1964), *Friendship*

The act of saving a comrade from death or capture while under enemy fire was long a staple of Victoria Cross deeds. This was exemplified during the South African War (1899-1902). Of 78 Victoria Crosses awarded, at least 16 involved mounted soldiers who turned back towards the enemy to retrieve comrades who had lost their horses. In two instances the rescuer gave his own horse over entirely to the stricken soldier, making a fighting retreat on foot. An Australian, Sergeant James Rogers, not only rescued his commanding officer, but having deposited that man safely returned to within 400 yards of Afrikaaner positions to retrieve two more soldiers (15 June 1901). The first VC awarded to a member of a Canadian unit involved just such a rescue (Sergeant Arthur Herbert Lindsay Richardson, Lord Strathcona's Horse, action at Wolwespruit, 5 July 1900).

A modern counterpart of this type of rescue was the pilot who landed his airplane close to hostile forces in order to pick up a comrade. While this deed has been performed frequently, it has been the subject of only two Victoria Crosses. This was probably due to the general tightening up of VC standards from the First World War onwards.

The first instance was on 19 November 1915 in the Balkans. No. 3 Squadron, Royal Naval Air Service, was bombing a bridge at Ferejik in Bulgaria. An aircraft piloted by Lieutenant Gilbert F. Smylie was hit by rifle fire and

Rescue Under Fire by an unidentified artist depicts one of several incidents in the Boer War when soldiers who had lost their horses were rescued by mounted comrades, which led to several awards of the VC. (Canadian War Museum)

force-landed near the target. He ran for cover, hiding from Bulgarian troops. Lieutenant Richard Bell-Davies, flying a Nieuport 10, went to his assistance. It was a particularly bold gamble, because he was uncertain as to the nature of the ground, whether solid or marshy, and the aircraft had little reserve power if it became bogged. As it turned out, he alighted on just about the only suitable terrain in what was otherwise a mixture of narrow channels and packed mud ruts. Smylie emerged from his hiding place, seized the Nieuport's wing and swung it around. He then ran alongside, steadying the aircraft while Bell-Davies manoeuvred between reeds until he could face the aircraft into the wind. Smylie boarded the aircraft, Bell-Davies opened the throttle, and with Bulgarian soldiers now in range and firing, managed to get airborne. Both men were decorated, Smylie with the Distinguished Service Cross, Bell-Davies with the Victoria Cross, both on 1 January 1916.

On 20 March 1917 in Egypt, during an aerial bomb attack, a pilot was forced to land behind enemy lines, with hostile Turkish cavalry approaching. Lieutenant Frank Hubert McNamara, No. 1 Squadron, Australian Flying Corps, perceived the situation and descended through heavy fire to the rescue. Although wounded on the approach, he landed about 200 yards from the damaged plane, and the pilot climbed into his machine. Owing to his injury, McNamara could not keep it straight and it turned over. The two officers extricated themselves, set fire to the machine and made their way to the damaged one, which they succeeded in starting. Finally, Lieutenant McNamara, although weak from loss of blood, flew the machine 70 miles back to his base. This resulted in the award of the Victoria Cross (*London Gazette*, 9 June 1917).

One month after McNamara's feat, 21 April 1917, another Australian pilot in the same squadron, Captain Richard Williams, also landed in enemy lines to retrieve a downed comrade. His exploit brought him a Distinguished Service Order (*London Gazette*, 17 August 1917). The elements of his being unwounded and the fact that he had not been hard pressed by the enemy undoubtedly affected the award for which he had been recommended. In time the frequency of such incidents resulted in awards of even lesser standing. Thus, the *London Gazette* of 21 September 1918, reporting a Distinguished Flying Cross to Lieutenant and Honorary Captain Hippolyte Ferdinand Delarue gave the following citation:

> *This officer, in a Short seaplane, accompanied by another, formed escort to machines carrying out a long-distance bombing raid. When nearing the objective both machines were attacked by a fast enemy scout, and the companion plane was forced to alight. Captain Delarue at once followed it down, picked up pilot and observer, and returned with the two additional passengers. A brave and meritorious action, for the risk he ran was great in such close proximity to the enemy, it being extremely doubtful if his machine would rise from the water with four on board.*

Nor was this an isolated case. Lieutenant Ronald A. Austin, No. 4 Squadron, Australian Flying Corps received a Military Cross on 26 March 1918 for work that included an exploit which earlier had earned his fellow countrymen a VC and a DSO. The citation (published in August 1918) read:

For conspicuous gallantry and devotion to duty. He was one of two pilots who carried out a remarkable series of photographs in one flight, which covered an area of 25 square miles. On an earlier occasion he alone had photographed in the completest detail an area of 20 square miles in spite of intense anti-aircraft fire. During recent operations he has led all important bombing raids and his skill and gallantry have been largely responsible for the excellent results attained. Previous to this he had landed in enemy country and rescued another pilot who had been forced to land through engine trouble.

In Mesopotamia, where flat desert country prevailed, these types of rescues appear to have become more common by 1918, if we judge by the awards granted. Captain Frank Nuttall, No 30 Squadron, was awarded a Military Cross on 24 August 1918 with the following citation:

For conspicuous gallantry and devotion to duty. Seeing another machine being driven down by hostile fire in the enemy's lines, he glided to the ground under heavy fire and dispersed the enemy with his machine gun. He took the stranded pilot on board and got safely away. By his prompt and courageous action he saved his comrade from being taken prisoner.

Another case, however, makes for horrendous reading – that of Flight Lieutenant Walter Fraser Anderson (pilot) and Flying Officer John Mitchell (observer), No. 47 Squadron, who in 1919 were supporting White Russian forces during the Russian Civil War. Red Army commanders had threatened to crucify any British fliers taken prisoner. This may have been more than an idle warning; photographic evidence proved ghastly atrocities committed during the Russo-Polish War.

On 30 July 1919, during a reconnaissance mission, a DH.9 was hit by ground fire and landed five miles behind Bolshevik lines. Hostile cavalry were closing in. The downed crew burnt their machine and held off the enemy with a Lewis machine gun, apparently intent on selling their lives dearly. Anderson and Mitchell rushed to the rescue. Their aircraft had already been damaged; a bullet punctured their fuel tank and Mitchell was on the top wing, somehow hanging on as he stanched the flow of petrol with his thumbs. Nevertheless, they chose to alight. The crew of the downed machine climbed aboard and Anderson took off again. However, with petrol leaking rapidly, desperate measures were needed. Flying Officer Mitchell remained atop the wing, slowing the loss of fuel. The engine exhaust stack nearby burned his legs. This ordeal lasted 50 minutes, and he was hospitalized immediately after landing.

On 9 August 1919, the commanding officer of No. 47 Squadron, Squadron Leader Raymond Collishaw, recommended that Anderson and Mitchell be decorated but did not specify what award should be made. The Officer Commanding, Royal Air Forces in Russia, Brigadier A.C. Maund, drafted two recommendations for the Victoria Cross. Instead, each man was awarded a Distinguished Service Order. The evidence is scanty, but it appears that Maund's submissions failed because statements corroborating their exploit were lost during a chaotic departure of British units from South Russia.[125]

During the period between the wars, several instances occurred during Britain's colonial campaigns of airmen being forced down in hostile country. Whether any were recommended for the Victoria Cross is unknown, but Flight Lieutenant John F.T. Barrett received a DSO;[126] Flying Officer Victor E. Groom received a Bar to his Distinguished Flying Cross (the original medal having been earned in 1918);[127] similarly, Flying Officer Dudley L. Evans received a Bar to an earlier DFC.[128]

Given the interwar treatment of pickups similar to this, it is not surprising to find a Victoria Cross recommendation for a similar deed downgraded. On 15 March 1941, Lieutenant Robert H.C. Kershaw, No. 3 Squadron, South African Air Force, broke off his attack on an Italian airfield in Libya to land and retrieve Captain E. Frost, whose Hurricane fighter had been shot down. Kershaw picked up his comrade under fire; Frost actually flew the aircraft home sitting on Kershaw's lap. Air Ministry substituted a DSO for the VC.[129] Subsequently several other similar desert rescues were made; if noticed by commanding officers, they might earn a DFC, but Flying Officer George Keefer, making such a rescue on 4 June 1942 received nothing more than the thanks of the family whose son he had saved. They may later have regretted Keefer's saving the man. As a POW he would almost certainly have survived the war. As it turned out, Lieutenant John Lane, South African Air Force, was killed in action on 22 October 1942.

The nature and complexity of modern combat aircraft has eliminated "return and recovery" episodes such as those described; Phantom and Tornado fighters are too heavy and expensive to alight in deserts or jungle clearings. Aerial rescues under fire are now the province of helicopter crews. No Victoria Cross or even Distinguished Service Order has been awarded to such aircrew, but several Distinguished Flying Crosses have gone to personnel executing remarkable feats of battlefield rescue and resupply.[130] In the Vietnam War, the United States conferred the Medal of Honor on at least eight helicopter pilots conducting rescues and evacuations under fire, and the accounts of their deeds, though not exact parallels of those by Bell-Davies and McNamara, make stirring reading.[131]

CHAPTER 10

THE SINGULAR CASE OF
WILLIAM AVERY BISHOP

Scholars dispute, and the case is still before the courts.

Horace (65-8 B.C.), *Ars Poetica.*

id William Avery "Billy" Bishop really perform the deed for which
he was awarded the Victoria Cross? Even if he did carry out the act,
should he have been awarded the Victoria Cross?

The questions that arise about aerial fighting on the Western Front during the First World War could be directed at more than one pilot. How exact
were claims for aerial victories? What standards were applied in determin-
ing whether enemy aircraft had been destroyed, damaged, or merely driven
away? The case of Albert Ball makes an interesting counterpoint to Billy
Bishop. Both were known as solo performers, given to patrols and combats
where friendly witnesses were not common. Bishop, however, was recommended for a Victoria Cross while alive on the basis of a single flight. By
contrast, Ball was first recommended for a VC on 3 October 1916; this was
downgraded to a second Bar to the DSO.[132] He was recommended again, this
time posthumously, for an extended series of actions (many of them witnessed), and specifically for seven combats between 23 April and 6 May 1917,
at least one of which had been in company with other pilots. Nevertheless,
the Officer Commanding, No. 9 Wing wrote, on 8 May 1917:

*Owing to the peculiar nature of the operations in which Captain Ball took
part, corroborative evidence is impossible.*

143

The day after this passage was written, Major-General Hugh Trenchard edited it to read "corroborative evidence is unavailable" – a subtle but significant change. Nevertheless, the condition of Ball's aircraft seemed to be deemed as corroboration of his deeds. Again, the submission from No. 9 Wing read, in part:

> *His machine was invariably out of action for a considerable period after each combat.*
>
> *He displayed the most remarkable energy and determination, and after returning from a combat with his machine badly damaged, had always to be restrained from getting into another machine and going out alone again immediately.*[133]

The VC awarded for Bishop's reported actions of 2 June 1917 has long been a staple of Canadian legend and iconography. In 1980 the first volume of the RCAF's official history repeated the oft-told story of his single-handed attack on a German airfield, but a footnote raised the first glimmer of academic doubt. "The location of the airfield Bishop attacked has never been definitely established," it said, and went on to emphasize that he had no idea at the time where he had been.[134]

The Bishop legend came under sustained attack in 1982 when the National Film Board of Canada produced *The Kid Who Couldn't Miss*, which even Bishop critic Brereton Greenhous described as shoddy and second rate. Nevertheless, the dust had been stirred. A retired RCAF officer, Philip Markham, began to probe more deeply. A portion of his findings appeared in 1994 in the *Journal of the Canadian Aviation Historical Society* and in 1995 in the American publication *Over the Front*. He had set out to prove the legend to be true; he was shocked when the evidence pointed in the other direction. He died shortly afterwards, but Greenhous took up where his friend had left off and in 2002 published *The Making of Billy Bishop*, which paid generous homage to Markham.

One fact appears to be undisputed. Billy Bishop is the only man ever to have been awarded the Victoria Cross solely on the basis of his own word. Corroborative evidence has disappeared – if it ever existed. German intelligence reports, which might have been expected to comment on a new British

Captain William A. "Billy" Bishop, DSO, MC, before being awarded the Victoria Cross. (Library and Archives Canada PA1990)

tactic (that of surprise low-level attacks on airfields) made no mention of the dawn strike that Bishop described, nor could any German casualties be tied to the event. Markham, concentrating on Bishop's career in 1917, concluded that an attack on a German airfield on 2 June 1917 *never happened*. Greenhous, agreeing with that thesis, explored Bishop's further career and stated that the famous pilot exaggerated his subsequent victory claims, "padding" a score which finally totalled 72 enemy aircraft destroyed; Greenhous believed a more accurate figure would be about 27.

The Making of Billy Bishop aroused a storm of controversy among aficionados of First World War aviation. A debate at the Air Force Historical Conference (Cornwall, June 2002) pitted Greenhous against aviation historian Colonel Dave Bashow. Wayne Ralph, whose own biography of ace William Barker virtually restored that pilot to the Canadian pantheon, disagreed with

Greenhous as to the events of 2 June 1917 but agreed on Bishop's subsequent dubious victory claims.

One might describe the current disputes over Billy Bishop as a "battle of footnotes." Those who defend the legend fall back on previous writings by earlier authors, good, bad and indifferent. Greenhous, citing many of these, nevertheless went back to as many primary sources as he could find. Both sides have been burdened with dubious gossip and unreliable recollections that have been added to the story over time. The sceptics are hobbled with the task of proving a negative – that Bishop did *not* do what he claimed to have done, because nobody witnessed or reported it. The acolytes argue that the award of a VC *proves* that confirming evidence was found, even though they cannot produce it themselves.

One thing is most interesting – a comparison of Bishop's Combat Report of 2 June 1917 and the citation for his VC. The latter is based almost solely on the former; the only significant difference is that the citation mentions an enemy mechanic "seen to fall" while the Combat Report does not. That detail was added by Bishop's commanding officer, Major Alan Scott. Overall, it is almost as if Bishop wrote his own citation.

Then there is the Caldwell report – a statement provided on 30 June 1917 by Captain Keith Logan Caldwell to Headquarters, No. 13 Wing. Caldwell was by then the acting commanding officer of No. 60 Squadron, Major Scott having been wounded. He answered questions that had been put to him by the senior formation. Supporters of Bishop declare that the Caldwell report proves that an investigation had been conducted and that it substantiated the VC recommendation, yet a close reading of it shows how inconclusive the investigation had been hitherto. Caldwell confirmed little more than Bishop's take-off and landing times and the state of his airplane on his return; he had no information about what Bishop had actually accomplished while flying alone.

Reference has already been to the wholesale destruction of First World War files dealing with Victoria Crosses. This has been used to explain the absence of corroborative documents, the argument being that since a VC *was* awarded then supporting evidence *was* found – *res ipsa loquatur* ("the thing speaks for itself"). The frailty of this defence becomes evident when we note that although the principal files relating to First World War Victoria Crosses have been lost, much documentation has survived in other files, including Royal Flying Corps dossiers of the period. The Victoria Cross recommendation for Sergeant Harry Mottershead (January 1917) was accompanied by witness statements by those who watched his burning airplane descend into British lines. When Brigadier J.F.A. Higgins (3 Brigade, Royal Flying Corps) recommended James B. McCudden for a VC (in February 1918) he was immediately advised to obtain eyewitness accounts of at least some of Mc-Cudden's air fights to "strengthen the case." Higgins promptly supplied two statements by officers commanding anti-aircraft guns and two by pilots who had flown with McCudden.[135] The recommendation for Ferdinand West's VC, submitted on 4 September 1918, was accompanied by statements by three witnesses – West's observer and two doctors who had treated West immediately after he was shot down; these testified not only to his wounds but to his determination to file a reconnaissance report before being hospitalized.[136] The contrast between these cases of corroborative evidence and the absence of similar confirmation in Bishop's case is striking.

Why then was this VC awarded when neither witnesses nor corroborative evidence were available four weeks after the events had supposedly happened? The "reason" most often cited by sceptics is that the RFC had been taking heavy losses, trench warfare had degenerated into stalemate, civilian morale needed a boost and the way to do it was to manufacture a hero (à la *The Blue Max*). It had been done before; Zeppelin killers Reginald Warneford and William Leefe Robinson were very timely heroes whose Victoria Crosses were awarded in record time from deed to gazetting – five and three days respectively – when German airships seemed to be invulnerable. Nevertheless, this "reason" cannot be proven because, simply put, we are never going to find a memo suggesting, urging or authorizing such a "production." Even had such a plot been afoot to create a "super hero," there were plenty of other potential candidates for elevation to the pedestal, including two fast-rising fighter pilots with impeccable "colonial" connections and numerous witnesses to their combats – Raymond Collishaw (Canada) and Robert A. Little (Australia), to say nothing of a famous actor and pioneer aviator (Robert Loraine). If authorities had decided to manufacture an aerial icon, they could easily have picked a person with better credentials than Bishop. The conspiracy theory fails both the tests of evidence and plausibility.

Contemporary letters and documents offer clues that suggest a much more political explanation, including senior officers railroaded against their better judgement to authorize a Victoria Cross. On 1 June 1917, in a letter to his fiancée, Margaret Burden, Bishop wrote, "I have just learnt that when I got my DSO, I was recommended for the VC."

Aside from evidence that Bishop had "VC on the brain", what do we make of this? Was Bishop telling the truth – or a whopper? Documents in Britain's Public Record Office (now their National Archives) show that he was recommended for a DSO (not a VC) on 7 May 1917.[137] One might assume, then, that Bishop was lying to the lady. But let us give him the benefit of the doubt and say that his commanding officer, Major Alan Scott, recommended a VC (in a document now lost) and that Wing or Brigade turned it into a DSO – the document now seen in the Public Record Office. What does this indicate?

One thing must first be made clear; Scott (or anyone else) had no business to inform Bishop in advance about the nature of his awards. Regulations were clear on this point; a memorandum circulated to all commanding officers on 23 September 1916 emphasized the avoidance of premature disclosure, especially to intended recipients:

> *The subject of recommendations for honours is to be treated as confidential and officers will not divulge at any time the recommendation they have made. There is no objection to cards of appreciation of services rendered being issued to officers and men, but the wording on such cards must not indicate, in any form whatever, that the services referred to will be brought to notice of higher authority.[138]*

Bishop's letter of 1 June 1917 indicates that, in matters pertaining to Major Scott, Bishop and/or No. 60 Squadron, the rules about confidentiality and discretion were ignored. Indeed, Bishop correspondence revealed a certain anxiety and impatience about the progress of the VC recommendation (which he should not have known about). Other later letters from Bishop to Margaret and to his father indicate that the public learned more, and faster, than anyone expected or deemed prudent. As early as 19 June 1917, the Toronto *Globe* was reporting that a "young British pilot" had "sat" over a German airfield, "smashing, one by one, four machines which came up to attack him." By early August word was afoot that a "colonial" pilot had been recommended for a Victoria Cross, and although no name had as yet been attached to this report, there were plenty of newspaper stories lauding Bishop for other deeds.

It was only a matter of time before the story would break, and authorities within the chain of command faced a dilemma. What would the press say if the VC never materialized? Worse still, how would the Dominions react if a VC were turned down? Canada alone had 400,000 troops in the field, a developing conscription crisis at home, and a Prime Minister (Sir Robert Borden) who was becoming more inquisitive about how the British were running the war. Bishop himself enjoyed the company of a chatty, upper-class London social circle that included Max Aitken (soon to be Lord Beaverbrook), press baron, propagandist for the Canadian war effort and political schemer.[139]

The following scenario is the author's own. It is unprovable – yet I am confident that the reader will find it as plausible as any other explanation of how Bishop came to be awarded a Victoria Cross without any collateral evidence. I suggest that, between 2 June 1917 (the date of the action in question) and 11 August 1917 (the date his Victoria Cross was gazetted) the following occurred:

Scott recommended a VC for Bishop on 2 June 1917, the day of the reported attack, trotting his protégé before senior officers to tell his story. They accepted it, but those who had to make the final decision were also duty bound to find witnesses or at least corroborative information. None could be expected from the Germans, so they must have scoured the front lines for persons who might have something to contribute. Late in June, they telephoned Captain Keith Caldwell, who was in temporary command of the squadron, Major Scott having been wounded. He, in turn, wrote a memo to Headquarters, 13 Wing, Royal Flying Corps, dated 30 June 1917. The answers he provided give a very clear idea of what the questions had been:

Reference our telephone conversation of today. Herewith information as requested:
1. *Time left aerodrome 3.57 a.m.*
   Time arrived at Hostile Aerodrome, 4.25 a.m.
   Time arrived back 5.40 a.m.

2. *Personal evidence only.*

3. *Damage done – 17 Bullet holes. Trailing edge of lower plane shot away in two bays.*

4. *Distance 30 miles. Aerodrome S. of Cambrai.*

Although the damage sustained, as described, might be considered severe, Bishop's logbook indicates that he flew the aircraft some 50 miles to visit friends at another airfield within hours of his famous sortie, indicating that it was easily repaired – probably no more than fabric punctures. The most important part of the report was the second response. Caldwell had been asked by superiors if there was any information other than what Bishop had supplied, and he confirmed their worst fears – *there was no more information*; the account (and hence the recommendation) were based on "personal evidence" and no more.

It was now nearly a month since the VC nomination had been made and the more authorities delayed a decision the greater were the risks of more leaks appearing. The process had acquired a momentum of its own. Lacking the normal corroboration, the authorities could have either stopped the train (fearing that newspapers would trumpet the story as "VC DENIED – COLONIAL OFFICER'S WORD NOT ENOUGH") or flag it through the station.

They blinked.

They waved it through the station.

They allowed, just once, the award of a VC based solely on the recipient's report, without witnesses or corroborative evidence.[140]

CHAPTER 11

SELF-SACRIFICE
OR INSANITY?

C'est magnifique – mais ce n'est pas la guerre.

Maréchal Bosquet, observing the Charge of the Light Brigade, 1854.

Is there such things as wise courage or foolish valour? Audie Murphy, America's most decorated combat soldier of the Second World War, on seeing a movie of his exploits (in which he played himself), is reported to have said, "I wasn't brave – I was nuts." Surgeon William Job Maillard, awarded a VC for heroism on Crete on 6 September 1898 (when a Muslim mob attacked Christian civilians and Royal Navy personnel), later stated that he should have been reprimanded rather than decorated because he was the only qualified medical man present to treat the wounded and should not have exposed himself to such danger. These may be taken as the statements of modest heroes (by all accounts, Murphy's acts contributed significantly to broader successes, while Maillard had been specifically ordered ashore in response to appeals from beleaguered sailors). [141]

On the other hand, Gordon Corrigan posed some interesting (although iconoclastic) questions about Captain Noel Chavasse, Royal Army Medical Corps, who was killed in the course of winning a Bar to the Victoria Cross (August 1917). In particular, he challenged the doctor's judgement in seeking out the wounded in No Man's Land in the course of his first VC exploit (August 1916). Corrigan pointed out that the task of bringing in the wounded was that of the stretcher bearers; the Regimental Medical Officer's place was at the Regimental Aid Post. Describing himself as a "cynical old soldier," Corrigan stated that had he been Chavasse's commanding officer he might have "awarded a rocket [reprimand] rather than a Victoria Cross."[142]

Corrigan's observations echo a memo written in 1943 to his officers by Major-General Guy Simonds, directing them how to approach the matter of recommending awards. Among other things, he noted that they should "discourage foolhardiness or the unnecessary and useless risk of lives and equipment" and that they should "strictly discourage any forms of 'medal hunting.'"

William Barker was no "medal hunter," yet he became Canada's most decorated military figure of the First World War. As a fighter pilot on the Western Front and in Italy he shot down 46 enemy aircraft. These successes owed much to his marksmanship, tactical skills – and calculation. Yet on the morning of 27 October 1918, under orders to deliver a Sopwith Snipe to an aircraft supply depot, he instead crossed the lines in an impromptu patrol and attacked an enemy reconnaissance machine, only to be attacked in turn by a succession of enemy fighters. His patrol ended in a few minutes with four enemy aircraft destroyed, the Snipe crash-landed in Allied lines and Barker near death from wounds that essentially left him a one-armed pilot for the rest of his life. The battle would lead to his being awarded the Victoria Cross.

Major William Barker with unidentified lady in 1919. His arm was still in a sling following his VC action of 27 October 1918 – a battle that left him virtually a one-armed pilot for the rest of his life. (Canadian War Museum M-839C)

Barker's biographer, Wayne Ralph, points out that he was far from proud of the action of 27 October 1918. Although he often spoke of his other wartime adventures, he declined to be interviewed about this one. A true professional, he regarded it as a foolish deviation from his normal practices, a crucial mistake:

> *All his leadership and tactical brilliance demonstrated in nearly three years of field service paled to insignificance against the "lone wolf" legend created on 27 October. He would always be remembered as the pilot who had fought single-handedly against 60 German machines. For someone so proud of his achievements, it was especially galling to know he had been the agent of his own undoing. His long fighting career was trivialized by a solo action in which he had been defeated.*[143]

On 18 June 1944, the *London Gazette* included in a long list of persons Mentioned in Despatches the name of Flying Officer Robert Bruce Tuff, Royal Australian Air Force. In Australia it was reported in the *Commonwealth Gazette* of 22 June 1944. Such awards were often posthumous and rarely accompanied by a citation, and the reasons for Tuff's recognition were unstated. Postwar declassification of records, however, revealed a remarkable story. He had committed an act of selfless gallantry or futile self-destruction, and the official debates as to the nature of his deed raise the question of whether courage, in some situations, is irrational and even self-indulgent.

A Typhoon pilot in No. 263 Squadron, Tuff had originally been recommended for a George Cross in the following terms:

> *On the 22nd February 1944, Flying Officer Tuff was returning from an armed shipping reconnaissance when he observed that his squadron commander (Squadron Leader G.B. Warnes, DSO, DFC) who had been compelled to alight on the sea some 20 miles northwest of Guernsey, was in difficulties and some 50 yards away from his dinghy. Flying Officer Tuff passed the information to his deputy leader by radio telephone and informed him that he intended to abandon his aircraft and go to the assistance of Squadron Leader Warnes, who also appeared to be injured. Flying Officer Tuff undoubtedly realized that, in view of the rough sea and poor*

visibility, it would be extremely unlikely that he would be able to alight on the sea close to Squadron Leader Warnes, and that to reach him he would probably have to swim a long distance in a perilous sea. He was a strong swimmer, however, and was evidently prepared if necessary to discard his own dinghy. Even if he reached Squadron Leader Warnes the chances of being picked up were extremely small in view of their distance from Guernsey and the roughness of the sea. Nevertheless, Flying Officer Tuff, in cold blood, took the risk in order to try and save the life of his squadron commander. In spite of every effort being made to locate Squadron Leader Warnes and Flying Officer Tuff they have not since been found. Flying Officer Tuff showed extreme bravery in attempting to help a comrade and his self-sacrifice was worthy of the highest praise.[144]

This particular incident drew considerable comment at the Air Ministry Awards Committee. Tuff had apparently baled out at 1,000 feet. An officer at Air Defence Great Britain described it as "a phenomenal case of quixotic bravery and devotion. Although opinions may differ on the wisdom of the Officer's action in abandoning his aircraft, his utter disregard for his life in a desperate effort to save his C.O. deserves a very high award." The committee, however, concluded (13 April) that "Flying Officer Tuff did not intentionally sacrifice his aircraft and his life in a vain effort to rescue his CO, but must have anticipated that there was a reasonable prospect of reaching safety. A posthumous award of the George Cross does not seem to be justified and a mention in despatches is the only alternative."

Another officer wrote (15 April 1944), "This heroic exploit is obviously a borderline case for the George Cross but I agree, albeit reluctantly, that the Awards Committee were right in concluding that F/O Tuff thought he had a fair chance of saving himself and his Squadron Commander. In other words, he did not deliberately accept an almost certain prospect of self-immolation. I therefore agree that a Mention is probably the best that we can do." The same officer nevertheless wished to investigate the possibility of an Albert Medal (for saving life at sea) and suggested approaches to the Admiralty for advice and information.

Yet another officer (apparently in the office of Chief of Air Staff) wrote (17 April 1944), "I am quite agreeable to P.U.S. trying to get a posthumous

Albert Medal for this pilot but I feel bound to mention that in spite of the extreme gallantry displayed for which I have the highest possible admiration his action was not justifiable on military grounds since he threw away an aircraft for an extremely improbable chance of saving his Squadron Leader's life." Although other minutes on file indicated hopes that an Albert Medal would be secured, yet another communication (24 April 1944, apparently by one Harries or Harris, DGPS) indicated that, since 1918, the Home Office had discouraged use of the Albert Medal for acts performed by Service personnel in the discharge of their duty, especially on active service. The minute read, in part:

> *In the case of No. 22 [the Tuff award] it seems to me that there is likely to be considerable difficulty in establishing eligibility for the Albert Medal under the present Warrant, since we have no evidence that Flying Officer Tuff actually engaged in any life-saving activities at sea. After the officer had informed the deputy leader of his intention to abandon his aircraft there was no visual contact with him. A Typhoon aircraft was seen to dive vertically into the sea from approximately 1,000 feet and the recommendation states, "it is thought that it can be accepted that this was the aircraft of Flying Officer Tuff after he had baled out." Whether he did bale out and what happened to him subsequently will probably never be known..*
>
> *There is also the point that to make an award of the Albert Medal to Flying Officer Tuff, which is bound to receive widespread publicity, would be to hold out his action as an example to other air crews, in contradistinction to CAS's view that this action was not justifiable on military grounds.*

Further correspondence apparently occurred with the Admiralty, which seems to suggest possible Royal Navy support for a posthumous award that would nevertheless be a step below that of a George Cross. However, the Chief of Air Staff himself appears to have scotched even this when he wrote, on 17 May 1944:

> *I had previously supposed that Tuff attempted to alight on the sea near the Squadron Leader; I now think the evidence of abandonment of the air-*

craft at or above 1,000 feet is more easily explained by the assumption that Flying Officer Tuff was under the influence of some kind of brainstorm than by attributing the act to the cold-blooded gallantry with which the recommendation credits him. Without further light on this point (which can presumably be obtained, if at all, only from his deputy leader) I should hesitate to go forward with the recommendation.[145]

If Tuff was a fool it was because he threw away his life (and a good airplane) on his own impulse and in a futile gesture. Other men fight and die in conditions almost as hopeless, yet they are heroes. The officers leading the Charge of the Light Brigade may have doubted the wisdom of their orders, but they did not openly question them, for military cohesion vanishes when instructions are debated, and no one can foresee whether the act he is called upon to perform will be successful or meaningful. Over 19,000 British and colonial troops died in the first day of the Battle of the Somme (1 July 1916), most of them probably unaware that they would be statistics in the bloodiest battle the British army ever fought. More than 7,200 Australian, British and Canadian soldiers were killed in the Third Battle of Amiens (8-11 August 1918), most without knowing that it would be a victory. The soldiers who stormed the Normandy beaches on 6 June 1944 carried no guarantee in their pockets that their sacrifices would achieve more than had occurred at Gallipoli. Yet in every case, the soldiers pressed ahead, some with confidence, some with only hope, that they were not being asked to go in harm's way for something trivial. One of the most remarkable things about the Western Front from 1914 to 1918 was that so few men deserted – on either side – notwithstanding horrendous casualties. When men gave up in whole battalions, as happened in Italy and Russia in 1917, it was not casualties but corruption that destroyed their cohesion. Even the French zouaves, rebelling in 1917, did not kill their officers; they merely refused to participate in any more offensives until such time as their attacks could have some hope of success and their deaths some significance beyond that of being numbers in an endless list. '

Sometimes men can see with their own eyes what is happening and why they are being asked to die. Those aboard HMS *Jervis Bay* knew what their job was – to protect a convoy – and on 5 November 1940 they could see that to save the ships in their care, the *Jervis Bay* must engage in hopeless, unequal battle with the German cruiser *Admiral Scheer*. They had no say in the matter; Captain Fogarty Fegen had chosen for them, and given a vote, few would have suggested anything different. From a crew of 255, a total of 187 perished, among them Captain Fegen, whose posthumous Victoria Cross was indeed a "token award given to a few in recognition of the bravery of the many."

Others, in great and imminent peril, did not have that comfort of certainty. The men who followed Wing Commander Hugh G. Malcolm into battle may have wondered what was to be accomplished, yet follow him they did.. Their final action was a small-scale aerial Balaklava, and even Air Ministry officials drew the parallel.

In late 1942 Wing Commander Malcolm commanded No. 18 Squadron in North Africa, flying Bisley aircraft (also known as the Blenheim V). The Bisley was an anachronism, an obsolete aircraft adapted ineffectively to a ground attack role. Like the Fairey Battle of 1940, it could survive only if it were operated in the context of total Allied air superiority. In December 1942, British and American air forces ruled North African skies only sporadically. By luck and good management, Malcolm had led successful attacks on enemy airfields on 17 and 28 November 1942 (incidents mentioned in the recommendation to his VC, evidently in an attempt to justify a "periodic" Victoria Cross). His luck ran out on 4 December. The squadron was ordered at short notice to attack an enemy airfield some 150 miles from base. The urgency of the order precluded any hope of providing fighter escort, but Wing Commander Malcolm took off anyway, leading 12 Bisleys to the target. They reached it unmolested, bombed the target, and then were beset by swarms of enemy fighters. He attempted to maintain the formation, as mutual supporting fire was their only hope, but one by one the Bisleys went down. Malcolm's machine was the last to go; he was shot down in flames and killed. It was subsequently learned that the initial orders had been issued with excessive haste; the target was less important than had been assumed, and a delayed take-off would have enabled a fighter escort to be assembled.

When the VC recommendation came before the Air Ministry committee, several references from Tennyson crept into the correspondence. At the same time, probing questions were posed. Did he know the risk of disaster? Was he justified in risking his squadron as he did? Was it a foolhardy undertaking from the outset? Were such losses attributable to the high degree of conscientiousness displayed by him? Did his courage justify the highest award?

It was generally agreed that Wing Commander Malcolm had received his orders and had no option but to obey them – "His not to reason why," as one officer noted. The Chief of the Air Staff himself wrote:

> *The fact that "someone had blundered" does not seem to me to distinguish the merit of this case from that displayed by, for instance, volunteers for an equally dangerous operation in which the risks had been recognized and properly assessed by the officer issuing the order. Of course it is quite possible through bad luck or incompetence for squadrons to be wiped out on operations which are no more hazardous than the average, and an award in this instance must not be taken as a precedent for decorating,* ipso facto, *leaders or survivors of operations that turn out disastrously.*
>
> *To sum up: I think the necessary degree of risk was present and was known to Wing Commander Malcolm, who faced it without question and from the highest sense of duty. I therefore consider that the VC should be awarded.*[146]

Wing Commander Malcolm's Victoria Cross was not the only one earned in a "forlorn hope" mission. The men who bombed the Maastricht bridges in May 1940 were equally doomed, as were the Swordfish crews led by Lieutenant-Commander Eugene Esmonde, attacking *Scharnhorst* and *Gneisenau* with their fighter umbrella (February 1942). The Augsburg raid of 17 April 1942 had a vital target (U-boat engine manufacturing plants) but only problematical chances of survival (7 of the 12 Lancasters engaged were shot down). Squadron Leader John D. Nettleton bombed the target, made it back to base and received a VC.

A one-aircraft mission by Squadron Leader Arthur S.K. Scarf on 9 December 1941 was as close to a self-imposed suicide mission as one can imagine. In Malaya, No. 62 Squadron had been ordered to bomb a Japanese airfield in Thailand. Scarf had just taken off in his Blenheim when enemy aircraft attacked his base, destroying or damaging all the other Blenheims that would have accompanied him. He could have abandoned the mission and landed; a single bomber could accomplish little, yet he chose to fly to the target. His rationale was that his gesture would restore the morale of his unit, whose members were at that moment watching their machines burn. Flak and fighter opposition was severe; he was mortally wounded in the running fight back to Malaya. He executed a successful forced landing and his crew survived, but he died shortly afterwards. Scarf's full story did not come out until 1945, when returned POWs testified to his actions, and his Victoria Cross was gazetted on 21 June 1946.[147]

The line between duty and blind obedience is not always clear, nor is that between self-sacrifice and self-indulgence. Flying Officer Tuff was deemed to have been driven by a "brainstorm" rather than bravery. Nevertheless, when reading of Scarf's mission one is reminded of Marshal Bosquet's assessment of Balaklava.

CHAPTER 12

REGIMENTAL
POLITICS

A medal glitters, but it also casts a shadow.

Winston S. Churchill (1874-1965)

No sane man joins the forces with the intention of winning the Victoria Cross or commits a gallant act with just such a reward in mind. Nevertheless, the prestige accruing to the VC has led units to seek awards for the honour of the regiment. This was demonstrated at the outset, for while some British commanders in the Crimea failed to submit any recommendations, others fairly swamped the War Office and Admiralty with submissions. The 55th Regiment alone sent forward 32 names for Crimean valour of whom two were finally given the award. The 57th Regiment recommended 31 men (two awards approved) while the 77th Regiment recommended 38 men (two awards).[148]

Once the significance of the award had dawned on various colonels, units scrambled to recommend soldiers. The attitude of the 58th Regiment demonstrated this admirably. Private Charles McCorrie's VC had been gazetted on 24 February 1857 but he died of natural causes on 8 April of the same year. His commanding officer immediately applied to the War Office to have another VC awarded from the lists previously submitted, so that the 57th might continue to have two VC recipients on its rolls.[149]

The story of Private Timothy O'Hea has been told often enough; as a member of the Rifle Brigade he fought a fire in an ammunition car on 9 June 1866 and was recommended for a VC which was gazetted on 1 January 1867. What is less well known is that the Rifle Brigade, having scored points with the O'Hea VC, soon attempted to repeat their success; early in 1867 they recommended Private William Berry for a VC "in consideration of his having saved the life of a child at the risk of his own, on the occasion of a Fire at Quebec on the 14th October last." On this occasion the War Office declined to forward the submission to the Queen, arguing that Berry's actions, though "very praiseworthy," were still inferior to those that would merit a VC. The more probable reason is that the Secretary of War deemed the Rifle Brigade to have gone to the well once too often.[150]

Once the status of the VC had been established, regimental officers were not above boasting of the number of times their unit had included a recipient. In February 1879, word reached Britain that the 24th Regiment of Foot had been almost entirely massacred by Zulus (Isandlwana, 22 January 1879), but that only hours later the same unit had mounted a spectacular defense at Rorke's Drift. In a letter to *The Times* on 21 February 1879, Major-General Thomas Ross, a former CO, wrote, in part:

> *Although the 24th Regiment have had hard knocks, they have also come in for their share of those rewards which are the soldier's greatest ambition. In the early part of 1868 I had the gratifying task of assembling the regiment to witness the decoration of one officer and four men with that most coveted prize, the Victoria Cross. Shall we be blamed if I confess that we were proud to think that no other regiment could show so high a number?*

Even as the 24th was engulfed in tragedy as well as triumph, others could not let that go, and the presumptions of the 24th were attacked the next day by one signing himself "Perthshire Light":

> *A Corps now serving in South Africa at one time bore on its roll a field officer, two doctors, two captains, two sergeants and two privates who all earned the "Cross of Valour" for acts performed under fire in the presence of an enemy. The five Victoria Crosses which at one swoop the 24th most gallantly carried off were awarded to a boat's crew for a deed of great daring but which was not performed under fire, and so under the original wording of the Victoria Cross Warrant would not in Crimea or Mutiny days have entitled the wearers to the coveted decoration.[151]*

Regimental "boosting" is difficult to document, but there is more than a hint of it in respect of Private Ernest Alva "Smokey" Smith. Following a bitterly fought action on the Savio River, Italy, on the night of 21/22 October 1944, the commanding officer of the Seaforth Highlanders of Canada, Lieutenant-Colonel Henry P. Bell-Irving, received a message from the General Officer Commanding, Eighth Army:

My congratulations on your gallant and successful action in the night crossing of the River Savio under the most difficult conditions. The maintenance and enlargement of your bridgehead in face of armoured counterattacks shows determination and skill of the highest degree. Your part in this attack made a decisive contribution to the army plan.

It is not clear if the GOC first suggested a VC to the Seaforths or if Bell-Irving pointed out that the expression "decisive contribution" merited one, but shortly thereafter the colonel met with his officers to examine several instances of brave acts from the night in question. Those performed by Smith, described later as close to being a one-man army, were chosen.[152]

The development of modern communications, including television (especially documentaries) and even the internet, has put tools at the disposal of lobbyists that have enabled many groups (notably regimental associations) to argue for their rights and champions to ever broader audiences. The modern case of Talaiasi Labalaba, Special Air Service (SAS, an elite tactical unit), is a fine example.

British forces had a long history of operations around the Arabian peninsula, even after the various sultanates had gained their independence. In 1972, they were active in Oman. A tribal group, the Dhofar Liberation Front, had risen against the Sultan in Dhofar, a southern province. On 19 July 1972, some 250 rebels attacked Mirbat, a coastal village ringed by barbed wire. They were intent on killing every one of its inhabitants and were armed with AK-47 assault rifles, grenades, mortars, anti-tank rifles and rocket launchers. The place was defended by one Omani artilleryman, 30 northern tribesmen armed with .303 rifles, some 25 policemen, and a nine-man SAS squadron commanded by Captain M.J.A. Kealy. The British troops had been training the Omani forces and were due to be airlifted out the following day. Instead, they were at the heart of a bitter battle over a dilapidated corner of a small desert kingdom.

The action lasted between two and three hours. The defenders had an 81-mm mortar and a Second-World War vintage 25-pounder, the latter in a gun pit outside the barbed wire. Sergeant Talaiasi Labalaba, BEM, a Fijian member of the SAS, ran 500 metres to the gun pit housing the 25-pounder. Labalaba was a well known figure in the SAS, having fought in Borneo and Aden, where he had led an undercover anti-terrorist plainclothes team. As the rebels attacked in waves, he manned the gun alone, firing repeatedly. At length he reported he had been wounded in the chin but that he was all right. Kealy suspected otherwise and sent another soldier under fire to check on Labalaba. This man realized the situation was critical and fetched the Omani gunner, who nevertheless was severely wounded just as they regained the 25-pounder gun pit. The two SAS men lowered the gun to 45 degrees, firing over open sights until Labalaba was hit by a bullet in the neck and rapidly bled to death. His comrade was also wounded. A third British soldier reached the gun pit, only to be mortally wounded.

The rebels came near to overrunning the defenders but, just in time, Omani Air Force fighters arrived and attacked the enemy. Soon afterwards, helicopters brought SAS reinforcements and evacuated the wounded. The rebels left 30 dead behind plus 10 men taken prisoner; the defenders suffered four dead and three seriously wounded. Sergeant Labalaba's gun shield was found riddled with bullet holes.

SAS veterans contend that the defenders of Mirbat should have been highly decorated and argue that, because the British government did not want to expose their involvement in Dhofar, gallantry decorations were not announced until three years after the battle. Captain Kealy was awarded the Distinguished Service Order. One man received a Distinguished Conduct Medal, two received Military Crosses, and Sergeant Labalaba was posthumously Mentioned in Dispatches. Thirty years after the fight, the campaign continues to have this upgraded to a Victoria Cross.[153]

But was one warranted? Could it be argued that he was bravely doing the job for which he had been trained and paid? Is there an element of regimental politics in Special Forces groups arguing so long after the event for a Victoria Cross? The reader may form an opinion. In the meantime, it may be worth while noting the frequency with which SAS personnel have been mentioned in conjunction with more recent events, including attempts to raise a VC for Lieutenant-Colonel Robert Blair Mayne (61 years after the events cited) and curious disclosures about events in Afghanistan and Iraq. On a website dedicated to the Victoria Cross (but unhappily now defunct) this author asked if retired SAS officers might have been lobbying on several fronts to get a VC for their formation, even to the point of reaching back to the Second World War; other contributors to the website declared that there had been no such campaign.

In March 2002 British newspapers carried reports that one, if not two, members of the Special Air Service had been awarded Victoria Crosses for action at Bora Bora. When no names or citations were released, it was claimed that the awards had been approved but that secrecy precluded their disclosure. One sceptic, commenting on these "hidden" Victoria Crosses, wrote, "I find it slightly ironic that the SAS, which prides itself on looking after secrecy, seems to leak like a sieve."

In the end, it was clear that no VC awards had been made for combat in Afghanistan. Commencing in 2003, British and Australian participation in the Iraq War opened up new speculation about Victoria Cross actions. In September 2004, another story appeared in the press, this time claiming that an SAS soldier had been recommended for a Victoria Cross but that it had been downgraded to a lesser award. Anonymous generals were quoted as deploring the situation with comments such as, "It would appear these days it is easier to achieve sainthood than to win a Victoria Cross while you are alive." The deed purportedly involved rescuing a wounded Australian SAS colleague under fire; but the story began to fall apart when Australian Defence Force spokesmen told an Australian newspaper there was "no record of an Australian SAS soldier being wounded in Iraq."

The publicity and controversy accompanying these reports contrasts markedly with the confidentiality and discretion with which a Victoria Cross was finally awarded – that to Private Johnson Gideon Beharry (see Appendix G).

CHAPTER 13

RIGHTING WRONGS
OR SETTLING SCORES?

I'll be reveng'd on the whole pack of you.

Malvolio, *Twelfth Night* by William Shakespeare (1564-1616)

T he history of the Victoria Cross is replete with "near misses," indicating that even to be recommended is a signal honour. *The Times* of 3 May 1904, reporting the death of General Sir Charles Shute, described his heroism as a young major in the Crimean War and stated, "He was recommended for the Victoria Cross, but was not among those eventually decorated." The same paper, on 11 April 1905, writing of General Sir William Traill-Burroughs, said of his exploits in the Indian Mutiny, "He was the first, or one of the first, through the breach at the storming of the Secundragh, and with some dozen men overpowered the gate guard. For this service, in which he received a slight tulwar cut on the hand, he was recommended for, but did not get, the Victoria Cross."[154] The death of Brigadier Edward Allen Wood led *The Times* (21 May 1930) to observe that he had been "twice recommended for the Victoria Cross," which may have been true, given his record as a Companion of the Order of St. Michael and St. George, awarded the DSO three times, "nine times mentioned in despatches, wounded five times, twice gassed, and once buried." Upon the death of Siegfried Sassoon ("Poet, fox-hunter, soldier and pacifist"), *The Times* of 4 September 1967 wrote, "After capturing some German trenches in the Hindenburg Line [in 1917], he remained in the enemy position reading a volume of poems, oblivious to the danger, and as a result was recommended for the Victoria Cross, but as the campaign eventually ended in a reverse, he only received a Bar to his Military Cross."

Should any of the cases of failed VC recommendations be revisited and Victoria Crosses substituted for previous lesser awards? Should people now long dead be granted Victoria Crosses who were valiant in their time and yet, for one reason or another, were never recommended for one? To what degree can we re-write the past? Is "re-writing" the record the same as "re-righting" or redressing old injustices? The questions are particularly relevant when groups now demand that governments pardon or exonerate long-dead figures like Louis Riel and Patrick Whalen, or apologize for assorted past actions – slavery, the deportation of the Acadians, the Irish Potato Famine, the Battle of Culloden, the Inquisition – and perhaps come up with hard cash to compensate the descendants of those who were enslaved, deported, exiled or burned at the stake. All this brings us to developments that have offered tantalizing prospects of overturning past decisions and thumbing noses at dead politicians – national honours created for one purpose but amenable to corrupt ends as well.

A distinct system of Canadian honours was proposed as early as 1868 (by the Governor General himself) and repeatedly discussed in decades that followed. The Canadian government ventured into a few campaign and service medals (such as one for troops and police serving in the Northwest Rebellion of 1885); it created a Memorial Cross for bereaved mothers and widows of First World War military fatalities (continued in subsequent wars and conflicts) and it devised a Canadian Volunteer Service Medal for all Second World War enlistments (1943). On the other hand, the government created a Canada Medal (1943) but dithered so much about who should be eligible that it was never awarded. It repeatedly ignored suggestions from Canadian generals and diplomats that a hierarchy of Canadian honours be created, distinct from those distributed in Great Britain.

In 1967 (Canada's Centennial year), spurred by Canadian nationalism, the Liberal government of Lester B. Pearson instituted distinct Canadian state honours. The system took some five years to evolve, but by 1972 the most important elements were in place. They included the Order of Canada in three categories (Companion, Officer, Member) for services to humanity, the nation or the community; the Order of Military Merit, also in three categories (roughly a service equivalent of the Order of Canada); plus a small pantheon of bravery awards (Cross of Valour, Star of Courage, Medal of Bravery) open to both military and civilian personnel. As of 2005 the Cross of Valour has been awarded 19 times (five times posthumously) and the standards of bravery have been very high indeed. The Star of Courage has been awarded less sparingly, but the Medal of Bravery has, alas, been distributed with a prodigality that has rendered it more equivalent to a Commendation for Brave Conduct than a true gallantry decoration.

The Commonwealth of Australia followed the Canadian example in 1975, but in 1991 that nation went one step further. They created a series of gallantry awards for military personnel alone, including an "Australianized" Victoria Cross. Canada then copied Australia and in 1993 instituted its own military valour decorations consisting of the Victoria Cross (Canadian), Star of Military Valour and Medal of Military Valour, for varying degrees of courage in the presence of an "enemy." None have yet been awarded, in large measure because the government has been reluctant to admit until recently that the Canadian Armed Forces abroad do anything more belligerent than to be Boy Scouts in camouflage uniforms and helmets.

The creation of an "Australian" VC might seem unremarkable, but it became the focus of a strange campaign, continuing to this day, to have the award bestowed posthumously on John Simpson, who was killed at Gallipoli in 1915. And thereby hangs a tale.

Australians have by turns (and sometimes simultaneously) had a love-hate relationship with Great Britain (not unlike Canadians vis-à-vis the United States). The Gallipoli campaign is still regarded with pride (much as the Battle of Vimy Ridge is deemed a Canadian triumph) and yet with resentment for which there is no Canadian counterpart. John Simpson was what Australians call a "larrikan" – a free spirit – who enlisted in the Australian Imperial Force and achieved fame in 1915 by traversing the Gallipoli battlefield with a donkey, bringing supplies to beleaguered troops, evacuating casualties and finally being struck down by an artillery shell. He is Australia's best known war hero; a statue of Simpson and his donkey stands outside the Australian War Memorial. He was Mentioned in Despatches – but he was not awarded a VC.

In 2001 the magazine *Medal News* carried the following item:

In an unprecedented move the Australian Government are planning to award the "Hero of Gallipoli," John (Jack) Simpson, the Australian Victoria Cross. Simpson was a stretcher bearer who rescued more than 300 men from the carnage of the battlefields of Gallipoli and is recognized as a national hero. He was recommended for the VC at the time of his death in 1915, but because he had originally deserted from the British Merchant Marine to enlist in the Australian Army under a new name, he was considered ineligible for the award. Numerous requests have been made to the British authorities over the years for the original decision to be overturned but have always been rejected. However, under the new rules Australian honours can now be awarded without reference to Westminster and Australians consider that this "national disgrace" can now be put right.

The idea that a VC might be used as a "sharp stick in the eye," rebuking the vile British for their unfeeling treatment of the case, seemed an odd way to use a national honour. This writer despatched a query to the Australian War Memorial itself. My questions were:

1. *Has this happened already?*
2. *Is there any documentation of the period indicating that Simpson was recommended for a VC?*
3. *If said recommendation is recorded, is the name of the officer making the recommendation known?*
4. *If the recommendation is on file, are the reasons (as stated in the news item) as described?*

The reply that I received on 29 March 2001 bears reproduction almost in full:

Subject: John Simpson Kirkpatrick
Dear Mr Halliday,
Our Internet Coordinator has asked me to reply to you regarding some of your queries about the possible award of a VC to Simpson.
    The Medal News *article is incorrect in most respects.*
    Simpson was never recommended for a VC, either in his lifetime, or posthumously. Although the fact that he was posthumously awarded an MiD is given as evidence that he was recommended for a VC, which was downgraded to a MiD, this is simply untrue, and is not supported by

our official honours recommendations (although there are other recorded instances in this series of the downgrading of VC recommendations to other awards – presumably because of the operation of the quota system). Simpson could only have been eligible for a VC or MiD because these were the only two awards at the time of his death that could be given posthumously.

Although there were no written rules about who should get a VC, in the First World War, nearly all recipients were involved in close combat, killing or capturing the enemy (in the Boer War VC winners had mostly rescued comrades, injured or otherwise, under fire- Simpson may well have qualified in this war. The "criteria" were different again in the Second World War). In the First World War stretcher bearers and other members of field ambulances and casualty clearing stations were occasionally awarded DCMs, and after 1916, many Military Medals, but never VCs. Simpson's actions might well have earned him a DCM had he lived.

The current Australian government is not planning to award Simpson a VC. There will be, however, a federal election this year, and as part of its run up to the election campaign the federal opposition (Labor Party) is claiming that it will award VCs to Simpson, and to Teddy Sheean,* a World War Two sailor. They've got no further than issuing this statement but it may be that they plan to make posthumous awards of the new (and so far unissued) Victoria Cross of Australia. Clearly this is just a political statement at this stage. Although Sheean has relatives in Australia, Simpson has not, and I suspect that no one has even stopped to think that, if a VC were to be awarded to him, a distant Scottish relative could legally claim it and have no obligation to see the medal housed in Australia.

There haven't been numerous requests over the years to "overturn" the decision not to award Simpson a VC because there was no decision to be overturned. However, there have been moves to secure a VC for him in the last fifteen years or so. The move to secure a VC for Sheean is even more recent. I am not aware of any formal approach to the British Government regarding the proposed awards.

---

* Ordinary Seaman Edward "Teddy" Sheean, Royal Australian Navy, died following the sinking of HMAS *Armidale*, 1 December 1942.

You should note that although what Simpson did was undoubtedly brave his actions at the time were not viewed with universal approbation by those on Gallipoli. Finding that he did not take kindly to orders, and preferred to "do his own thing" his commanding officer let him do just that. Some independent observers also thought that his actions drew unnecessary Turkish fire on to Australian positions. It was also alleged that Simpson carried a rifle when he should not have been seen to be a combatant.

Simpson and his donkey were used after his death for propaganda purposes for the war effort, and later in the century as an example of true Australian "digger spirit" whatever that may be. Public sentiment has generally overturned any attempts at a critical evaluation of his life and work.

Yours sincerely,

Jane Peek

Curator, Military Heraldry

The lobbying to award Simpson a Victoria Cross continues to this day; the website that promotes the cause (<http://www.diggerhistory.info/pages-heroes/simpson.htm>) insists that he was "twice recommended for the Victoria Cross." It blames "red tape and bungling" for having "denied Simpson due recognition." Nevertheless, the campaign may well have run out of steam.

New Zealand, that most "loyal" of all British Dominions, instituted its own Victoria Cross in 1999. It, too, has become the centre of a debate (less passionate than that surrounding Simpson) about posthumous awarding to a historical figure. As early as 1997 a campaign had begun to upgrade a DCM awarded to Lance Sergeant Haane Manahi to a Victoria Cross. The cause was initially promoted by a committee headed by Sir Charles Bennett, a former commander of the Maori Battalion, and supported by Tuariki Delamere, a New Zealand cabinet minister who came from the same tribe as Manahi. On 20 December 2005, the Wellington *Dominion Post* reported that two Maori bodies, the Te Arawa Trust Board (a tribal council) and the Waitangi Tribunal, were urging that a submission be put to the Queen for the grant of a Victoria Cross to Manahi. As a Maori body examining and recommending land settlements and other claims dating to the earliest days of European settlement in New Zealand, the Waitangi Tribunal spoke with a particularly loud voice, especially when it suggested that refusal of a VC might somehow offend native sensibilities and be in breach of settler-aboriginal treaties. A spokesman for the New Zealand First party regarded the campaign as "eminently sensible," although the Returned Services Association (a veterans' organization) was only cautiously supportive, noting that the campaign "could result in similar cases being advanced."

Lance Sergeant Manahi (who died in 1968) was indeed recommended for a VC following an attack on a position in North Africa on the night of 19/20 April 1943. The submission survived the scrutiny of senior officers including (then) General Bernard Law Montgomery, whose pen later turned several Canadian VC recommendations into DSO and DCM awards. Nevertheless, the War Office in London turned Manahi's VC into a DCM. His supporters claimed that the decision had been unfair and arbitrary, based more on award quotas than on the measure of his gallantry.[155] Be that as it may, he did not go unrewarded, and he was in good company when one observes other cases of VC recommendations reduced to DCM awards.[156]

Even before the campaign on behalf of Manahi, another New Zealander was the focal point of a campaign to raise (not revive) a VC recommendation years after the events concerned. Warrant Officer John Horan was air gunner in an Air/Sea Rescue Sea Otter aircraft of No. 292 Squadron. On 9 January 1945, it was on a mission off Akyab, Burma, when six Japanese Ki.43 "Oscar" aircraft attacked. When Horan reported he was hit, the navigator went aft to find the gunner unconscious and with his left hand blown off. He revived as he was being dragged back into the fuselage, then insisted that he be returned to his post. Horan jammed his guns against his chest and continued to hold off the fighters, although wounded again in the head. The Sea Otter had been reduced to a shambles, but the pilot managed to force-land in the water and beach his machine. He subsequently insisted that "Horan's supreme sacrifice" had saved the lives of the crew.

As early as 1 March 1945, Group Captain Keith Caldwell, RNZAF, was writing Air Command South East Asia to inquire about a possible VC recommendation for Horan. Caldwell was quoting from a colourfully worded press officer's account of the action. Six weeks later, the same headquarters replied in the negative. It appeared that they had received conflicting reports about what had happened; the press officer had mentioned eight "Oscars" (contradicted by the pilot's first report) and the initial accounts on file had indicated that Horan had died after the second or third burst of enemy fire. He was, however, Mentioned in Despatches.

The matter rested there until 1953, when an officer who had known Horan in 1941-42 wrote to a British organization, the Air Gunners Association, inquiring about his former associate, wondering why he had received no more than a Mention in Despatches, and raising an emotional red herring – that Horan had left a widow and child who deserved "something more tangible as a Memorial." The association in turn published an account of the action and asked the same question. Unfortunately for the cause of clarity, the letter writer had not even been in the Far East in 1945, and his narrative could only be described as "enhanced" – the aircraft was now a Blenheim, the enemy fighters were A6M Zeros and there were 13 of them. The Air Gunners Association newsletter, *The Turret*, used such phrases as "not sufficient recognition" and "shamefully neglected."

British newspapers soon took up the cry and Air Ministry was called upon to review the surviving records. These showed considerable discrepancies even at the time. The Operational Record Book of No. 292 Squadron referred to only two Japanese fighters, although it did confirm that a wounded Horan had returned to his post and kept on fighting to the end. No. 67 Squadron, which had scrambled Spitfires to intercept the "Oscars," mentioned four enemy fighters, joined later by a fifth.* Inquiries did confirm that no Victoria Cross recommendation had been drafted, much less submitted at the time. The officer who had decided at the time to recommend a Mention in Despatches was Air Chief Marshal Sir Keith Park – RAF by profession, New Zealander by birth and upbringing. The idea of proposing a VC nine years after the event faded away, although it has been revived by members of Horan's family at least twice.[157]

The scramble to resurrect VC claims on behalf of dead champions exercises persons in England itself. Such movements have even found their way to the floor of the British House of Commons, where the following motion was tabled on 14 June 2005 by MP Ian Gibson:

---

* There was a Canadian angle here; the Spitfires shot down all five "Oscars"; two of these were destroyed by Squadron Leader Robert R.W. Day, RCAF.

That this House recognizes the grave injustice meted out to Lieutenant-Colonel Paddy Mayne, of 1st, Special Air Service, who won the Victoria Cross at Oldenburg in North West Germany on 9th April 1945; notes that this was subsequently downgraded, some six months later, to a third bar DSO, that the citation had been clearly altered and that David Stirling, founder of the SAS has confirmed that there was considerable prejudice towards Mayne and that King George VI enquired why the Victoria Cross had "so strangely eluded him"; further notes that on 14th December it will be 50 years since Colonel Mayne's untimely death, in a car accident, and this will be followed on 29th January 2006 by the 150th anniversary of the signing of the Royal Warrant to institute the Victoria Cross; and therefore calls upon the Government to mark these anniversaries by instructing the appropriate authorities to act without delay to reinstate the Victoria Cross given for exceptional personal courage and leadership of the highest order and to acknowledge that Mayne's actions on that day saved the lives of many men and greatly helped the allied advance on Berlin.

The movement to replace Mayne's fourth DSO with a VC relied on some highly questionable statements; the claim of "prejudice" was never convincingly explained or proven, while the assertion that King George VI had been a Mayne "booster" was equally unprovable (no royal correspondence was produced, nor was it likely to be forthcoming). The Parliamentary resolution generated heated discussions in newspapers and on-line. When, in January 2006, the British government declined to reopen the case, the Blair Mayne Association declared itself ready to continue the campaign, one supporter swearing "to fight until his dying breath to have the VC reinstated."

The very heat of the argument puzzles a North American. One contributor to the on-line debates declared that the "revisionist" campaign was rooted in Ulster's sectarian rivalries. Only one Ulster citizen had been awarded a Victoria Cross during the Second World War – and that a working-class West Belfast Catholic (James Magennis). Indeed, five Victoria Crosses had been awarded to citizens of Eire who had joined the British forces, notwithstanding that country's neutrality. Mayne having been a prewar athletic star and bona fide war hero, extreme Protestants were embittered that no VC had been forthcoming for "their" man and so lobbied to have history revisited. Another contributor, writing privately to this author, disputed the sectarian theory, declaring that "95 per cent of the [Ulster] population ... are moderate, sensible people who go about their lives in the same way as most of us in the UK or Canada." That may be true, although 5 per cent of any group determined to make life miserable for the majority can be very strident indeed, be they Islamic fundamentalists or soccer hooligans.

By way of comparative history, it is interesting to note that in January 2001 the Americans awarded a Medal of Honor to Teddy Roosevelt 101 years after the Battle of San Juan Hill and 82 years after his death. They have also retroactively awarded Medals of Honor to racial minorities of both world wars to redress perceived slights of those days. The Roosevelt award climaxed years of lobbying by many (including descendants of the former president). The House of Representatives and United States Senate both unanimously supported a 1998 resolution for the award (who would publicly scoff at the idea?). Significantly, a website lauding the move admitted:

> *The opposition to awarding the Medal of Honor to TR came particularly from elements within the U.S. Army. The Army has opposed in general the repeal of the statute of limitations on military decorations and the award of what might be called historical medals. Moreover, some in the Army thought that Roosevelt simply did not deserve the Medal of Honor. While no public statement was made on the case, it is widely believed that some historians in the Army think that TR was no more outstanding than many other brave officers in the battle of July 1, 1898 in Cuba, who did not receive the Medal of Honor either.*[158]

Americans may do what they like with their history; Canadians have a duty to their own. The idea of retroactive and retrospective VC awards, simply because they were recommended by Commonwealth citizens and frustrated within a largely British chain of command, ignores the fact that British personnel as well as "colonials" were the subject of failed recommendations, and nobody will speak for them while Canadians, Australians and New Zealanders busily inflate their VC lists.

To look back and retroactively award Victoria Crosses would create a new class of VC, awarded out of a sense of grievance, bestowed on those fortunate enough to have current lobbyists. Such "revisionism" simply cheapens the award, making it less honorable even to future nominees. It has been estimated that, if all requests for retrospective Victoria Crosses were accepted, over one thousand such awards would be granted for Second World War deeds alone – more than five times the number actually awarded during that war.[159]

Another reason for not revisiting and upgrading old recommendations can best be explained with the question, "Where do you stop?" For if failed Victoria Cross submissions are modified, why not failed DSO, MC, DCM, DFC, DFM or similar recommendations? Consider the following cases from hundreds that can be found in Canadian files (doubtless there are more in Australian, South African or New Zealand dossiers):

On the morning of the 19th May 1944, the Royal 22e Regiment was attacking the Adolf Hitler Line in the area Map Reference 732194. Major Joseph Oliva Garceau was commanding "D" Company, one of the forward companies.

After the forward companies had reached the intermediate objective the two reserve companies were pushed through to the Battalion objective. One of these companies, "B" Company, had advanced 400 yards towards their final objective when it came under intense machine gun fire and accurate sniping. All the officers and non-commissioned officers of the company became casualties. When this situation was reported to Major Garceau, he went forward to "B" Company and found that a Corporal was in command of the company. Realizing the very critical tactical situation in which the company was placed, Major Garceau began to reorganize it. With complete disregard for his own safety and under continuous enemy fire, he ordered more favourable positions to be taken up, visiting each platoon position in turn. He ensured the evacuation of the wounded and by his words and encouragement to the remaining Non-Commissioned Officer and his men he soon restored their fighting spirit which had been badly shaken by the loss of all their leaders. Shortly after this, the forward companies were ordered to withdraw.

Throughout this action Major Garceau showed inspiring leadership and devotion to duty and it was due largely to his efforts that the withdrawal was carried out successfully and that more lives were saved.

Major Garceau had been recommended for a DSO and received no award whatsoever. Should his case be reopened?

On the afternoon of 22 May 1944, 4 Canadian Reconnaissance Regiment (4 Princess Louise Dragoon Guards) were probing the defences of the enemy's Adolf Hitler Line in the area MR 7215 to the south of Pontecorvo.

C.4505 Trooper John Wesley Emigh of "A" Squadron led a three-man patrol against a German outpost. In spite of heavy mortar and machine gun fire this trooper manoeuvred his men into position. They then charged and overran the outpost. So successful was the assault that twelve prisoners were captured. Six of these were taken by Trooper Emigh alone when he entered a German pill box.

This trooper's cool bravery and disregard for his own safety were an inspiring example to other members of his troop.

Trooper Emigh had been recommended for a Military Medal and received no award at all. Should his case be reopened?

On 21 May 1944 the West Nova Scotia Regiment were in a forward position facing the Adolf Hitler Line at Map Reference 753187. Lance Sergeant (Acting Sergeant) Hugh Allan MacLeod was acting as Signal Platoon Leader.

During this period the unit was heavily mortared and shelled for 24 hours. "C" Company Headquarters including its two signalers all became casualties. Although the Signal Platoon was under strength, Acting Sergeant MacLeod sent his only two remaining signalers to that company, taking over the duties of an operator at battalion headquarters in addition to his normal duties.

Absolutely disregarding personal safety he made his way from Battalion Headquarters to "C" Company through mortar and shell fire carrying batteries and signal equipment essential to the continued maintenance of communications.

It was largely due to this Non-Commissioned Officer's personal efforts that signal communications were maintained at a critical phase in the battle. He performed his duties in an exemplary manner, well beyond the normal call of duty.

Lance Sergeant MacLeod had been recommended for a Distinguished Conduct Medal and received only a Mention in Despatches. Should the decisions of his contemporaries be set aside and a DCM substituted based on perceptions of those who were not even born when these events took place?

On 27 January 1945, Flying Officer Leonard Joseph Kearney (RCAF) of No. 410 Squadron was recommended for a Mention in Despatches as follows:

This officer served as a pilot with this squadron on Mosquito night fighter aircraft from the 11th November 1943 to the 10th December 1944 on which date he was posted for repatriation to Canada on completing three years service overseas. Throughout his service with this squadron, Flying Officer Kearney displayed consistently good flying ability and invariably carried out his duties with keenness and efficiency, during the course of which he completed 70 operational sorties involving 139 operational hours. On the 28th May 1944 when operating from Hunsdon he engaged a Ju.88 at a height of 4,000 feet and shot it down in flames, the enemy aircraft being last seen going down as a ball of fire from a height of 800 feet in the Lille area (France). Again on the 13th June 1944 he destroyed an He.177 fifteen miles northeast of Le Havre, shooting down the enemy aircraft after intensive evasive action. At the conclusion of this combat both engines started to go bad, one had to be feathered as it was on fire and the pilot had to land immediately on an emergency strip on the beachhead, evading a balloon barrage bordering the strip.

No award, not even a humble MiD, was forthcoming. Should this too (and others) be the subject of revision and supposed restitution?[160]

There are those who would argue that awards of the Victoria Cross were arbitrary and hence unfair. If one agrees with that, without reservation, then two possible conclusions might be drawn:

(a) That all failed VC recommendations should be upgraded to Victoria Crosses, *or*

(b) That all awards of the Victoria Cross should be revoked, the medals recalled and melted down, the records burned.

However, even the argument of "unfairness" fails when we look at reality. No one emerging from the womb is presented with a certificate guaranteeing that life will be "fair." If our world was "fair," then everyone would be born into wealth equivalent to that of the average Canadian, or born into the poverty that is the lot of the average Sudanese. Shall we spend our time rewriting history to square with our concepts of justice – or strive to mould the future in conformity with our present ideals? The past is both an inspiration and a warning. It ceases to be either when we mutilate it to match our current prejudices and perceptions.

The past happened. Get used to it.

CHAPTER 14

MYTHS, FACTS
AND FOOTNOTES

History is a distillation of rumour.

Thomas Carlyle (1795-1881)

This is the West, sir. When the legend becomes fact, print the legend.

Carleton Young as Maxwell Scott, *The Man Who Shot Liberty Valance* (1962)

I
n the age of print there is more to history than rumour, but the line
between fact and legend is not necessarily easy to define. Modern historians are confronted with information and misinformation, facts and
propaganda, sometimes filtered through ideologies or special interests. They
would prefer to draw upon the most reliable sources – eyewitness accounts,
contemporary documents – but with so much to cover and only limited time
to research, they often fall back on the earlier writings of others, hoping that
their predecessors got it right. Sometimes they did not.

Footnotes and endnotes are relatively modern devices (neither Plutarch
nor Francis Parkman used them), but they are excellent measures of diligence. M.J. Crook's *The Evolution of the Victoria Cross* is an example of such
diligence; his own footnotes refer to specific documents in Britain, and as
such his book may be assumed to be a reliable source. Yet an array of footnotes that refer only to previously published books (rather than documents
or recent scholarly studies) invites A.J. Balfour's observation, "History does
not repeat itself. Historians repeat each other."

Accepted facts may remain facts, but sometimes they are revealed as errors. Even so, the mistakes may be perpetuated because authors do not fol-

low the most recent findings. The story of the Japanese submarine *Ro.32* demonstrates how difficult it can be to set the record straight. When, in the late 1940s, the Royal Navy was compiling its Official History, Captain William Roskill included *Ro.32* in an appendix listing Japanese vessels sunk; it had supposedly been destroyed by an RCAF aircraft and American ships off the coast of Alaska. When evidence to the contrary was brought to him – that *Ro.32* was still afloat as a training vessel in 1945 – Roskill published a revised listing in a succeeding volume. The original error had appeared in a 1949 RCAF publication, *Chronology of the RCAF*, but had been dropped from a 1975 edition produced by the Canadian War Museum. The correction was also noted by Larry Milberry in *Sixty Years: The RCAF and CF Air Command, 1924-1984*. Nevertheless, the original (and erroneous) account has been repeated in at least two more recent books (*All the Fine Young Eagles* by David L. Bashow, 1996; *The History of the Royal Canadian Air Force* by Christopher Shores, 1984) whose authors had missed the correction. No doubt, somebody plagiarizing from Bashow or Shores 10 or 20 years hence will again "sink" the unsunk *Ro.32*.

It is not surprising to find on occasion that events and personalities associated with the Victoria Cross have been invented, distorted, exaggerated or simply misunderstood. Sometimes it seems as though popular writers did so for no better reason than the need to dramatize what were otherwise bare facts. Alan McLeod's Victoria Cross action of 27 March 1918 is a case in point. The citation to this award takes up 213 words in the *London Gazette*. Among other things, it states merely that, in the fight with eight enemy aircraft, he enabled his observer (Arthur Hammond) to shoot down three of their attackers "out of control." Two documents relating to the recommendation for the award (which, incidentally, started as a suggested Mention in Despatches) do not add materially to this aspect of the fight; indeed, the greater part of the documents deals with a wounded McLeod stepping out on the wing of his burning aircraft and sideslipping it to the ground, then rescuing his gunner.[161]

McLeod and Hammond were too badly injured to file a combat report, although both wrote personal letters to describe the day's events. That from McLeod to his father was especially long, although it did not detail the aerial combat, and since he died of influenza in November 1918, he offered no

Bill Wheeler's art depicts Alan A. McLeod's VC action of 27 March 1918, as McLeod stands on the wing of his burning FK-8 aircraft and brings it down under control while his gunner, Arthur Hammond, continues to battle enemy aircraft. (Canadian War Museum and William J. Wheeler, artist)

further accounts of the deed. Twelve years later, however, George Drew, in *Canada's Fighting Airmen,* had expanded the account. From the first brush with enemy fighters to the crash in British lines, he provides approximately 650 words of description, including details of how the enemy aircraft went down ("By skillful maneuvering McLeod put Hammond in position, and after three short burst of fire the German machine went over on its back, then into a spin, and crashed to the ground immediately below ... Hammond opened fire. The force of the bullets hitting the German machine was so great that the body of the triplane broke off at the pilot's seat and the wreckage immediately burst into flames. One of the Germans, evidently thinking that the British machine was hopelessly out of action, dived so close that Hammond could see the features of the pilot.... Hammond again manned his gun and shot the German machine down in flames."

As of 1980, Ron Dodds in *The Brave Young Wings,* had not been able to add substantially to Drew's questionable account and indeed recounted the fight in more reserved language, even allowing that Hammond, firing on the third German fighter "drove him down" – no flames. Dodds' narrative took some 264 words from first encounter to final crash. In 1990, however, Dan McCaffery wrote of the battle in terms that can only be described as "Drew Plus" – a rock-em' sock-em' fantasy of aerial gore. He stated that, before being engaged by German fighters, McLeod and his observer had stalked and shot down a German observation balloon. Quite simply, this never happened (although McLeod and another observer had shot down a balloon on 14 January 1918). Drew had written of a German aircraft getting so close that Hammond could "see the features of the pilot"; the newest version was more lurid: "One attacker, obviously contemptuous of the old two seater, came too close and Hammond blew his head off." [162] The "old two seater" was, in fact, an Armstrong-Whitworth FK.8, a rugged, near-state-of-the-art army cooperation aircraft

The accounts by Dodds and McCaffery, drawing from little beyond the overheated Drew, are best contrasted with the work of Carl Christie, who consulted many original and contemporary sources, most notably the McLeod correspondence held by the Canadian War Museum, supplemented by letters written by Hammond into the 1920s. Significantly, Christie wrote a character study of McLeod that noted he "must have been a good ambassador for Canada" in that both of his wartime observer/gunners immigrated to Canada after the war. Equally striking is Christie's spare, subdued description of the VC action itself; as a professional historian he was not in the habit of making things up.[163]

Academic historians have not been immune from error, although mistakes are sometimes compounded by uncritical writers who follow. The story of Timothy O'Hea and his Victoria Cross is a case in point. The first account appeared in the Montreal *Gazette* of 11 June 1866:

SPECIAL TELEGRAM FROM RICHMOND
Richmond, June 9

A car containing over 2,000 pounds of ammunition on its way from Quebec to Kingston, under charge of Sergeant Hill and the guard of the 4th Battalion, Rifle Brigade, was, on reaching Danville Station, discovered to be on fire. The car was immediately shoved down the line, away from the station, and the alarm given. The people living in the vicinity ran from their homes in fear of the explosion. Private O'Hay [sic] of this guard, ran down to the car, forced open the door, removed the covering from the ammunition, discovered the source of the fire, ran for water, and succeeded in extinguishing it. A braver or more daring act it is impossible to imagine. A subscription was immediately set on foot, and a purse handed to the noble fellow. The fire originated from a spark from the engine.

This account was repeated by other papers, including the *Quebec Mercury* of 12 June 1866. Little appeared in the English-language press thereafter. However, a French-language newspaper, the *Journal de Lévis*, carried a story that was subsequently repeated in other papers. It differed in some degree from the *Gazette*'s account, both in details and in attributing credit (author's translation follows):

Saturday, towards two o'clock in the afternoon, two wood freight trains [deux trains en bois] were stopped in Danville waiting for a "Mixed Train" bound for Montreal with 350 emigrants. Among the freight of this latter train was a car filled with gun powder for the Militia.

Suddenly it was found that one of the cars of the "Mixed Train" was on fire and unhappily it was the car with the powder. Cinders had set the roof of the car on fire.

It is almost impossible to describe the scene that followed. The alarm was raised and everyone – employees, passengers and onlookers, sought safety in flight. There was general confusion. An explosion seemed inevitable, and would have encompassed the destruction of all three trains, neighbouring property, and the deaths of all passengers and other persons present.

One man was sufficiently brave [hardi] to risk his life and save all. Having obtained a key to the car, he procured two water buckets, entered the car, and after unprecedented efforts, extinguished the fire, which had spread through the roof and was separated from the powder only by the blankets covering the barrels themselves. A minute more and the fire would have reached the powder, blowing everything up.

The crowd took up a collection and heartily cheered their saviour. The name of this young man is Albert Marquette, a "Baggage man" employed by the Grand Trunk Company on the Montréal-Lévis and the Rivière-du-Loup lines.

The company should be happy to have such a capable and devoted employee. Let us hope that the Grand Trunk directors and the Militia Department do not lose sight of his actions and reward him.[164]

There was, however, a witness to these events who put a very different spin on what had happened. On the very day of the fire, Captain Henry Hanning, Danville Volunteer Rifles, despatched a letter to the commanding officer of the regiment, Lord Alexander George Russell, at Quebec:[165]

I have the honour to draw your attention to the gallant conduct of Private Timothy O'Hea of the First Battalion of the P.C.O. [Prince Consort's Own] Rifle Brigade on the occasion of the car loaded with ammunition taking fire at Danville Station this day, causing an immediate panic in the neighbourhood, and but for his prompt and courageous conduct, imitated by a young Brake man whose name is Marquette, the consequences to the locality, and loss of about five hundred Emigrants attached to the train would have been fatal.

Captain Hanning's letter began the process by which Private O'Hea would be recommended for the Victoria Cross. This entailed the gathering of statements by other witnesses, of whom there were many including a railway conductor, a telegrapher, and the sergeant who had commanded the guard detail assigned to the train. The bulk of this evidence confirmed that O'Hea had been the principal mover in fighting the fire. Even Albert Marquette, describing himself as a brakeman, confirmed this, although he was clearly the person who first isolated the ammunition car ("I disconnected it at once and left it"). Nevertheless, it was also clear that, following O'Hea's lead, others (including Marquette) had

Private Timothy O'Hea was the central figure in the only VC action performed in Canada (at Danville, Canada East, 9 June 1866) (Library and Archives Canada C20671)

joined in establishing a bucket brigade and fighting the fire. One J. McKie of the Grand Trunk Railway wrote, "The rest of the Escort, no doubt stimulated by the example set them worked vigorously to save the ammunition but O'Hay [sic] was the leading spirit in the whole affair."[166]

On 1 January 1867, the *London Gazette* announced that Private O'Hea had been awarded the Victoria Cross with the following citation:

> *For his conspicuous conduct on the occasion of a fire which occurred in a railway car, containing ammunition, between Quebec and Montreal, on 9 June 1866. The Sergeant in charge of the escort states that when, at Danville Station, on the Grand Trunk Railway, the alarm was given that the car was on fire, it was immediately disconnected, and, whilst considering what was best to be done, Private O'Hea took the keys from his hand, rushed to the car, opened it, and called out for water and a ladder. It is stated that it was due to his example that the fire was suppressed.*

As has been noted earlier, this was a remarkable award – the only Victoria Cross presented for an event in Canada, and rare in that it was issued under the authority of a warrant that permitted awards for valour *not* in the face of the enemy. O'Hea was invested with his Victoria Cross on 26 April 1867 in the presence of the garrison at Quebec and a small group of civilians. The ceremony was duly reported in the local press, whose stories added little to the previous accounts. The *Quebec Mercury*, however, sourly reported that Marquette, not O'Hea, had been the true hero:

> *Documents put into our hands today show that the Grand Trunk authorities paid ten dollars gratuity to Mr. A. Marquette, the baggageman of the train, for his gallantry in rushing at once to the burning car and remaining in it till he had extinguished the fire. And we are told by his friends that the soldier honoured got to the car only after the flames had been extinguished. The soldier's position when he heard the news of the fire was not, they admit, that of such proximity as the baggageman, and his arriving later than Marquette does not detract from his courageous and brave act. While admitting the perfect propriety of the action of the military authorities, we nevertheless regret that some notice could not be officially taken by the civil power of the meritorious conduct of Marquette the baggageman who in France would justly have received the Legion of Honour.[167]*

This slur on O'Hea was promptly answered by a letter to the editor:

> *TRUE ACCOUNT OF THE DANVILLE POWDER CAR AFFAIR*
> To the Editor of the Mercury:
> *Sir – I have just read the account of the "Military Parade" as it appears in the Mercury of the 26th inst. My object is to do justice to O'Hea. The last paragraph in the account must have been suggested by someone who knew or who pretended to know nothing about O'Hea's conduct on the 9th June last.*
> *I write with some confidence for I happen to be the only eye-witness of that young man's splendid and heroic exertions from beginning to end. The circumstances of the case are simply these. – On the car containing the ammunition arriving at Danville, it was discovered to be on fire.*

Immediately it was sauve qui peut *(run for your life) with everybody who was aware there was powder in the car. Not suspecting what the car contained, I walked up to within ten feet of it and remained, regarding with interest O'Hea's superhuman exertions to subdue the flames which were bursting out through the roof of the car. In this he was assisted by some men who brought buckets of water from a neighboring well, but be it remembered that O'Hea was the only man who ventured on and into the car, for he opened the doors himself and scrambling over the boxes of powder, dashed the water on to the flames. After they were extinguished he turned and quietly remarked to me, "I have saved the ammunition." This was the first intimation I had of what the car contained, otherwise no doubt I would have scampered off with the rest. On it being known that all danger was past, the escort, railway officials and others gradually approached the scene of the action. O'Hea was thanked and cheered and a collection taken up on the spot and presented to him.*

If you think these facts worth publishing on O'Hea's account, you are welcome to them, from

The only eye-witness
Danville, April 30.[168]

For years published accounts of the events at Danville scarcely went beyond the account in the *London Gazette*; they did not even mention Marquette, much less the bucket brigade. The basic story remained unembellished until about 1905, when it acquired additional trappings and details. The ammunition car had become such a secret that only the highest officials of the Grand Trunk Railway knew of it. The train was now carrying "800 German immigrants"; these had been locked in the coaches and were thus helpless if an explosion occurred. O'Hea had made exactly 19 trips to fetch water while all others stood back and watched. All these "facts" appeared in Australia, where Timothy O'Hea had supposedly died in 1874, having been discharged from the army in March 1868 as medically unfit. Albert Marquette had vanished from the narrative, along with the bucket brigade that had assisted O'Hea.

What can only be called "the Australian version" was published in the 30 May 1951 issue of *The Times* (when O'Hea's VC was being transferred to the

Rifle Regiment Museum in Britain). It gained further exposure in 1972 when Volume X of the *Dictionary of Canadian Biography* carried an entry on O'Hea written by Charles Thompson, "800 German immigrants" included, and a bald assertion that the soldier had "single handedly put out the blaze."

Publication of this in the *Dictionary of Canadian Biography* lent authority to the account, as other contributors to that volume included such prestigious authors as Courtney Bond, Edwin Guillet and George Stanley. Charles Thompson, however, was described as "graduate student in history, Duke University," and he had shown singular laxness in research. He cited numerous secondary sources, none of them earlier than 1875, and apparently took no account of the Quebec newspapers of 1866- 1867. He had, moreover, ignored an important primary source, the official citation itself ("… due to his *example* that the fire was suppressed") to confirm the Australian version that made O'Hea the sole hero.

When this writer began compiling the present book, he immediately suspected the established version, simply because locomotive technology and contemporary railway roadbed construction would have rendered impossible an 800-passenger train. He soon discovered that other authors had added yet more details. One had miraculously succeeded in reconstructing the verbal instructions that had been given to the guard detail. At least two authors had explained the astounding assertion of passengers locked in the coaches as being either as a security step during a Fenian threat or as a quarantine measure. The former was dubious, given the distance of the rail line from the American border, while the latter was ridiculous given that immigrant quarantines were conducted at Grosse Isle, downstream from Quebec, long before the people were released into the general population.

Just as this writer began to research the anomalies in the O'Hea story, he discovered that Elizabeth Reid of Yale, British Columbia, had been researching the same subject, sniffed out the inconsistencies and published a book.[169] Miss Reid generously provided copies of much of her research material, including the War Office correspondence with witness statements. Hers is a remarkable work, encompassing as it does O'Hea's entire life and the history of his Victoria Cross, which included a cast of characters much larger than O'Hea himself. Perhaps her most startling revelation was that most of the "facts" added in the Australian version could only have been derived from a man who likely knew Timothy O'Hea well but was not O'Hea himself, and who was not present at the events of 9 June 1866. Even this man's accounts were filtered through a third party before they appeared in print in 1905.

A close comparison of the foregoing with Miss Reid's account will indicate some differences between herself and this writer (who is less certain than she about the actual composition of the train and the number of lives at stake). Moreover, this author has reservations about her use of reconstructed dialogue. Nevertheless, her book is a cautionary tale to those who accept history as carved in stone and who would denounce anyone correcting the accounts as a vile revisionist. Researchers and writers such as Elizabeth Reid (dealing with O'Hea) and Brereton Greenhous (dealing with Billy Bishop) demonstrate the value of informed scepticism over unquestioning repetition of ancient tales.

The story of Private Richard Rowland Thompson and the Queen's Scarf is yet another example of a minor historical event twisted and misinterpreted. A Canadian Army press release, issued in 1964, parroted and may even have invented some of the myths, including reference to a fictional Australian army order equating the Victoria Cross with the Queen's Scarf; much of this was repeated in an article published that same year in the *Canadian Military Journal.* Even the most respectable military historians were subsequently taken in. J.L. Granatstein, David Bercuson and Carman Miller may be forgiven in that their works were serious studies of the Canadian role in the Second South Africa War, better known as the Boer War (1899-1902), in which Thompson was a minor figure scarcely deserving of probing research. Nevertheless, in giving the authority of their reputations to old misconceptions, they helped ensure the power of repeated legends over accurate stories.[170] Two historians, Brian Reid and Cameron Pulsifer, latterly set out to discover the facts. Unhappily, their well-documented findings were published in two relatively obscure journals, not likely to be read by those who have already imbibed of the traditional myths as per Granatstein, Bercuson and Miller.[171]

The Queen's Scarf bears explanation. It was an honour unique to the Boer War. Queen Victoria, driven by the same interest in her soldiers that had inspired creation of the Victoria Cross, undertook to demonstrate her concern for them in several other ways. One was a gesture at the close of 1899 in which she sent to every soldier in South Africa a box of chocolates embossed with her portrait and a signed message, "I wish you a happy New Year." Many recipients never opened the boxes, preferring to treasure them as Imperial souvenirs. Another royal gesture was to knit a series of scarves for presentation to outstanding soldiers. "Knitting for the troops" was a time-honoured tradition, common to many nations, whereby mothers, daughters, sisters and sweethearts linked themselves to the fighting front. The Queen maintained her own link through this symbolic activity.

She began by knitting four scarves which she despatched to Field Marshal Lord Roberts, commanding the largest British field force (but not the only one) then engaged with the Boers. They were to be given to private soldiers of the Colonial units who had in some way distinguished themselves. Lord Roberts had four Colonial contingents under his command at that time, from Australia, Canada, New Zealand and the South African colonies themselves, and by July 1900 a member of each force had been designated to receive a scarf. The manner in which the recipients were chosen was apparently left to Roberts, who in turn delegated the selection to regimental commanding officers; no royal warrant governed the award. At least one recipient was clearly chosen by his regimental comrades (Trooper Leonard Chadwick, Roberts' Horse, which had been raised from local inhabitants).* With respect to Private Richard Thompson, 2nd (Special Service) Battalion, Royal Canadian Regiment, the evidence is contradictory; he may have been elected by his fellow soldiers but there is greater evidence to suggest that he was recommended by his commanding officer acting on advice of other regimental officers. In the cases of the Australian and New Zealand recipients, the process of selection is unknown.

The Queen knitted four more scarves, which she despatched to her grandson, Major Prince Christian Victor, for presentation to members (not necessarily privates) of regular British units. He selected a single formation, the 2nd Brigade, 5th Division, then operating in Natal independently of Roberts' forces, and had one scarf issued to each of the four battalions in that brigade. There is no sign of award by election with these scarves; all four went to colour sergeants (senior non-commissioned officer in rifle companies). Whatever the personal qualities of these men, they received their Queen's Scarves by virtue of their appointments rather than through any specific deeds in the field.

---

* Chadwick must have been an interesting fellow. An American by birth, he had been awarded a Medal of Honor during the Spanish-American War and had clearly moved on to South Africa seeking further adventures.

The Queen's Scarf presented to Private Richard Thompson, though knitted by a queen, could pass for any scarf produced by a mother or grandmother. ("Queen's Scarf of Honour," © Canadian War Museum)

The rarity of a Queen's Scarf led some to equate it with a Victoria Cross, but this was not the case. The absence of a fixed procedure for bestowal indicated an *ad hoc,* haphazard distribution. There was no provision for any approval higher than that of the Army Commander – no War Office committee and certainly no personal approval by the Queen. No pension accompanied a Queen's Scarf, nor was a recipient entitled to postnominal letters (such as "VC" or even "QS") after his name. At least one recipient (Private Alfred Henry Dufrayer, New South Wales Mounted Rifles) did try to have it classed as an award comparable to the Victoria Cross, but he was unsuccessful. The campaign waged by him and his family, which continued until 1956, probably led to much of the confusion surrounding the Queen's Scarf.

Who, then, was Richard Rowland Thompson, and how did he become associated with a Queen's Scarf?

His biography has been muddled by various writers, but Reid and Pulsifer agree that he was an Irish-born medical student who made his way to Canada in the late 1890s and enlisted in the Royal Canadian Regiment upon the outbreak of the Boer War. He accompanied that unit to South Africa under the command of Lieutenant-Colonel William D. Otter. The deeds which gained him the attention of his commanding officer were subsequently set out in a scroll dated 24 December 1908 given to his family, which described in general the manner in which he was selected for a Queen's Scarf and the deeds which made him eligible to receive it:

This is to certify that Private R.R. Thompson late "D" Company, 2 Royal Canadian Regiment, was awarded the Queen's Scarf for bravery during the recent South African Campaign, under the following circumstances:-

In July 1900, official notification was received by Colonel W.D. Otter, C.B., A.D.C., Commanding the 2 Royal Canadian Regiment, that Her Majesty the late Queen proposed awarding to a non-commissioned officer or man in each of the Colonial Contingents, who might be nominated as having performed the bravest act during the War, a scarf worked, or made, by herself. The regiment was then stationed on the Line of Communication at Springs, and Colonel Otter at once had the Staff and Officers Commanding Companies brought together for the selection of the non-commissioned officers or man to represent the Royal Canadian Regiment. After considerable discussion the decision was made in favour of Private R.R. Thompson, late "D" Company, 2 Royal Canadian Regiment, and his name was forwarded accordingly. The scarf was in due time received and given to Private Thompson.

The particular acts upon which Private Thompson was selected were as under: First, Having on the night of the Eighteenth-Nineteenth February 1900, kept Private Bradshaw, who was left dangerously wounded at Paardeberg, alive by the care and attention bestowed upon him, until he could be properly attended to. Second, Having twice left the trenches on the morning of the capture of the Boer Laager at Paardeberg, the Twenty-Seventh February, 1900, at the imminent risk of his own life, for the purpose of assisting wounded comrades, lying some distance in front of the trenches.[172]

Thompson was a regular private with the Royal Canadian Regiment (not a stretcher bearer, as some accounts have it). Although the official account is sparse, some details can be added. "Private Bradshaw" was James Bradshaw of Picton, Ontario, who later wrote that he had been wounded by a bullet that struck him "just behind the left jugular, and it went clear through coming out just behind the right jugular." A Private Bull had also been instrumental in Bradshaw's survival, though in what role or degree was not stated. Contemporary letters make clear that Thompson was very brave indeed. On the first occasion (18-19 February 1900) he lay for more than seven and one-half hours, stanching the blood from Bradshaw's wound, all the while under Boer fire that carried away his helmet. On 27 February, after a failed night attack on Boer positions, he volunteered to retrieve a wounded comrade. Thompson crossed 300 yards of open ground under fire, only to have the man die as he reached him. "I was heartily complimented by the officer commanding," wrote Thompson to his brother. "I think now [it was] pure foolishness."

The Thompson legends have it that he was recommended for the Victoria Cross at least once, possibly twice, but that he received the Queen's Scarf instead. Brian Reid has written that, had Thompson been recommended for a Victoria Cross in February or March 1900,he would have stood an excellent chance of receiving it. Nevertheless, he was not so recommended at that time. Lieutenant-Colonel Otter was an austere officer not given to praise or reward. The most formal recognition that members of the Royal Canadian Regiment would receive was 17 Mentions in Despatches, one of them for Otter himself. Having received instructions on 21 April 1900 that a Queen's Scarf nominee should be brought to Lord Roberts' attention, he put forward the name of Private Thompson, who had already left the regiment, felled by disease and sunstroke. He proceeded back to England, then to North America. Thompson was staying in Buffalo, New York, when, late in 1900, he received the scarf, mailed to him by Colonel Otter. There was no fanfare or formal investiture.

Precisely what happened next is unclear. Either Thompson or his family may have felt he deserved more. In March 1901, now back in Canada, Lieutenant-Colonel Otter wrote to the Adjutant General, Canadian Militia, belatedly recommending Thompson for the Victoria Cross. This got as far as the Governor General (Lord Minto) who wrote in May 1901 suggesting a second application with an explanation as to why no recommendation had been made at the time of the events described. Otter complied, gathered up evidence of Thompson's deeds (including a statement from Captain S.M. Rogers, former commander of "D" Company), and despatched the submission through the Governor General on 18 July 1901. It then progressed through British channels. At the War Office it was reviewed by Lord Roberts himself, now wearing the hat of Commander-in-Chief. The decision came back through the Governor General and Adjutant General, the latter writing to Otter on 6 March 1902:

The Commander-in-Chief has gone carefully into the case and regrets that he does not feel justified in submitting Pte. Thompson's name for the Decoration in question.

> *The War Office Despatch states further: "the fact of his having been selected by his gallant comrades of the Royal Canadian Regiment is ample proof of his courage, but His Lordship does not consider that the recommendations contain conclusive proof of such conspicuous bravery as is necessary under the provisions of the Victoria Cross Warrants."*

Discharged from the Royal Canadian Regiment, Thompson returned to South Africa, first as a police officer, then as an employee of De Beers. He moved on to Buffalo again, where he died of appendicitis in 1908. His widow, a native of Gatineau, Quebec, arranged to have his body taken there. Thompson's grave, in Chelsea, Quebec, is a minor shrine in the community. His scarf is in the possession of the Canadian War Museum.

The stories of O'Hea and Thompson demonstrate the manner by which first-hand information can be supplemented by suppositions and errors perpetuated through repetition and dissemination. Mel Gibson's depiction of William Wallace in the movie *Braveheart* is a travesty of historical truth, ridiculed even in Scotland, but in popular mythology he will now always be a Highlander (not an Ayreshireman) fighting to create a nation that had, in fact, existed for centuries. Marie Antoinette never said, "Let them eat cake," but how many people believe that she did? The ringing command, "Sink her! Blow her! Don't give up the ship!" (Captain William Lawrence, USS *Chesapeake*, 1 June 1813) was followed by the surrender of the vessel; the rhetoric is remembered by many; the aftermath is forgotten by all but a few. Leonard Birchall, shot down and taken prisoner in April 1942 after reporting a Japanese fleet approaching that island, was dubbed "the Saviour of Ceylon," although the enemy had neither the intention nor the means of invading; what he *did* save was a weaker British fleet which, with proper warning, was able to retire out of range of Japanese aircraft and survive to fight another day, thus denying the enemy the more limited objective they had sought. Generations of Americans will henceforth believe that some of the 9/11 terrorists came from Iraq and entered the United States via Canada, notwithstanding the contrary findings of the Congressional Commission that investigated the tragic events of that day. Legends are difficult to dispel, even with facts.[173]

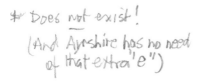

✱ Does not exist!
(And Ayrshire has no need of that extra "e")

CHAPTER 15

EPILOGUE:
DISTINCT CANADIAN AWARDS

When they had been running half an hour or so, and were quite dry again,
the Dodo suddenly called out "The race is over !" and they all crowded
round it, panting, and asking, "But who has won?"

This question the Dodo could not answer without a great deal of thought,
and it sat for a long time with one finger pressed upon its forehead (the
position in which you usually see Shakespeare, in the pictures of him), while
the rest waited in silence. At last the Dodo said, "EVERYBODY has won,
and all must have prizes."

Charles Lutwidge Dodgson, alias Lewis Carroll (1832-98), *Alice in Wonderland*

The evolution of distinct Canadian bravery awards has been outlined earlier. To what degree have they held up as badges of courage? Assessing this is difficult because many of the state papers that would explain policies and deliberations remain closed to the public for another 30 to 50 years. We may read the citations, compare awards with experience in other countries, and look at how things have been handled in the past. Nevertheless, any conclusions at this time must be deemed subjective. The reader is warned.

When the Cross of Valour was first discussed in official Canadian circles, the standards envisaged were very high. Records show that the first recipients had been chosen in advance – two crewmen who had sacrificed their lives aboard HMCS *Kootenay* whilst saving both ship and shipmates in a 1969 fire at sea. Indeed, consideration was given to naming this honour the "Kootenay Cross."[174]

In one of the best known photographs from the Second World War, David Currie, pistol in hand, talks with another member of the South Alberta Regiment as German soldiers surrender, St. Lambert-sur-Dives, 19 August 1944. (Photo by D.I. Grant. Library and Archives Canada PA111565)

A review of the 19 Cross of Valour awards made, as of September 2005, is convincing proof that the standards have been kept very high, very close to those for the George Cross. One of these was particularly memorable – that to René Marc Jalbert. The citation to his award scarcely does justice to his achievement:

In a rare display of coolheadedness and courage, René Jalbert, Sergeant-at-Arms at the Quebec National Assembly, subdued a man who had killed three people and wounded thirteen more on the morning of 8 May 1984. The man had entered a side door of the National Assembly building and immediately opened fire with a submachine-gun; moments later he climbed the main staircase toward the assembly chamber, known as the Blue Room, shooting repeatedly, and then burst into the chamber. As bullets peppered the wall, Mr. Jalbert entered the Blue Room and with icy calm convinced the man to allow several employees to leave the premises. Then he invited the heavily armed man into his downstairs office, in effect setting himself up as hostage while removing the man from the scene. At extreme personal risk, but with unflinching authority, Mr. Jalbert spent four hours persuading the man to surrender to police. The audacity of this retired Major of the Royal 22nd Regiment, a Second World War and Korean War veteran, almost certainly prevented a higher death toll.

In *The Victory Campaign*, a volume in the official history of the Canadian Army in the Second World War, C.P. Stacey included a photograph of Major David Currie, pistol in hand, conversing with a comrade while Germans surrendered. The caption stated that this was as close as anyone could come to being photographed in the act of winning a Victoria Cross. The first 50 minutes of Jalbert's encounter with Bernard Lortie were captured on the cameras that normally covered the proceedings in the National Assembly – a unique instance of a national gallantry award being photographed, at least in part, "live."

The Jalbert episode was notable for the cool professionalism of its principal player. The office of Sergeant-at-Arms included responsibility for security in the parliamentary precinct, and in 1983-84 many authorities were worried about terrorists and hostage-takers; it was, after all, an age that included the Symbionese Liberation Army. Several weeks before the incident, a meeting had been held attended by Canadian and American sergeants-at-arms (or their equivalents) to learn about means of dealing with such individuals.

René Marc Jalbert was formidable in the official dress of the Sergeant-at-Arms of Quebec's National Assembly, but even in a trenchcoat he could dominate an armed and highly strung Bernard Lortie.

Jalbert never dreamed that he would be applying his lessons so soon, but when the crisis came he was both improvising and remembering.*

The most recent awards of the Cross of Valour involved a joint award to Master Corporal (later Sergeant) Keith Paul Mitchell and Master Corporal Brian Keith Pierce illustrating the hazards faced by Search and Rescue personnel in Canada's north:

On November 12, 1996, Search and Rescue Technicians Mitchell and Pierce carried out an unprecedented night parachute jump into freezing Arctic waters to provide medical aid to a critically ill fisherman onboard a Danish trawler near Resolution Island, Northwest Territories. Tasked initially as back-up to another air rescue team, the Hercules aircraft with Master Corporals. Mitchell and Pierce on board arrived first on the scene only to learn that the stricken seaman had taken a turn for the worse. There was no time to waste so they elected to attempt a risky parachute descent. With inadequate flare illumination and the promised Zodiac boat not yet launched from the Danish trawler, they jumped in extremely strong winds that carried them away from the vessel. As they entered the three-metre waves, Master Corporal Mitchell became entangled in the shroud lines under his partially collapsed chute canopy, while Master Corporal. Pierce's chute remained inflated and dragged him face down through the water farther away from the ship. Although equipped with dinghies, they could not paddle nor swim to the trawler because of heavy seas and severe icing. Struggling to stay afloat, they battled the onset of hypothermia for 15 minutes before the crew of an ice-encrusted Zodiac picked them up and delivered them to the ship where they carried out medical procedures that saved the patient's life.

The Canadian Cross of Valour invites comparison with its Australian counterpart, which was established in 1975 with terms of reference virtually

---

* This writer, as an employee of the Canadian War Museum, was visiting the Citadel in Quebec (headquarters of the Royal 22e Regiment) a week after the incident and spent an afternoon in the company of Lieutenant-Colonel Lucien Turcotte (Director of the Regimental Museum) and his good friend René Jalbert. Needless to say, both Lieutenant-Colonel Turcotte and I were agog at Jalbert's matter-of-fact account of events.

identical to the Canadian version. In 30 years the Australians have awarded it four times, most recently to an off-duty policeman for heroism following terrorist bombings in Bali (2002). Even allowing for differences in population (Australia has about two-thirds the people that Canada has), it is evident that awards have been more stringently scrutinized and distributed. This becomes even more apparent when one compares the numbers for second- and third-level awards for bravery. As of September 2005, Canada has awarded 398 Stars of Courage and 2,190 Medals of Bravery, compared to 60 and 307 of the "down under" counterparts. Radical changes in British gallantry awards make comparisons difficult, but since 1947 there have been 42 awards of the George Cross, generally regarded as the model for the Australian and Canadian Crosses of Valour. This figure does not include an award of the GC to the Royal Ulster Constabulary as a whole in 2002, similar to a collective award of the GC to the island of Malta in 1942.

Does Canada award bravery decorations too freely? It may appear callous to question any specific award, but this writer is haunted by doubts. Should people be decorated for saving or attempting to save members of their own families from fires or drowning? Should they be decorated in those circumstances only if they lose their own lives in the process? Should a man be awarded a Medal for Bravery if he first puts his own daughter in peril, then is badly burned as he tries vainly to save her?

That said, even the sceptic is sometimes challenged when faced with specific cases. Cynthia Corlett-Parolin may have been denied a Cross of Valour for her heroism on behalf of her own children, but her posthumous Star of Courage, announced 31 October 1997, commemorated fortitude and devotion to which any parent would aspire:

On August 19, 1996, Cindy Parolin died to save her six-year-old son from a vicious cougar attack near Princeton, British Columbia. Mrs. Parolin was horseback riding with three of her children when her youngest son was thrown by his frightened horse and attacked by the cougar. Mrs. Parolin jumped to the ground and provoked the cat with a stick, until it released her child. The enraged beast then pounced on her. As she wrestled with the animal, she ordered her children to take their injured brother and run for help. When rescuers arrived, over one hour later, they found her still

alive in the underbrush where she had been dragged by the cougar. The
animal was still crouched over her savagely mauled body. A man fired a
shot in the air and unleashed his dog to scare the cougar off. The animal
was then shot.

Once one begins to inquire as to measurements of courage (how much? how calculated? on whose behalf?) one begins to grasp the questions that troubled various Victoria Cross committees, weighing duty against valour and calculated courage against indefensible rashness.

The Medal of Bravery was almost certainly compromised on 8 September 1994 when the *Canada Gazette* reported the award of 183 such medals to rescue workers in the aftermath of the Westray mine disaster. The citation, which covered all these men, vividly described the hazards:

After a massive explosion inside the Westray Coal Mine at Plymouth,
Nova Scotia, on May 9, 1992, two hundred and one men attempted to
rescue twenty-six miners trapped underground. For the next five days,
rescue teams searched around the clock for survivors. Despite the peril-
ous mixture of highly volatile gases, they repeatedly went underground,
beneath a largely unsupported and unstable roof structure. They crawled
around twisted pieces of steel that had once been supporting arches,
passed machinery that was no longer useful or recognizable, climbed
over rockfalls and debris, and waded through brackish water. The teams
moved cautiously and silently, fearing that the slightest noise or vibra-
tion would cause further rockfalls or explosions. Rescue efforts were finally
abandoned after more than a kilometre of the mine had been searched,
with no sign of survivors. The rescuers recovered the bodies of fifteen of
the twenty-six victims.

But did no individuals stand out in terms of leadership? Doubtless every man who received a medal was proud to have it – but did the award on this scale simply reduce the Medal of Bravery to a "hazardous occupation badge?" To what degree did the Canadian Chancellory promote this mass distribution? Or was political pressure applied? The Westray mine disaster was complicated by charges of political interference affecting mine safety and litigation to prosecute (unsuccessfully) mine owners and managers. Did somebody think that a distribution of medals would somehow mitigate the controversies?

Sadly, successive governments have created a veritable jumble of awards for both courage and service. The Order of Canada (in its three grades) has been deemed to be the most prestigious of service awards, and it has over-shadowed another type of civic award, the Meritorious Service decorations (Cross and Medal). Meanwhile, the Canadian military has its own honours (Order of Military Merit, in three grades, Meritorious Service awards in two). Confusing matters further, several military Meritorious Service awards have appeared closer to rewards for gallantry than distinguished service in and of itself. Furthermore, although uniformed personnel have always been eligible for the Cross of Valour/Star of Courage/Medal of Bravery (and have been decorated frequently in all three categories), there have been, since 2001, Military gallantry decorations exclusively for "combat" with an "enemy," the latter defined broadly as a "hostile armed force" that includes "armed muti-neers, armed rebels, armed rioters and armed pirates." None have as yet been awarded, since to do so would be an admission that Canadian troops actually do engage in combat occasionally, contrary to idealistic notions that they are exclusively "peace keepers."

If these were not enough, there have been created, over the years, numer-ous awards recognizing long service in hazardous or socially important oc-cupations; the Police Exemplary Service Medal, the Corrections Exemplary Service Medal, the Fire Services Exemplary Service Medal, the Canadian Coast Guard Exemplary Service Medal, the Emergency Medical Services Exemplary Service Medal and the Peace Officer Exemplary Service Medal (similar to that for police, but awarded to peace officers in service depart-ments such as Parks Canada or the Department of Fisheries and Oceans). All recognize 20 years of meritorious service in high-risk professions related to public protection.

To further complicate and clutter the scene, every province has created its own specific Order, and since 1991 these have been recognized by Govern-ment House as having equal status with national awards. They are pretty baubles which allow provincial Premiers to stroke the egos of numerous folk, who are happy enough to place letters like "OBC" (Order of British

Columbia) or "AOE" (Alberta Order of Excellence) after their names. Unhappily, they also feed the ambitions of premiers who seek wider stages – even international recognition – at the expense of a national outlook. A particularly unfortunate (because it was undignified) example was that of Céline Dion. On 6 January 1998, Government House in Ottawa announced that she had been appointed an Officer in the Order of Canada. The government of Quebec scrambled to appoint her an Officer in the *Ordre national du Québec* and succeeded in having her invested with that honour (and being photographed wearing its insignia) before the investiture with the Order of Canada in Ottawa the very next day.

Christopher McCreery has warned of a "balkanized" honours system and noted that the federal government has tolerated provincial orders principally to avoid exacerbating federal-provincial tensions. He contrasts the "honours vacuum" that existed decades earlier with the complex system of today, cautions against creating more (and unnecessary) awards, and urges the establishment of a museum that would display Canadian honours in their full array and context.[175] This writer concurs wholeheartedly.

A MID-WAR CONSIDERATION
OF POSTHUMOUS AWARDS

The Committee on the Grant of Honours, Decorations and Medals in Time of War was a multi-departmental body which weighed matters ranging from campaign medals to gallantry decorations. Essentially, it recommended policies rather than awards to specific individuals. Commonwealth governments were informed of its deliberations, which meant that copies of many committee records were supplied to Wellington, Canberra, New Delhi, Ottawa and Pretoria, although each was free to pick and choose what was most appropriate to their geographical and political realities.

The following document is transcribed as it was found in the file (Governor General's records, file 19 AK-39, National Library and Archives of Canada, Record Group 25-G.1, Volume 1885), except that this writer has emphasized some passages which are particularly relevant by virtue of their realism. The Committee was not to be stampeded by pressure from either the Prime Minister (Churchill) or his deputy (Clement Atlee).

CONFIDENTIAL

H.W.479

COMMITTEE ON THE GRANT OF HONOURS, DECORATIONS
AND MEDALS IN TIME OF WAR

1939-1942

EIGHTY-NINTH REPORT

POSTHUMOUS MILITARY AWARDS

1. The Prime Minister's request for review.

The Prime Minister recently asked that the question of having, for services in action with the enemy, some other Honour besides the V.C. which may be granted posthumously, should be again considered. Mr. Churchill said that he had the D.S.O. particularly in mind.

2. <u>Minute submitted to the Prime Minister by the Chairman of the Committee.</u>

Following is a copy of the minute dated 9th June furnished by the Chairman of the Committee.

"A question on the subject of posthumous Honours was addressed to the Prime Minister on 20th May and Mr. Atlee replied as follows:-

"This question was reviewed in October 1939 by the Committee on the grant of Honours, Decorations and Medals in time of war, and in February this year by the Chiefs of Staff Committee. The *main purpose of decorations is to reward the living*, and it has always been felt to be fitting and dignified that posthumous grants should be limited to the very highest awards for gallantry. Moreover, a high proportion of fatalities occur when acts of heroism leave no surviving witnesses. To extend the system to other Honours would make it extremely difficult to justify in the eyes of next-of-kin the great numbers of necessary exclusions."

The matter was reviewed on several occasions during and after the Four Years' war,* again in 1938, and subsequently, as mentioned in the reply above.

One of the main problems which has faced those concerned is the difficulty of selection when a vessel either in the Fleet or the Merchant Navy has gone down after a gallant action and no survivors, or very few, remain. It is, in practice, impossible to make a selection on good grounds from among all of the dead; in fact the selection might again and again be in favour of the wrong man.

Much the same applies to aircraft crews. Frequently all members of a crew are lost together. To grant a posthumous award by selection without justification and without knowledge of the circumstances from among all the dead would be a matter of the greatest difficulty.

If posthumous awards were to be made in such circumstances, perhaps by rank or blindly with a pin, the result, it has been thought, would ultimately be to cause far more dissatisfaction than gratification among next-of-kin. *Clearly, the number of recipients would only be a fraction of the total of the bereaved.*

Another difficulty which would arise is some new practice were authorised now in the middle of this war would be *the demand for the examination of all past cases.* Requests would be made for the consideration of the circumstances of the death of all those killed in action, so that those who have already given their lives would be treated on the same basis as those who are killed during the remainder of the war.

With regard to the D.S.O., which is particularly mentioned, *it would clearly be unwise to make a concession of this kind only to commissioned ranks.* An essential consequence, therefore, is an alteration in the conditions of award for the D.S.O. would be that a similar

---

* The First World War; it was only late in 1942 before terms like "The Great War" and "The Four Years War" were superseded by the currently accepted name, it being accepted by then that the most recent conflict was indeed a global one – a true "Second World War."

principle should be applied to more or less equivalent awards for other ranks, that is the C.G.M. in the Navy, the D.C.M. in the Army, and for the upper ranks of awards for the D.F.M. in the Royal Air Force. It would be necessary, also, to alter similarly the conditions of award for the George Medal which is granted to military as well as civil personnel, and ranks in the degree of bravery next to the highest of the George Cross.

It would therefore be no inconsiderable change in the Honours system as a whole.

The Canadian Government grant forthwith to the next-of-kin a small silver Memorial Cross hanging from a narrow purple mourning ribbon of miniature width. This was the practice in Canada in the Four Years' war, and the Canadian Government are using now exactly the same design.

They and the other Dominions, India and the Colonies are all using the Royal Message of Condolence. It has not been thought desirable to consider the institution here as yet of any permanent memorial other than the Royal Message. In respect of services in the last war the next-of-kin received in addition to the commemorative campaign medals, a bronze plaque some six inches across and an inscribed memorial message. It has been considered up to now that before venturing on presentations of this kind, we should await events to discover what the volume of casualties is likely to be, and how far casualties in the Merchant navy, in civil defence and so forth should be included in any such scheme. This course has been approved. There are obvious objections at the present time to the use of the metal, the labour in production, and so forth.

The Royal Message of Condolence is, therefore, at present the permanent memento for retention by the next-of-kin.

It is important to realize that a Mention in Despatches may be granted posthumously, and that the appropriate Honours which always become the property of the next-of-kin, in the case of death in action or during hostilities, are the commemorative campaign medals which may be awarded.

The arguments against an alteration in the arrangements for posthumous award are of great weight and it would seem wiser to leave the system unaltered.

H.J.W.

Treasury Chambers

----

3. The Prime Minister agreed. As the question is raised from time to time from one quarter or another, we consider it desirable that the reaffirmation of the existing practice should be recorded in this Report and submitted for approval.

(signed) H.J. Wilson
(on behalf of the Committee)

Treasury Chambers
Whitehall, S.W.1
26th June 1942.

COMPARING W.A. BISHOP'S COMBAT
REPORT AND VC CITATION

The Combat Report:

Squadron: 60   *Date: June 2nd, 1917*

Armament: one Lewis Gun   *Time: 4.23–5 a.m..*

Pilot: Capt. W.A. Bishop, DSO, MC   *Duty: H.A.*

Observer: none   *Height: 50 ft–7,000 feet*

Locality: Either Esnes aerodrome or Awoignt

I fired on 7 machines on the aerodrome, some of which had their engines running. One of them took off and I fired 15 rounds at him from close range and 60 ft. up and he crashed. A second one taking off, I opened fire and fired 30 rounds at 150 yards range, he crashed into a tree. Two more were then taking off together. I climbed and engaged one at 1,000 feet finishing my drum, and he crashed 300 yards from the aerodrome. I changed drums and climbed E [East]. A fourth H.A. [hostile aeroplane] came after me and I fired one whole drum in to him. He flew away and I then flew 1,000 feet under 4 scouts at 5,000 feet for one mile and turned W. [West] climbing. The aerodrome was armed with one or more machine guns. Machines on the ground were 6 scouts (Albatros type I and II) and one two-seater.

(Signed) W.A. Bishop, Capt.

Further annotated by Major Scott (commanding officer, No. 60 Squadron) as follows:

Capt. Bishop had been encouraged to catch the H.A. referred to in VII Corps Daily Intelligence Summary No. 151. His method was not quite what I intended. He was several times at a height of 50 feet over this enemy aerodrome at least 17 miles E. [East] of the lines. His machine is full of holes caused by machine gun fire from the ground.

The Victoria Cross citation (*London Gazette,* 10 August 1917):

For conspicuous bravery, determination and skill.

Captain Bishop, who had been sent out to work independently, flew first of all to an enemy aerodrome; finding no machine about, he flew to another aerodrome about three miles south-east, which was at least twelve miles the other side of the line. Seven machines, some with their engines running, were on the ground. He attacked these from about fifty feet, and a mechanic, who was starting one of the engines, was seen to fall. One of the machines got off the ground, but at a height of sixty feet Captain Bishop fired fifteen rounds into it at very close range, and it crashed to the ground.

A second machine got off the ground, into which he fired thirty rounds at 150 yards range, and it fell into a tree.

Two more machines then rose from the aerodrome. One of these he engaged at the height of 1,000 feet, emptying the rest of his drum of ammunition. The machine crashed 300 yards from the aerodrome, after which Captain Bishop emptied a whole drum into a fourth hostile machine, and then flew back to his station.

Four hostile scouts were about 1,000 feet above him for about a mile of his return journey, but they would not attack.

His machine was very badly shot about by machine gun fire from the ground.

A GENERAL'S VIEW OF HONOURS
AND AWARDS

The following memorandum has been found in several files, most notable Canadian Army file 1 CDR/6-7 (3), "Honours and Awards" (National Library and Archives Canada Record Group 24 Volume 10917). Although prepared by Major-General Guy Simonds, it probably reflected the thinking of contemporary senior officers as to "who should get what and why." It is a sometimes harsh outlook, reflecting primary concern with battle results; it is also realistic, particularly with the respect to the soldier's trade ("a risky business") and the soldier's obligations ("to do his duty and serve his country").

Headquarters, 1 Canadian Division
25 October 1943

TO ALL COMMANDERS AND COMMANDING
OFFICERS 1ST CANADIAN DIVISION

HONOURS AND AWARDS

1. The correct allocation of honours and awards is of great importance, since it affects morale. If decorations are distributed too freely they lose their value in the eyes of the Army as a whole and to the recipients. Conversely the recognition of valuable service by the award of a decoration is a just encouragement to others and in the best interests of the Service – particularly when considered in relation to promotion which must be based upon the promise of ability to perform a task in a higher sphere and NOT upon past services rendered.

2. The regulations governing honours and awards are given in Royal warrants and official publications. The views and policies given below are intended to guide and assist commanders and commanding officers in submitting recommendations. They will provide the basis upon which I will scrutinise all recommendations when passing for consideration by higher authority.

3. Soldiering is a risky business and the normal performance of duties, varying in each sphere and with the role of the Army, is inseparable from the element of risk. Commanders must bear in mind that the purpose of the campaign medal is to give recognition to the performance of normal duties in a Theatre of Operations where risks form part of the day to day business of soldiering. The idea that special honours should be liberally awarded to individuals for normal performance of their duties "because it is all they get out of it," cannot be entertained, for it cuts across the fundamental principle of military service. A soldier serves to do his duty and serve his country – not "for what he gets out of it." On the other hand the soldier who bears the responsibility and runs the risks of actual combat with the enemy deserves some distinction to show he has withstood the test.

4. A proper allocation of honours and awards should -

(a) Give recognition to exceptional acts, or duties performed with outstanding ability, or recognition of exacting duties performed unfailingly during a difficult or long period.

(b) Encourage aggressiveness and skill and the offensive spirit.

(c) Discourage foolhardiness or the unnecessary and useless risk of lives and equipment. I look to every Commander and Commanding Officer to strictly discourage any forms of "medal hunting."

(d) To give recognition to acts of such outstanding gallantry that they are an example to the Army for all time.

5. <u>The value of the service rendered is the first consideration in any award.</u> The service rendered may be measured in terms of effect against the enemy or in terms of outstanding gallantry affording an example and inspiration to the whole Army, or in terms of a valuable contribution, effecting the efficiency or well-being of the Army, or the general war effort.

6. <u>Awards for Services in Combat with the Enemy (VC, DSO, MC, DCM, MM).</u>

(a) With the exception of personnel of the Medical or Chaplain's Services which are dealt with under a separate heading below, recommendees by their act or acts must have made, or contributed directly to, an effective blow against the enemy – the direct contribution to the success of the battle, on the battle field – is the standard by which such recommendations will be judged. Except in most extra-ordinary circumstances, acts of gallantry NOT directly contributing to damage to the enemy (such as rescuing of our own personnel, salvage of equipment, extricating a unit or sub-unit from a difficult position will <u>NOT</u> be considered for these awards even if performed in the presence of the enemy and under fire.

(b) The act or acts forming the basis of recommendations must be in the line of duty (for example, an artillery F.O.O. who, in the heat of battle, leaves his O.P. and joins in the infantry fight may put up a very gallant show, but if it was possible for him to have continued giving support to forward troops by remaining at his O.P. then he should not be considered for an award. To give an award in such a case encourages foolhardiness as opposed to performance of duty.

(c) The act or acts for these awards must have been carried out under fire and the citation must so state.

(d) Except in very special and extraordinary circumstances and for Chaplains and Medical personnel, the above rules exclude the award of these decorations to personnel of the Services whose duties do not require them to <u>directly</u> deal a blow against the enemy. This should be realised by the personnel of such Services when it is decided that their contribution is best made in their service rather than in a unit which takes direct action against the enemy, and accords with the principle that a soldier's duty is to render the service for which he is best fitted by experience and training. The Provost Service is an exception in that control of traffic in the forward area at difficult diversions or bottlenecks, under hostile fire, contributes directly to a blow at the enemy in that such blow may be dependent upon the forward movement of supporting arms.

(e) Chaplains and Medical personnel are eligible for these decorations, for their primary duties are concerned with the physical and spiritual welfare of casualties on the battlefield. Acts of rescue under fire are legitimate cases for awards to officers and soldiers of these Services as it is in their "line of duty." Commanders and Commanding Officers must remember however combat personnel. There have been instances where the enemy have obviously refrained from firing at soldiers or vehicles bearing the Red Cross, and in assessing acts by medical personnel and clerics, this must be borne in mind.

(f) Except for the VC, recommendations for the above decorations may be either "immediate" or "periodical." The immediate recommendation is for a single act and the majority of deserving cases can be covered by the immediate award. Certain categories of Staff Officer, through a long period of valuable service in the area of contact may be recommended for a periodical award.

(g) As a guide (except in the case of medical officers or chaplains) to ear the DSO the act or acts for which an officer is recommended must have contributed directly to the success of the battle, at least and unmistakably on the brigade level, and more usually on the divisional level.

(h) In the case of the VC the act must be so outstanding as to provide an example to the Army for all time and its effect in damage to the enemy and furtherance of operations must be marked beyond question and of the first importance. Whenever a case is considered for a recommendation for the VC, as far as operational circumstances permit, the Brigade Commander concerned should visit the ground accompanied by the eyewitnesses of the act. Each eyewitness should be called forward, out of hearing of others, and describe to the Brigadier, on the ground, exactly what he saw. These accounts should be taken down at the time and eventually attached to the recommendation.

(i) It is quite legitimate to give recognition to outstanding work of a unit by an award to its commanding officer, for there would be no question as to who would bear the responsibility if it did badly.

7. Awards for Gallantry for Acts not in Combat with the Enemy (GC, GM, Commendations for Gallantry.

Passive acts of gallantry, not directly contributing to damage to the enemy, or outside the area of contact, may be rewarded by the GC or GM and recommendations should be submitted accordingly.

8. Awards not requiring an Element of Gallantry (CB, CBE, OBE, MBE, BEM, CM, Mention in Despatches.

These awards are intended for recognition of valuable service rendered NOT necessarily in combat with the enemy. Those who have not had the opportunity of directly contributing to damage to the enemy may nevertheless have rendered exceptional service, and should receive first consideration for these awards. Anyone, providing they qualify within the regulations laid down for each decoration, is eligible to earn, for exceptional services, a periodical award of one of these decorations.

9. It must be remembered that, in their final form citations are published in the Gazette. They must be accurate as to fact, include essential details such as date, time and place and be worded in good, simple English. Citations for immediate awards must be based on one or two specific acts during a particular phase and if drafted to cover a period will not gain acceptance. Carelessness in submitting citations results in delays to collect details, in rewriting and in getting signature on redrafted documents when there is always the possibility that original initiators may have become casualties. It is important that deserving cases should be rewarded certainly and without delays.

10. Commanders and Commanding Officers should be careful to see that outstanding acts by individuals of supporting Arms and Services, working under commander in support, are brought to the attention of the Commander of the Arm or Service concerned, otherwise there is always the possibility that deserving cases may be overlooked.

11. I would particularly caution Commanders and Commanding Officers against submitting recommendations for individuals who rendered them personal services, such as their drivers or orderlies. Commanders must bear in mind that these individuals are very much "under their eye." They must compare their services with those of the infantry section leader who during a period of operations may daily lead his

section into battle in the forward area. The place for individuals of the former type to earn decorations is serving with their units, and I would again remind you that such personnel are eligible for a general campaign medal. I do not mean that such individuals should be excluded if, in very exceptional circumstances, they carry out an act of gallantry beyond their duties. But it has an adverse effect on morale of fighting troops if those in positions of little or no responsibility but close to the Commander and under his personal observation seem to come by decorations more easily than the front line soldier.

12. The final criterion of a good or bad award is the reaction of the troops. If the troops feel it is a good award, it is a good award. If awards are criticised by the fighting troops they are bad awards. Before forwarding any recommendation, at each level, the Commander should ask himself the question "would the front line soldier, if he knew the facts, consider this well deserved."

(Signed)
G.G. Simonds
Major-General
GOC 1 Canadian Division

SUCCESS AND VALOUR ARE
NOT ENOUGH

Captain Jack Birnie Smith, Royal Canadian Regiment, was recommended for a Victoria Cross but received no honour greater than a posthumous Mention in Despatches (*Canada Gazette*, 26 May 1945). The VC submission, including witness statements, was found in Canadian Army file 1 CDR/6-7-4 (2), National Library and Archives of Canada, Record Group 24 Volume 10919.:

Reference Map Italy 1:100,000, Sheet 101-11, Rimini

At San Lorenzo in Strada (MR 904913), at 0400 hours, 6 September 1944, Captain Jack Birnie Smith, commanding "A" Company, The Royal Canadian Regiment, was ordered to prepare his company for a dawn assault. The objective was a strongly held enemy position on rising ground, astride the Ancona-Rimini road. Captain Smith moved his company, which had already suffered 35 per cent .casualties and was almost exhausted by three days hard fighting, into the FUP. The assault of three companies went in at 0600 hours, Captain Smith being among his leading elements. The advance had progressed to within 150 yards of the objective when it came under murderous machine gun cross fire. In spite of it, this gallant officer placed himself at the very head of his company and led it against strongly fortified houses and dug-in positions held by troops of the redoubtable First German Parachute Division. The enemy fire inflicted many casualties, but in the face of this, and showing supreme contempt for danger Captain Smith kept going steadily forward, urging his men on, to within 35 yards of the enemy strong point. Determined to achieve his object and carry out his commanding officer's intention, notwithstanding the danger, this officer continued to display courage of the highest calibre. By this time the company was reduced to half its normal establishment, and was coming under withering fire from three sides; however, rallying the remnants, personally hurling hand grenades at the enemy, Captain Smith kept leading his men forward. When last seen alive he was standing erect only a few yards from the final objective throwing grenades in the face of point-blank fire. Hit on the head by a German stick-grenade he fell, mortally wounded. So effective was the leadership and personal valour of this officer that his shattered company advanced steadily, inflicting casualties according to the best infantry traditions, and he was personally instrumental in destroying many of the enemy by his own hand. The efforts of "A" Company so employed the enemy that the remainder of the assaulting troops were saved from complete annihilation, and were able to reorganise as fighting companies.

Captain Smith's conduct on this occasion, as on others in the previous fighting in this area, was such as to be an example to the Canadian Army for all time.

His superb bravery and personal leadership kept a physically exhausted company fighting forward in the forefront of battle. The morning before, when it was suggested by his Commanding Officer that a rest was his due, he asked permission to remain with his company, choosing to share with them what might arise.

The magnificent performance of this officer places him in the highest rank as a leader and a brave man.

This was accompanied by three witness statements:

STATEMENT OF P.16467 CSM (WO II) I.A. MacDONALD, RCR, REGARDING THE ACTION OF "A" COMPANY, RCR, 6 SEPTEMBER 1944.
The company attacked with 7 Platoon on the left and 8 Platoon on the right, the company consisting of two platoons only, the remnants of 9 Platoon being split between 7 and 8 Platoons. Captain Smith, the company commander, went forward leading 8 Platoon. When within 150 yards of the objective the company came under enemy machine gun fire from three directions. Captain Smith immediately rushed over to No. 1 Section, 7 Platoon, which was a bit forward of the rest of the company, and ordered Private Rogers into a position where he could fire into an enemy post not more than 35 yards away. Captain Smith then engaged the enemy with his rifle, and shortly afterwards while throwing grenades fell wounded. I believe the Bren gunner who Captain Smith placed knocked out one enemy machine gun post as it remained silent following a burst. The company charged up the slope with fixed bayonets at 0605 hours behind the company commander.

STATEMENT OF H.9286 PRIVATE ROGERS, E.P., RCR, REGARDING THE ACTION OF "A" COMPANY, RCR, 6 SEPTEMBER 1944.
Captain Smith called for a Bren gunner to come forward and when I came up he showed me where to fire and told me to stay there and continue firing which I did. During the next few minutes the butt of the Bren was nicked by a bullet and one magazine was shot off. The No. 2 man was killed beside me and Captain Smith was also killed close by. I saw him standing up throwing grenades at the enemy position before he fell dead.

STATEMENT OF H.14314 PRIVATE SANDERSON, E.P., RCR, REGARDING THE ACTION OF "A" COMPANY, RCR, 6 SEPTEMBER 1944.

We were held up by a machine gun position right beside a pole at the edge of the road. It seemed about 35 yards away from w here our section was pinned down. The ground was a cultivated field with short vines and there was practically no cover. I saw Captain Smith throwing hand grenades at the machine gun near the pole as I was crawling back to the Company Sergeant-Major with a message for him from Captain Smith.

"PADDY" MAYNE: SPECTACULAR,
BUT NO VC

The following VC recommendation for Robert Blair Mayne was obtained from a website, <http://en.wikipedia.org/wiki/Paddy_Mayne#Reputation>, quoting this as the citation to his fourth DSO. The text refers to orders being received from "General Officer Commanding 4th Canadian Armoured Division," who at the time was Major-General Chris Vokes. Canadian Army file 4 AD/6-7-1/1 (formerly Directorate of History and Heritage file 245C.4 docket 5), in National Library and Archives RG 24 Volume 10934 contains some additional correspondence from Vokes dated June 20, 1945, by which time he had assumed command of 3 Canadian Infantry Division which had been selected for Occupation duties in Germany. The original submission was raised by Brigadier R.W. McLeod and supported by Brigadier J.M. Calvert. Vokes, for his part, could not produce any Canadian eyewitnesses to Mayne's personal acts of bravery, but following a visit to the SAS unit he observed the respect given Mayne by his officers and men. Vokes concluded, "In my opinion this officer is worthy of the highest award for gallantry and leadership."

On Monday April 9th 1945, Lieutenant-Colonel R.B. Mayne was ordered by the General Officer Commanding 4th Canadian Armoured Division to lead his Regiment (then consisting of two armoured jeep squadrons) through the British lines and infiltrate through the German lines. His general axis of advance was N/East towards the city of Oldenburg, with the special task of clearing a path for the Canadian armoured cars and tanks, and also causing alarm and disorganisation behind the enemy lines. As subsequent events proved the task of Lieutenant-Colonel Mayne's force was entirely and completely successful. This success however was solely due to the brilliant military leadership and cool calculating courage of Lieutenant-Colonel Mayne who, by a single act of supreme bravery drove the enemy from a strongly held key village thereby breaking the crust of the enemy defences in the whole of this sector.

The following is a detailed account of the Lieutenant-Colonel's individual action which called for both unsurpassed heroism and cool clear sighted military knowledge.

Lieutenant-Colonel Mayne on receiving a wireless message from the leading squadron reporting that it was heavily engaged by enemy fire and that the squadron commander had been killed immediately drove forward to the scene of the action. From the time of his arrival until the end of the action Lieutenant-Colonel Mayne was in full view of the enemy and exposed to fire from small arms, machine guns, sniper rifles and Panzerfausts. On arrival he summed up the situation in a matter of seconds and entered the nearest house alone and ensured the enemy here had either withdrawn or been killed. He then seized a Bren gun and magazines and single handedly fired burst after burst into a second house, killing or wounding the enemy there and also opened fire on the woods. He then ordered a jeep to come forward and take over his fire position before returning to the forward position where he disposed the men to the best advantage and ordered another jeep to come forward. He got into the jeep and with another officer as rear gunner drove forward past the position where the Squadron Commander had been killed a few minutes previously and continued to point a hundred yards ahead where a further section of jeeps were halted by intense and accurate enemy fire. This section had suffered casualties and wounded owing to the heavy enemy fire and the survivors were unable at that time to influence the action in any way until the arrival of Lieutenant-Colonel Mayne. The Lieutenant-Colonel continued along the road all the time engaging the enemy with fire from his own jeep. Having swept the whole area with close range fire he turned his jeep around and drove down the road again, still in full view of the enemy. By this time the enemy had suffered heavy casualties and had started to withdraw. Nevertheless they maintained intense fire on the road and it appeared almost impossible to extricate the wounded who were in a ditch near to the forward jeeps. Any attempt of rescuing these men under those conditions appeared virtually suicidal owing to the highly concentrated and accurate fire of the enemy. Though he fully realised the risk he was taking Lieutenant-Colonel Mayne turned his jeep round once more and returned to try and rescue these wounded. Then by superlative determination and displaying gallantry of the very highest degree and in the face of intense enemy machine gun fire he lifted the wounded one by one into the jeep, turned round and drove back to the main body. The entire enemy positions had been wiped out, the majority of the enemy having been killed or wounded leaving a very small percentage who were now in full retreat. The Squadron having suffered no further casualties were able to continue their advance and drive deeper behind the enemy to complete their task of sabo-

tage and destruction of the enemy. Finally they reached a point 20 miles ahead of the advance guard of the advancing Canadian Division thus threatening the rear of the Germans who finally withdrew. From the time of the arrival of Lieutenant-Colonel Mayne his gallantry inspired all ranks. Not only did he save the lives of the wounded but he also completely defeated and destroyed the enemy.

MANY BRAVE DEEDS
ARE NOT ENOUGH

Flight Lieutenant John Alan Anderson of Winnipeg, Manitoba, was award-ed a Distinguished Service Order on 6 February 1945 for services with No. 419 Squadron, RCAF. The published citation was considerably shorter that the original recommendation that had been drafted on 23 October 1944 by Wing Commander D.C. Hagerman, who recommended a Victoria Cross. At the date of the submission, Anderson had flown 22 sorties (127 hours 25 minutes of operational time), considerably less than that logged by other "periodic VC" nominees.

Flight Lieutenant Anderson has completed 22 day and night operations against the enemy, during the course of which his outstanding devotion to duty and complete contempt of personal danger have been most remarkable. His determination to press home his attacks in spite of the fiercest opposition the enemy can put up has earned him the utmost admiration from all ranks.

On no fewer than ten attacks his aircraft has been badly damaged by enemy action but his enthusiasm to operate remains undiminished.

On July 28th, 1944, when detailed to attack Hamburg, his starboard inner engine failed when crossing Flamborough Head en route to the target. Although Flight Lieutenant Anderson was aware that he would probably lose height and be late on the target, he nevertheless, without hesitation, carried on, arriving on the target six minutes late and bombing from 8,000 feet below the main stream. On the return journey, when thirty miles off Heligoland, his aircraft was attacked by two FW.190s, one dropping fighter flares while the other made no fewer than five attacks. These were all successfully evaded and the attacking aircraft was so badly damaged by his gunners that it broke off the attack and was last seen in flames going down in a steep turn. This officer then brought his aircraft safely back to base, still on three engines.

On 25th August 1944, when detailed to attack Russelheim, his aircraft was badly damaged by flak on the way into the target. Many holes were made in the fuselage; nevertheless he pressed home his attack and, on his return, was diverted to Great Orton after ten hours 50 minutes flying. Again, on 27th August 1944, when attacking Mimoyecques, his aircraft was again hit by heavy flak over the target area, no fewer than 37 large flak holes being counted on his return to base. On 29th August, when attacking Stettin, his GEE and H2S equipment became unserviceable while crossing the English coast on the way out, but he proceeded on D/R navigation to the target, where he again suffered heavy damage from flak. While in the target area, his aircraft was coned for some considerable time while on the bombing run and was attacked by a Ju.88. Nevertheless he brought his aircraft safely back to base.

On 6th September 1944, when attacking Emden, his aircraft was hit by heavy flak while on the approach, but this did not prevent him from making an excellent bombing run and returning with a first-class picture of the aiming point. On 12th September, when attacking Dortmund, his aircraft was hit by concentrated heavy flak, many large holes being torn in the fuselage, but again he returned safely to base. On the 6th October, while attacking Dortmund, his aircraft was again hit by flak while on the bombing run and, after bombing, he was attacked by no fewer than five fighters, all of which were successfully evaded. On the 8th October, when attacking Bochum, 27 large flak holes were torn in his aircraft and, during an attack by two fighters, a cannon shell exploded in the fuselage, short-circuiting the entire electrical system and causing all the navigation lights to burn. With great skill and coolness, he successfully evaded the fighters which were attracted by his lights and successfully returned to base with his aircraft in a badly damaged condition. On the 14th October, when attacking Duisburg in daylight, his aircraft was again hit by predicted flak and a "scarecrow" but again he succeeded in returning to base with a badly damaged aircraft.

This officer's most outstanding feat was performed during a daylight attack on the oil refinery at Bottrop on the 27th September. On arriving at the target it was found that this was obscured by 9/10th cloud cover. The target was sighted through a gap in the clouds too late to afford an accurate bombing run. Anti-aircraft fire was very heavy, but without hesitation, Flight Lieutenant Anderson decided to do an orbit to ensure an accurate bombing run be made. At the beginning of the orbit, the aircraft was repeatedly hit by shell fragments and both port outer and inner engines were put out of action. The port outer engine was also set on fire, the hydraulic system was rendered unserviceable and the controls were damaged to such an extent that he had to call on the assistance of two members of his crew to pull manually on the rudder controls. With complete disregard of the heavy opposition, and the difficulty in controlling his crippled aircraft, Flight Lieutenant Anderson completed the orbit and made a steady bombing run, enabling his Air Bomber to attack the target very accurately.

Shortly after leaving the target, it was found that the starboard inner engine had also been badly damaged and was giving less than half power. Through superb planning, crew co-operation and flying skill, Flight Lieutenant Anderson successfully flew his crippled aircraft back to this country, with only full power from the starboard outer, half power on the starboard inner engine, and made a masterly landing without causing further damage to his aircraft or crew.

I consider Flight Lieutenant Anderson's great courage, whole-hearted enthusiasm to press home his attacks in the face of whatever opposition he may meet, and his brilliant flying skill and crew Captaincy, fully merit the award of the Victoria Cross.

THE VICTORIA CROSS TO PRIVATE JOHNSON GIDEON BEHARRY

The Victoria Cross is now so rarely bestowed that it is worth recording the citation for the most recent recipient of this honour, Private Johnson Gideon Beharry, First Battalion, Princess of Wales' Royal Regiment, announced in the *London Gazette* of 25 March 2005, for gallantry at Al-Amarah, Iraq, on 1 May and 11 June 2004.

Private Beharry carried out two individual acts of great heroism by which he saved the lives of his comrades. Both were in direct face of the enemy, under intense fire, at great personal risk to himself (one leading to him sustaining very serious injuries). His valour is worthy of the highest recognition.

In the early hours of the 1st May 2004 Beharry's company was ordered to replenish an isolated Coalition Force outpost located in the centre of the troubled city of Al Amarah. He was the driver of a platoon commander's Warrior armoured fighting vehicle. His platoon was the company's reserve force and was placed on immediate notice to move. As the main elements of his company were moving into the city to carry out the replenishment, they were re-tasked to fight through a series of enemy ambushes in order to extract a foot patrol that had become pinned down under sustained small arms and heavy machine gun fire and improvised explosive device and rocket-propelled grenade attack.

Beharry's platoon was tasked over the radio to come to the assistance of the remainder of the company, who were attempting to extract the isolated foot patrol. As his platoon passed a roundabout, en route to the pinned-down patrol, they became aware that the road to the front was empty of all civilians and traffic – an indicator of a potential ambush ahead. The platoon commander ordered the vehicle to halt, so that he could assess the situation. The vehicle was then immediately hit by multiple rocket-propelled grenades. Eyewitnesses report that the vehicle was engulfed in a number of violent explosions, which physically rocked the 30-tonne Warrior.

As a result of this ferocious initial volley of fire, both the platoon commander and the vehicle's gunner were incapacitated by concussion and other wounds, and a number of the soldiers in the rear of the vehicle were also wounded. Due to dam-

age sustained in the blast to the vehicle's radio systems, Beharry had no means of communication with either his turret crew or any of the other Warrior vehicles deployed around him. He did not know if his commander or crewmen were still alive, or how serious their injuries may be. In this confusing and dangerous situation, on his own initiative, he closed his driver's hatch and moved forward through the ambush position to try to establish some form of communications, halting just short of a barricade placed across the road.

The vehicle was hit again by sustained rocket-propelled grenade attack from insurgent fighters in the alleyways and on rooftops around his vehicle. Further damage to the Warrior from these explosions caused it to catch fire and fill rapidly with thick, noxious smoke. Beharry opened up his armoured hatch cover to clear his view and orientate himself to the situation. He still had no radio communications and was now acting on his own initiative, as the lead vehicle of a six Warrior convoy in an enemy-controlled area of the city at night. He assessed that his best course of action to save the lives of his crew was to push through, out of ambush. He drove his Warrior directly through the barricade, not knowing if there were mines or improvised explosive devices placed there to destroy his vehicle. By doing this he was able to lead the remaining five Warriors behind him towards safety.

As the smoke in his driver's tunnel cleared, he was just able to make out the shape of another rocket-propelled grenade in flight heading directly towards him. He pulled the heavy armoured hatch down with one hand, whilst still controlling his vehicle with the other. However, the overpressure from the explosion of the rocket wrenched the hatch out of his grip, and the flames and force of the blast passed directly over him, down the driver's tunnel, further wounding the semi-conscious gunner in the turret. The impact of this rocket destroyed Beharry's armoured periscope, so he was forced to drive the vehicle through the remainder of the ambushed route, some 1500 metres long with his hatch opened up and his head exposed to enemy fire, all the time with no communications with any other vehicle. During this long surge through the ambushes the vehicle was again struck by rocket-propelled grenades and small arms fire. While his head remained out of the hatch, to enable him to see the route ahead, he was directly exposed to much of this fire, and was himself hit by a 7.62mm bullet, which penetrated his helmet and remained lodged on its inner surface.

Despite this harrowing weight of incoming fire Beharry continued to push through the extended ambush, still leading his platoon until he broke clear. He then visually identified another Warrior from his company and followed it through the streets of Al Amarah to the outside of the Cimic House outpost, which was receiving small arms fire from the surrounding area. Once he had brought his vehicle to a halt outside, without thought for his own personal safety, he climbed onto the turret of the still-burning vehicle and, seemingly oblivious to the incoming enemy small arms fire, manhandled his wounded platoon commander out of the turret, off the vehicle and to the safety of a nearby Warrior. He then returned once again to his vehicle and again mounted the exposed turret to lift out the vehicle's gunner and move him to a position of safety. Exposing himself yet again to enemy fire he returned to the rear of the burning vehicle to lead the disorientated and shocked dismounts and casualties to safety. Remounting his burning vehicle for a third time, he drove it through a complex chicane and into the security of the defended perimeter of the outpost, thus denying it to the enemy. Only at this stage did Beharry pull the fire extinguisher handles, immobilising the engine of the vehicle, dismounted and then moved himself into the relative safety of the back of another Warrior. Once inside Beharry collapsed from the sheer physical and mental exhaustion of his efforts and was subsequently himself evacuated. .

Having returned to duty following medical treatment, on the 11th June 2004 Beharry's Warrior was part of a quick reaction force tasked to attempt to cut off a mortar team that had attacked a Coalition Force based in Al Amarah. As the lead vehicle of the platoon he was moving rapidly through the dark city streets towards the suspected firing point, when his vehicle was ambushed by the enemy from a series of rooftop positions. During this initial heavy weight of enemy fire, a rocket-propelled grenade detonated on the vehicle's frontal armour, just six inches from Beharry's head, resulting in a serious head injury. Other rockets struck the turret and sides of the vehicle, incapacitating his commander and injuring several of the crew.

With the blood from his head injury obscuring his vision, Beharry managed to continue to control his vehicle, and forcefully reversed the Warrior out of the ambush area. The vehicle continued to move until it struck the wall of a nearby building and came to rest. Beharry then lost consciousness as a result of his wounds. By moving the vehicle out of the enemy's well chosen killing area he enabled other Warrior crews to be able to extract his crew from his vehicle, with greatly reduced risk from incoming fire. Despite receiving a serious head injury, which later saw him being listed as very seriously injured and in a coma for some time, his level-headed actions in the face of heavy and accurate enemy fire at short range again almost certainly saved the lives of his crew and provided the conditions for their safe evacuation to medical treatment.

Beharry displayed repeated extreme gallantry and unquestioned valour, despite intense direct attacks, personal injury and damage to his vehicle in the face of relentless enemy action.

BIBLIOGRAPHY

There are numerous books and articles dealing in whole or in part with the Victoria Cross and George Cross. This listing concentrates on those notable for accuracy, originality or insights.

Abbott, P.E. and Tamplin, J.M.A., *British Gallantry Awards* (London, Nimrod, 1981).

Arthur, Max, *Symbol of Courage: The Men Behind the Medal* (London, Pan Books, 2005 edition).

Billière, General Sir Peter de la, *Supreme Courage: Heroic Stories from 150 Years of the Victoria Cross* (London, Little, Brown, 2004).

Blatherwick, Francis John, *1,000 Brave Canadians: The Canadian Gallantry Awards, 1854-1989* (Toronto, Unitrade Press, 1991).

Boileau, John, *Valiant Hearts: Atlantic Canada and the Victoria Cross* (Halifax, Nimbus, 2005).

Boyer, Chaz, *For Valour – The Air VCs* (London, William Kimber, 1978).

Crook, M.J., *The Evolution of the Victoria Cross* (Tunbridge Wells, Midas Books, 1975).

Glanfield, John, *Bravest of the Brave: The Story of the Victoria Cross* (Phoenix Mill, Sutton Publishing, 2005).

Greenhous, Brereton, *The Making of Billy Bishop* (Toronto, Dundurn Group, 2002).

Jordan, Alan and Mulholland, John, *Victoria Cross Bibliography* (London, Spink, 1999).

Peter D. Mason, Peter D., Nicolson, *VC: The Full and Authorised Biography of James Brindley Nicolson* (Ashford, Geerings, 1991).

McCreery, Christopher, *The Canadian Honours System* (Toronto, Dundurn Press, 2005).

Ralph, Wayne, *Barker VC* (Toronto, Doubleday, 1997).

Reid, Elizabeth, *The Singular Journey of O'Hea's Victoria Cross* (Yale, Leamcon Press, 2005).

Revell, Alex, *Victoria Cross: World War I Airmen and Their Aircraft* (Cornwall, Flying Machine Press, 1997).

Smyth, Rt. Hon. Sir John, *The Story of the George Cross* (London, Arthur Barker, 1968).

Stanistreet, Allan, *Heroes of the Albert Medal* (Honiton, Token Publications, 2002).

Swettenham, John (editor), *Valiant Men: Canada's Victoria Cross and George Cross Winners* (Toronto, Hakkert, 1973).

Tancred, George, *Medals and Honorary Distinctions Conferred on the British Navy, Army and Auxiliary Forces From the Earliest Period* (London, Spink, 1891).

ENDNOTES

You will find it very good practice always to verify your references, sir !

Martin Joseph Routh (1755-1854), "Memoir of Dr. Routh,"
published in the *Quarterly Review,* July 1878.

1. The internet is a true river of information, including that on the *Param Vir Chakra* (<http://www.bharat-rakshak.com/HEROISM/PVC.html>). Browsers may also wish to consult <http://faculty.winthrop. edu/haynese/medals/Pakistan/pakistan.html> for information of the *Nishan-i-Haider,* the VC equivalent for Pakistan (13 awards, 8 of them posthumous). Sadly, most of these high honours have been earned in wars that pitted the two countries against each other. Other websites deal with Israel's *Itur HaGvuah* or Medal of Valour (<http://www.yairmalachi.org/MedalsOfIsrael/Decorations.htm>). Whilst browsing, the surfer may also wish to consult <http://www.bienejer.mil.ar/veteranos/condeco.asp> for the seven *Cruz "La Nación Argentina al Heroico Valor En Combate"* (four of them posthumous) awarded in the 1982 *Guerra de las Malvinas* (aka the Falkland Islands War). Valour is seldom the property of one side only in a war.
2. See Reg H. Roy, *Sinews of Steel: The History of the British Columbia Dragoons* (Charters Publishing, Toronto, 1965), pp. 300-303.
3. M.J. Crook, *The Evolution of the Victoria Cross* (Tunbridge Wells, Midas Books, 1975), pp. 10-19 and 52.
4. The situation was not unique to the Victoria Cross; in the United States the Medal of Honor was distributed generously in the absence of other awards; no fewer than 26 were spread among the 200 survivors of the Battle of the Little Bighorn (1876). On 11 May 1898, a three-hour raid on a cable station in Cuba brought the Medal of Honor to 48 men, and in the brief Spanish-American War no fewer than 111 Americans received this honour. See John Pelzer, "False Invasion Repelled," *Military History,* June 1993, pp. 66- 73. A failed three-week show of force against Korea in 1871 resulted in the award of 15 Medals of Honor; see Michael D. Haydock, "America's Other Korean War," *Military History,* April 1996, pp. 38-44.
5. Crook, *op. cit.,* pp. 254-256.
6. Website of Dix-Noonan-Webb (medal dealers), <http://www.dnw.co.uk/> (auction of 2 March 2005, Lot 45).
7. *Orders, Decorations and Campaign Medals,* a Christie's (London) catalogue for an auction held on 2 November 1983, p. 25. The catalogue entry referred to a book, *Napier's Rifles* by H.G. Rawlinson. Two other officers named Forbes and Little, engaged in the rescue of the soldier, were also reported as having been recommended for the VC.
8. The qualification created a problem in that the Maori Wars continued following withdrawal of British regular forces. As the fighting progressed, Governor G.F. Bowen authorized a New Zealand Cross which was a near-lookalike of the Victoria Cross (March

1869). It was awarded 22 times. See George Tancred, *Medals and Honorary Distinctions Conferred on the British Navy, Army and Auxiliary Forces From the Earliest Period* (London, Spink, 1891), pp. 385-399; P.E. Abbott and J.M.A. Tamplin, *British Gallantry Awards* (London, Nimrod, 1981), pp. 230-236.

9. The exclusion of Indian troops until 1911 was based on political fictions rather than a colour bar. Before that date, three blacks, all of them enrolled in British units, had been awarded the Victoria Cross – William Hall (Royal Navy, service in the Indian Mutiny, VC gazetted 1 February 1859; Samuel Hodge, 4th West India Regiment, 1866 service in the Gambia, VC gazetted 4 January 1867; William James Gordon, West India Regiment, 1892 service in the Gambia, VC gazetted 9 December 1892.

10. Crook, *op. cit.*, pp. 248-250.

11. The name of "Captain Groves" was later corrected to "Captain Cafe."

12. Brereton Greenhous, Directorate of History. As of this writing (10 February 2006), this has not been confirmed by documents.

13. The original recommendation by Lieutenant-Colonel Burke appeared (edited) in *Aeroplane* of 4 February 1933.

14. Public Record Office Air 1/1479/204/34, document dated 2 July 1916 and submitted by Brigadier General D. de G. Pitcher, Commanding 1st Brigade, Royal Flying Corps.

15. Public Record Office Air 1/993/205/5.

16. Obituary to Brigadier-General Arthur Asquith, *The Times*, 26 August 1939.

17. *Aeroplane*, 1 September 1915.

18. Public Record Office Air 2/5686

19. Crook, *op. cit.*, pp. 184-185

20. Danial G. Dancocks, *The D Day Dodgers: The Canadians in Italy, 1943-1945* (Toronto, McClelland and Stewart, 1991), pp. 363-364.

21. *The Times* of 13 October 1921 reported the arrest in Cleveland, Ohio, of Sydney Breese, who had made free use of British uniforms, claimed to have won a VC with the 11th Hussars, and had "no difficulty in persuading banks and hotel keepers to trust him." The same newspaper (22 September 1923) carried an account of James Thomas Hazen, convicted of having received a stolen automobile. Suave and multilingual, Hazen had claimed to have been twice recommended for the VC; the records showed he had been cashiered in 1918 following conviction by court martial on charges of theft and being absent without leave. *The Times* of 14 December 1928 reported that Gilbert Jackson had been sentenced to prison for defrauding a lady of £394; he had previously been sentenced to two months in jail for wrongly wearing a Victoria Cross. In the United States, false claimants to the Medal of Honor have been ruthlessly exposed and a person may be fined up to $100,000 for claiming or wearing an unauthorized Medal of Honor. A judge was driven from the Bench for having made such a fraudulent claim.

22. Canon William Murell Lummis, *Honour the Light Brigade* (London, Hayward and Son, 1973). p. 128.

23. Lummis, *op. cit.*.

24. As reported in *The Times*, 31 March 1897, 15 February 1972, 5 March 1982 and 28 April 1983.

25. "A Hero's Medal," *Legion Magazine*, August 1974.

26. John Glanfield, *Bravest of the Brave* (Sutton, London, 2006), pp. 23-36.

There were precedents for casting medals using guns captured from the enemy. On 4 January 1844 the Governor General of India, celebrating a victory over a native prince, announced there was to be presented "to every general and other officer, and to every soldier engaged in the battles of Maharajpore and Punniar, an Indian Star, of bronze, made out of the guns taken at those battles, and all officers and soldiers in the service of the Government of India will be permitted to wear the Star with their uniforms." Tancred, *op. cit.*, p. 274.

27. Canadian Army file 1 CDR/6-7 (3) "Honours and Awards, Recommendations" in National Library and Archives, RG 24, Vol. 10917,

28. John Boileau, *Valiant Hearts: Atlantic Canada and the Victoria Cross* (Halifax, Nimbus, 2005), p. 213.

29. P.S. Newton, Army and Navy Club, writing to *The Times*, 8 November 1985. This quote now appears in almost every reputable history of the Victoria Cross, but even Crook admits he has been unable to locate the original correspondence stating the King's views.

30. *London Gazette*, 26 September 1924.

31. C.K. Bate and M.G. Smith, *For Bravery in the Field* (London, Bayonet Publications, 1991), pp. 14-15.

32. *Canada Gazette* dated 3 March 1945 (announcing the award); *Canada Gazette* dated March 16, 1946 (rescinding the award); Canadian Army file HQ 54-27-94-25, "Honours and Awards – USA – Decorations Policy," Vol. 3 (National Archives of Canada RG 24, Vol. 2229).

33. The formula in such forfeitures is demonstrated in a rare example involving a Canadian: "The King has directed that the appointment of Philip Henry Tedman, late Lieutenant-Colonel, the Royal Canadian Artillery (Canadian Army Active) to be an Officer of the Military Division of the Most Excellent Order of the British Empire, dated 7th July 1945, shall be cancelled and annulled, and his name erased from the Register in consequence of his having been dismissed from His Majesty's service by sentence of a Field General Court Martial. (The cancellation to be dated 1st November 1947)." – *London Gazette*, 25 November 1947.

34. *Queen's Regulations and Orders (Canada)*, Chapter 24, section 24.15 (a), iv.

35. Crook, *op. cit.*, p. 46.

36. *Ibid.*, pp. 169 and 258. See also website of Dix-Noonan-Webb (medal dealers), <http://dnw.co.uk/> (auction of 28 July 1993, Lot 277).

37. "Vetus," *The Times*, 5 November 1891, who claimed to be quoting Lord Wolsely.

38. Ronald G. Haycock, *Sam Hughes: The Public Career of a Controversial Canadian, 1885-1916* (Ottawa, Canadian War Museum, 1986), pp. 90, 93 and 154. It is easy to ridicule the eccentric and egotistical Hughes, but on the night of 29/30 May 1900 he certainly distinguished himself in organizing and directing the defence of a bivouac during a surprise attack by 600 Boers. Lieutenant-General Sir Charles Warren initially praised Hughes for this and other actions. He turned against Hughes when he discovered that the Canadian had written letters (which were published in newspapers) criticizing Sir Charles in his strategy and choice of bivouac sites. If Hughes had performed a VC action, he promptly antagonized the one person who could have promoted one on his behalf.

39. Randolph S. Churchill, *Winston S. Churchill*, Vol. I, "Youth" (London, Heinemann, 1966), pp. 526-527.

40. Gordon Corrigan, *Mud, Blood and Poppycock: Britain and the First World War* (London, Cassels, 2003), p. 286. An interesting case of a man demanding (and getting) a Victoria Cross is found in Indian Mutiny history. On 15 April 1858, Private Samuel

Morley and Farrier Michael Murphy went to the aid of a Lieutenant Hamilton, who had been wounded and unhorsed. Murphy was awarded the VC in May 1859. On learning of this, Morley complained to his superiors that he was equally deserving of one. They reviewed the evidence, agreed, and Morley's VC was gazetted in August 1860; Christopher John, "Did You Know?" *Medal News*, September 2005.

41. Crook, *op. cit.*, pp. 261-264.

42. Canadian Army file 6-20/A, "Awards – Policy," in National Library and Archives of Canada, Record Group 25 Vol. 10950. The memo in question did concede that battlefield rescues could be used to justify "periodic" gallantry awards. This policy probably explains the non-award of a Victoria Cross to Lieutenant Kenneth Pillar, 50th Royal Tank Regiment.

43. Crook, *op. cit.*, p. 259.

44. Public Record Office Air 2/5686.

45. John Frayne Turner, *VCs of the Air* (Shrewsbury, Airlife, 1993), describes the action as involving two runs by Trigg. The eyewitnesses stated only one run was made; *"U 468,"* *Interrogation of Survivors*, prepared by Royal Naval Intelligence Branch, October 1943. (Canadian Armed Forces Directorate of History and Heritage, Document 80/582, dossier 85).

46. Public Record Office Air 2/4890. Further details were published in the Admiralty's *Monthly Anti-Submarine Report* for August and October 1943 (copies consulted at the Directorate of History and Heritage, Canadian Forces Headquarters).

47. *Ibid.* There was certainly no discrimination against Keen on grounds of origin; he was a British-born member of the Royal Air Force who happened to be one of many non-Canadians serving in an RCAF squadron.

48. *Ibid.* The final text of Petrie's CGM (Flying) is in the *London Gazette* of 4 June 1943.

49. *Ibid.*

50. Canadian Army file 215C1 D-80, National Library and Archives of Canada, RG 24, Vol. 10572; Department of National Defence Directorate of History and Heritage file 73/1321. The theory that somebody had gone too far when writing a letter of condolence cannot be either proved or disproved, as Griffin's service file does not include correspondence sent to his family at the time he was killed.

51. Canadian Army file 215C1 (D.88), in National Library and Archives RG 24, Vol. 10572.

52. Public Record Office Air 2/4890, referring to the Addis VC recommendation.

53. Canadian Privy Council Orders PC.8601 dated 23 September 1942 (recommending the Victoria Cross), PC.9802 dated 27 October 1942 (revoked PC.8601), and PC.9805 of 27 October 1942 (substituting the CGM). See also Robert C. Fisher, "Heroism in the North Atlantic," *Legion Magazine*, May/June 2002.

54. *London Gazette*, 16 March 1943. See also A.F.C. Layard, "Algiers – 8 November 1942," *Naval Review*, April 1978.

55. Naval Staff History, Second World War, Battle Summary No. 17, *Naval Operations of the Campaign in Norway* (London, Admiralty, 1951), pp. 12-13.

56. *Ibid.*, pp. 128-129.

57. The correspondence cited is found in the Public Record Office, ADM 178/334.

58. Public Record Office ADM 1/24300.

59. John Sweetman, *Tirpitz: Hunting the Beast* (Phoenix Mill, Sutton Publishing, 2000), pp. 81-82; Errol W Martyn, *For Your Tomorrow*, Vol. II (Christchurch, Volplane Press, 1999), p. 266; S.D. Waters, *The Royal New Zealand Navy* (Wellington, War History Branch,

1956), pp. 515-516. Errol Martyn also provided documents from Richardson's file which included statements by senior officers.

60. *Orders, Decorations, Campaign Medals and Militaria*, a Spink (London) catalogue for an auction held on 24 November 2005, pp. 75-76, specifically the sale of William Courtney's Crimea Medal.

61. Corrigan, *op. cit.*, pp102-103.

62. "Officers – Recommendations for Raid, March 1st, Vimy Ridge," Victor Odlum Papers, National Library and Archives of Canada, MG.30 E.300, Vol. 20.

63. Canadian Army file 1 CDR/6-7 (4), National Library and Archives of Canada, RG 24, Vol. 10917 and file 1 CDR/6-7-2 (3), RG 24, Vol. 10418..

64. National Library and Archives of Canada, file 239C1 (D15) "Honours and Awards – Sicily," in RG 24, Vol. 10916; service files of Private Cousins, RG 24, Vol. 25652.

65. National Library and Archives of Canada, file 239C1 (D15) "Honours and Awards – Sicily," in RG 24, Vol. 10916. Gagnon's personal file is devoid of detail, although early in 1943 he was being considered for duty with an army concert party; the project was cancelled and he went on to combat duty and his death. In 1946 his family inquired as to whether he had been recommended for any bravery award. They were told that none was on record, which was true because the failed VC submission had never found its way into his official service documents!

66. National Library and Archives of Canada, file 239C1 (D15) "Honours and Awards – Sicily," in RG 24, Vol. 10916

67. Canadian Army file 1 CDR/6-7 (4), "Honours and Awards," in National Library and Archives Canada RG 24, Vol. 10917 has a letter dated 29 December 1944 from Major-General H.W. Foster (General Officer Commanding, 1 Canadian Division) to the Military Secretary, 1 Canadian Corps, stating that he is forwarding statements by the commanding officer of the PPCLI, Officer Commanding 2 Canadian Infantry Brigade, and witness statements, all bearing on VC recommendations for Acting Corporal McGrath and for Lieutenant W.D.L. Roach, plus a draft citation. None of these documents seem to have survived.

68. As with McGrath, the supporting documents have not yet been located. However, it seems unlikely that authorities would have allowed two Victoria Crosses to the same regiment for the same action, and the submissions would most likely have been downgraded to lesser awards at the level of 1 Canadian Corps. The PPCLI seem to have been grasping for VC awards.

69. Canadian Army file 21/Dieppe/1 "Honours and Awards, Dieppe," National Library and Archives RG 24, Vol. 12730; Canadian Army file 109/Honours/3 (MS), "Honours and Awards, Dieppe Operation," National Library and Archives RG 24, Vol. 10571.

70. Canadian Army file 1 CDR/6-7-4 (2), National Library and Archives of Canada, RG 24, Vol. 10919.

71. To this list might be appended two other names. Sergeant Yvon Piuze, MM, Royal 22e Regiment, killed in action on 15 September 1944, was reportedly recommended for the Victoria Cross; see Jean Victor Allard, *The Memoirs of General Jean V. Allard* (Vancouver, University of British Columbia Press, 1988), pp 64, 70, 92-93. Captain Robert Marsh, a Canadian officer on attachment to the British Army (under a scheme known as CANLOAN) was reportedly recommended for a posthumous Victoria Cross following a night action in Holland on 24 October 1944; see Wilfred I. Smith, *Code Word CANLOAN* (Dundurn Press, Toronto, 1992), pp. 138, 180 and 254, in turn citing *A Short*

History of the 6th (Cameronian and Anglesey) Battalion, The Royal Welch Fusiliers in North West Europe, June 1944 to May 1945. Michael Glover, *That Astonishing Infantry: Three Hundred Years of the History of the Royal Welch Fusiliers* (Leo Cooper, London, 1987) also mentions a VC recommendation for Marsh, again without citing sources. Both men were posthumously Mentioned in Despatches. As of this writing (10 February 2006) this writer has found no documentary evidence of any of these recommendations, although the Mentions in Despatches point strongly to some such submission. Allard was Piuze's commanding officer.

72. See Joseph Allan Snowie, *Bloody Buron: The Battle of Buron, 8 July 1944* (Erin, Boston Mills Press, 1984), pp. 67-68, 92-93, 111. The diary of the Highland Light Infantry of Canada (National Library and Archives of Canada, RG 24, Vol. 15076) has the recommendation for his Victoria Cross, raised by Major G.A.M Edwards, with three witness statements.

73. Canadian Army file 215C.1 in National Library and Archives of Canada, RG 24, Vol. 10571.

74. Website of Dix-Noonan-Webb (medal dealers), <http://www.dnw.co.uk/> (auction of 4 July 2001).

75. Claude Smith, *The History of the Glider Pilot Regiment* (Leo Cooper, London, 1992), pp. 110-118.

76. Canadian Army file 1 CDR/5-2 (2), "Honours and Awards, Recommendations, Sicily and Italy," in National Library and Archives of Canada, RG 24, Vol. 10916.

77. CFHQ Directorate of History and Heritage, Document Collection 96/47, "Honours and Awards Collection," folio 2 ("Recommendations for Awards – Korea").

78. CFHQ Directorate of History and Heritage file 229C1 (D36), now held in the National Library and Archives of Canada (RG 24, Vol. 10827).

79. Canadian Military Headquarters file 21/Dieppe/1, "Honours and Awards – Dieppe," held by National Library and Archives of Canada, RG 24, Vol. 12730.

80. Canadian Army Headquarters file HQC-54-27-94-21, National Library and Archives of Canada RG 24, Vol. 2225.

81. CFHQ Directorate of History and Heritage document 181.009 D.1516, National Library and Archives of Canada Record Group 24 Vol. 20601 (Reichert); CFHQ Directorate of History and Heritage document file 181.009 D.1552; National Library and Archives of Canada Record Group 24 Vol. 20601 (McHarg); Public Record Office Air 2/5010 (Sargent).

82. CFHQ Directorate of History and Heritage document file 181.009 D.3386 (National Library and Archives of Canada RG 24, Vol. 20638), Daily Diary, P.1d.

83. Peter D. Mason, *Nicolson, VC: The Full and Authorised Biography of James Brindley Nicolson* (Ashford, Geerings, 1991), pp. 51-54. See also Public Record Office Air 2/5686.

84. Chaz Bower, *For Valour: The Air VCs* (London, William Kimber, 1978) outlines the circumstances of all Victoria Crosses awarded to air force personnel. Although he hints darkly at the validity of Bishop's award (he was writing before Bishop's record had come under scrutiny; on the other hand he may not have gone further simply out of courtesy), Bower does not explore the processes of awarding Victoria Crosses.

85. Policy about awards and the standards attached to them was published in several circulars distributed to Command, Group and Station levels. See for example Base Linton-on-Ouse file BL/S221-5, "Recommendations for Honours and Awards – Policy," CFHQ Directorate of History and Heritage document reference 181.009 (D1512), National Library and Archives of Canada RG 24, Vol. 20600.

86. Public Record Office Air 2/5686.

87. Public Record Office Air 2/5867.

88. Such, at least, were the numbers quoted in a memorandum of 25 September 1942; Public Record Office Air 2/4890.

89. Public Record Office Air 2/4890.

90. Public Record Office Air 2/4951

91. Public Record Office Air 2/4890.

92. Public Record Office Air 2/4890

93. Public Record Office Air 2/5867. A book on the Amiens prison raid states that French civilians erected a cross on Pickard's grave giving his awards as "VC, DSO, DFC, Bar," suggesting that the French, at least, believed he had merited the award. The Commonwealth War Graves Commission presumably replaced the cross with a regulation headstone which would have omitted reference to a VC. See Jack Fishman, *And the Walls Came Tumbling Down* (Toronto, General Paperbacks, 1982), p. 490.

94. Public Record Office Air 14/4115.

95. Public Record Office Air 2/5010.

96. *Ibid.*

97. Public Record Office Air 2/5867.

98. Watson's service files included numerous sworn statements by his comrades and associates. Much of this is also found in Public Record Office Air 14/4115. There can be little doubt that an award for him was very much sponsored by his peers.

99. Public Record Office Air 2/4890.

100. See Marc La Terreur (editor), *Dictionary of Canadian Biography*, Vol. X (Toronto, University of Toronto Press, 1972), p. 558 (O'Hea). Douglas has escaped the attention of Canadian encyclopedia authors.

101. M.J. Crook, *op. cit.*, pp. 137-148.

102. Allan Stanistreet, *Heroes of the Albert Medal* (Honiton, Token Publications, 2002).

103. *Ibid.*, p. 18.

104. P.E. Abbott and J.M.A. Tamplin, *British Gallantry Awards* (London, Nimrod, 1981), pp. 16-24; John Blatherwick, *1,000 Brave Canadians: The Canadian Gallantry Awards, 1854-1989* (Toronto, Unitrade Press, 1991), pp. 99-112. He lists 27 (omitting the case of AB Barber) and gives full details of each exploit.

105. *London Gazette*, 14 June 1910.

106. Randolph S. Churchill, *op. cit.*, pp. 462-468 and 526-527. In 1942, following one of Churchill's lengthy wartime excursions abroad, General Douglas MacArthur was moved to write, "If disposal of all the Allied decorations were today placed by providence in my hands, my first act would be to award the Victoria Cross to Winston Churchill. No one of those who wear it deserve it more. A flight of 10,000 miles through hostile and foreign skies may be the duty of young pilots, but for a Statesman burdened with the world's cares, it is an act of inspiring gallantry and valour." Quoted by Martin Gilbert, *Road to Victory: Winston St. Churchill, 1941-1945* (London, Stoddart, 1986), p. 217.

107. Abbott and Tamplin, pp. 131-137; Blatherwick, pp. 113-116.

108. Public Record Office Air 2/5038.

109. Canadian Army file 1 CDR/6-7-2 (4), in National Library and Archives of Canada, RG 24, Vol. 10918. Private Smalley was awarded a British Empire Medal. John Blatherwick, in a rare instance of second-guessing, declares that Mulherin's award *should* have been a George Cross.

110. Memorandum of Inter-Service Awards Committee, 12 May 1955, in Canadian Armed Forces Directorate of History and Heritage file 75/601, folio 18.

111. Memorandum of Inter-Service Awards Committee, 11 October 1963, in Canadian Armed Forces Directorate of History and Heritage file 75/601, folio 23.

112. A website dedicated to the George Cross, <http://www.gc-database.co.uk/alpha.htm>, previously provided scholarly and thorough material, but in 2006 reduced its on-line coverage in order to market the material as books.

113. Admiral Cunningham briefly describes their actions in his memoirs, *A Sailor's Odyssey* (London, Hutchinson, 1951), pp. 445-446, but without mentioning the dispute over awards and his own part in the debate.

114. Website <http://www.gc-database.co.uk/alpha.htm> lists several other George Cross awards that involved direct interaction with the enemy, see the headings for Captain Matreen Ahmed Ansari, Sergeant Arthur Banks, Captain Mahmood Khan Durnani, Captain Douglas Ford, Flight Lieutenant Hector Bertram Gray, Captain Lionel Colin Matthews, and Lieutenant-Colonel Lanceray Arthur Newnham (all Second World War prisoners and all posthumous awards); Fusilier Derek Geoffrey Kinne, Private Horace William Madden, and Lieutenant Terence Edward Waters (prisoners of war in Korea, Madden and Waters awarded the GC posthumously); Captain Robert Laurence Nairac (kidnapped, tortured and murdered by the IRA); John Alexander Fraser (a civilian captured at Hong Kong in 1941 and awarded a posthumous GC); Captain Mahmood Khan Durani (POW, survived), plus numerous cases of service and civilian personnel engaged in espionage – Lieutenant-Commander Albert-Marie Edmond Guerisse (alias Patrick Albert O'Leary); Lieutenant-Colonel Arthur Frederick Nicholls*, Odette Marie Celine Sanson, Lance-Corporal David Russell*, Violette Reine Elizabeth Szabo*, and Wing Commander Forest Frederick Edward Yeo-Thomas; those marked with an asterisk were posthumous awards. In addition, the posthumous George Crosses to Privates Benjamin Gower Hardy and Ralph Jones inform and remind us that even guard duty could entail great risks; they were killed during a mass breakout of Japanese prisoners from a camp in Australia.

115. See George H. Ford, *The Making of a Secret Agent: The Pickersgill Letters* (Toronto, McClelland and Stewart, 1978).

116. David Pugliese, "Inquest Hails Canadian Bodyguard for Saving Lives in Iraqi Ambush:, Ottawa *Citizen*, 1 February 2006.

117. The *Journal of the Canadian Aviation Historical Society* issue of June 1984 was dedicated to the Mynarski story.

118. The story of Hornell and his crew is related in the U-Boat Attack report (UBAT) which went into meticulous detail of both the attack and the subsequent ordeal by water; see Directorate of History and Heritage, document 181.003, D.880.

119. The author is in possession of a list of awards, obtained in 1973 from Norwegian authorities, which states that Lieutenant Krafft had been awarded a Commonwealth DFC. Nick and Carol Carter, in their excellent book *The Distinguished Flying Cross and How it was Won, 1918-1995* (London, Savannah Publications, 1998) do *not* list him among Norwegian recipients. Awards such as this to non-Commonwealth personnel are difficult to trace, and the thought that Krafft, with one U-boat kill to his credit plus his role in the Hornell story, would receive no award challenges credulity.

120. All quotations are from Public Record Office Air 2/8784.

121. CFHQ Directorate of History and Heritage file 181.009 D.1730, in the National Library and Archives of Canada, RG 24, Box 20607..

122. CFHQ Directorate of History and Heritage file 181.009 D.1719, National Library and Archives of Canada, RG 24, Box 20606.
123. *Ibid.*
124. Public Record Officer Air 2/4890.
125. Documentation for this is in the Public Record Office, Air 1/1957/204/260/12 and Air 1/448/15/303/48, copies of which have been copied and deposited in the National Library and Archives of Canada, MG.40 D.1 Vols. 30 and 8 respectively.
126. See Don Neate and Air Britain, *The Scorpion's Sting: The Story of No. 84 Squadron, Royal Air Force* (Air Britain, 1994), p. 24 and Public Record Office Air 30/72.
127. *London Gazette*, 19 August 1921 and *Aeroplane* , 24 August 1921.
128. *London Gazette*, 7 June 1921.
129. *London Gazette*, 11 April 1941 and Public Record Office Air 2/5686.
130. See for examples Captain James D. Campbell (Australian Army in Vietnam, citation in the *London Gazette* of 16 April 1968, Flying Officer David T.J. Collinson (RAF in Borneo, *London Gazette* of 1 June 1965), Captain John G. Greenhalgh (British Army, Falkland Islands, citation in *London Gazette* of 8 October 1982) and Lieutenant Richard J. Nunn (Falkland Islands, citation in *London Gazette* of 8 October 1982).
131. The website <http://www.medalofhonor.com> dedicated to the Medal of Honor, is an excellent reference point to explore the achievements of Major William E. Adams, Major Patrick H. Brady, Chief Warrant Officer Frederick E. Ferguson, Captain James P. Fleming, Lieutenant (N) Clyde E. Lassen, Chief Warrant Officer Michael J. Novosel, Major Stephen W. Pless and Captain Gerald O. Young.
132. Public Record Office file Air 1/1032/04/4./1434, "Immediate Honours and Awards, Foreign Decorations, August 1916 to January 1917," correspondence dated 3 October and 3 November 1916.
133. Public Record Office Air 1/1032/204/5/1434, "Honours and Awards, Immediate Awards, January 1917 to September 1917".
134. S.F. Wise, *Canadian Airmen and the First World War* (Toronto, University of Toronto Press, 1980), pp. 412-414.
135. Public Record Office Air 1/1032/204/5/1434, "Honours and Awards" – overlapping volumes covering immediate awards from August 1916 to March 1918 and October 1917 to March 1918.
136. Public Record Office Air 1/1030/204/5/1433, "Honours and Awards," covering immediate miscellaneous immediate awards, June to December 1918.
137. Public Record Office Air 1/1515, recommendation sent by Commander, 3rd Brigade, Royal Flying Corps to Headquarters, Royal Flying Corps, 7 May 1917.
138. "Memorandum Regarding Recommendations for Honours and Awards" dated 23 September 1916, found in Public Record Office Air 1/1031/204/5/1434. These strictures were repeated frequently in succeeding orders; see Public Record Office, files Air 1/1255/204/8/39 and Air 1/1479/204/36/131.
139. Aitken's awesome propaganda efforts on behalf of the Canadian troops included extensive photography, battlefield cinematography, books, front-line newspapers and Canada's first war art program. See Maria Tippett, *Art at the Service of War* (Toronto, University of Toronto Press, 1984).
140. Philip Markham, "The Early Morning Hours of 2 June 1917," *Over the Front*, Vol. 10 No. 3 (Fall 1995); Brereton Greenhous, *The Making of Billy Bishop* (Toronto, Dundurn, 2002). One of the most curious aspects of Bishop's VC is that, when gazetted, it was

reported to be with effect from 27 June 1917 – three days *before* the Caldwell report.

141. *Orders, Decorations and Campaign Medals*, Christie's (London) catalogue for an auction held on 18 November 1986, p. 58.

142. Corrigan, *op. cit.* .p. 106.

143. Wayne Ralph, *Barker VC* (Toronto, Doubleday, 1997), p. 168.

144. Public Record Office Air 2/9219.

145. *Ibid.*.

146. Public Record Office Air 2/4890.

147. See Christopher Shores, Brian Cull and Yasuho Izawa, *Bloody Shambles: Volume One: The Drift to War to the Fall of Singapore* (London, Grub Street, 1992), pp. 105-107.

148. Crook, *op. cit.*, p. 44.

149. *Ibid.*, p. 45.

150. *Ibid.*, pp. 145-146.

151. *The Times*, 21 and 22 February 1879.

152. Reginald H. Roy, *The Seaforth Highlanders of Canada, 1919-1945* (Vancouver, Evergreen, 1969), p. 368; conversation, John Blatherwick with Lieutenant-Colonel Bell-Irving, recounted to Hugh Halliday, and hence, admittedly, a third-hand anecdote.

153. This account is based upon the April 2004 auction list of Medals Archives (Hornchurch, Essex), and a website, *Britain's Small Wars, 1945-2003*, found at <http://www.britains-smallwars.com>.

154. Traill-Burroughs' VC recommendation arose from a storming incident on 17-18 November 1857 which nevertheless resulted in 13 Victoria Crosses being awarded (nine of them being elected). Simultaneous events elsewhere around Lucknow brought the award of a total of sixteen Victoria Crosses – the most for any date.

155. "Maori Injustice?" *Medal News*, December 1997/January 1998. The magazine was dismissive of the claim. A search of the internet, using only the words "Haane Manahi," turns up numerous sites reporting on this campaign. The argument that he was denied a VC because of quotas might have some merit, as Second Lieutenant Moana-Nui-a-Kiwa of the same unit received a posthumous VC for actions performed only weeks before those of Manahi. However, such decisions to approve or downgrade were common.

156. Other than Canadian cases mentioned in this book, the following instances of VC nominations reduced to DCM awards have been identified (*London Gazette* dates in brackets): Sergeant Richard I. Andrews, West Surrey Regiment (4 May 1943), Trooper Jack Barlow, 7th Queen's Own Hussars (25 April 1941), Battery Quartermaster Sergeant Arthur J. Batten, Royal Horse Artillery (18 July 1941), Corporal Harry L. Bell, Royal Inniskilling Fusiliers (18 October 1945), Lance Sergeant Charles V. Calistan, the Rifle Regiment (14 January 1943), Private Kenneth Carter, Duke of Cornwall's Light Infantry (7 December 1944), Sergeant Roland A. Clark, Oxfordshire and Buckinghamshire Light Infantry, Lance Corporal Ronald F.C. Coles, Royal Berkshire Regiment (23 March 1944), Fusilier Donald Dixon, Royal Welch Fusiliers (8 February 1945), Sergeant Roy Finch, Welch Regiment (12 July 1945), Corporal Alan G. Guise, Rifle Brigade (13 August 1942), Private George Jackson, Essex Regiment (22 July 1943), Lance Corporal Alexander R. Leitch, King's Own Scottish Borderers (12 April 1945), Private Charles R. McCallum, 2/14 Australian Infantry Battalion (4 February 1943), Lance Corporal William J. McQuoid, Royal Fusiliers (22 July 1943), Fusilier John E. Mercer, Royal Scots Fusiliers (20 July 1944), Staff Sergeant Stanley G. Miller, 2/1 Australian Infantry Battalion (22 April 1944), Sergeant Frank C. Mitchell, Royal Fusiliers (12 February 1942), Warrant Officer

Hendrick C. Nolte, South African Armoured Car Regiment (31 December 1942), Lance Corporal Joseph Penn, York and Lancaster Regiment (21 December 1944), Trooper Richard Piper, 107th Regiment, Royal Armoured Corps (22 March 1945), Pipe Major Robert Roy, Royal Highland Regiment (24 February 1942), and Corporal Arthur E. Smith, Royal Fusiliers (18 October 1945); Philip McDermott, *For Distinguished Conduct in the Field: The Register of the Distinguished Conduct Medal, 1920-1992* (Polstead, Hayward and Son, 1994). McDermott also lists many cases of Military Medal recommendations that were *upgraded* to Distinguished Conduct Medals, but no one complains when a potential medal is "promoted".

157. Public Record Office Air 2/12422, which is dedicated entirely to the Horan case.

158. <http://www.theodoreroosevelt.org/life/MedalofHonor%20Quest.htm>

159. Richard Doherty, "Why I believe Blair Mayne didn't deserve the VC," *Belfast Telegraph*, 27 January 2006.

160. The recommendations for Garceau, Emigh and MacLeod are taken from a single document – Canadian Army file 1 CDR/6-7 (5) "Honours and Awards, Recommendations" in National Library and Archives, RG 24, Vol. 10917.

161. Public Record Office Air 1/1255/204/8/39..

162. George Drew, *Canada's Fighting Airmen* (Toronto, Maclean, 1930), pp. 215-233; Ron Dodds, *The Brave Young Wings* (Stittsville, 1980, pp. 175-179); Dan McCaffery, *Air Aces: The Lives and Times of Twelve Canadian Fighter Pilots* (Toronto, James Lorimer, 1990, pp. 49-57.

163. Carl Christie, "Alan Arnett McLeod, VC: Canada's Schoolboy Hero," *Journal of the Canadian Aviation Historical Society*, Vol. 34, No. 1 (Spring 1996); see also his entry for McLeod in *Dictionary of Canadian Biography*, Vol. XIV (Toronto, University of Toronto Press, 1998), p. 725-726.

164. The original issue of the *Journal de Lévis* has been lost; the story was reprinted in another paper, as yet unidentified.

165. Hanning appears to have been a very industrious part-time soldier. He had acquired a First Class Military Certificate from one of the pre-Confederation Military Schools (23 February 1866). As of 23 October 1866 he would be promoted Major in the newly-formed 53rd Battalion of Infantry, later transferring to the 54th Battalion. On 26 October 1871 he would be promoted Lieutenant-Colonel (*Annual Volunteer and Service Militia List of Canada*, 1867, 1871 and 1877, printed in Ottawa). He retired on 16 April 1875.

166. Public Record Office WO 32/7372.

167. *Quebec Mercury*, 26 April 1867,

168. *Quebec Mercury*, 1 May 1867. The reader should not be surprised that different witnesses gave slightly different accounts. This author recalls testifying at a trial involving a person charged with dangerous driving. Several persons who had seen the accident gave statements; each differed in some detail or another. These discrepancies probably arose from the fact that nine months had elapsed between the accident and the court hearing.

169. Elizabeth Reid in *The Singular Journey of O'Hea's Cross* (Yale, British Columbia, Leamcon Press, 2005)

170. J.L. Granatstein and D.J. Bercuson. *War and Peacekeeping: From South Africa to the Gulf – Canada's Limited Wars* (Toronto: Key Porter Books, 1991). p. 58; Carman Miller, *Painting the Map Red: Canada and the South African War, 1899-1902* (Montreal: Canadian War Museum and McGill-Queen's, 1993), p. 108.

171. Cameron Pulsifer, "Richard Rowland Thompson and his Queen's Scarf: An Historical Investigation," *Canadian Military History*, Vol. 6, Number 1 (Spring 1997); Brian Reid, "Queen Victoria's Scarves," *Pro Patria* (annual publication of the Royal Canadian Regiment), Special Paardeberg Centennial Edition, 2000.

172. Department of National Defence file 2801-19, "Honours and Awards – Queen Victoria's Scarf," National Library and Archives of Canada, RG 24, Accession 83-84/167, Vol. 4843. Thompson's service files, also in the National Library and Archives of Canada (microfilm T-2087) confirm the belated recommendation for a VC, almost one year *after* he had left South Africa.

173. For those prepared to have their historical assumptions challenged, two books constitute excellent points of departure: *The Invention of Tradition*, edited by Eric Hobsbawm and Terence Ranger (Cambridge, University Press, 1983) and *They Never Said It* by Paul F. Boller, Jr. and John George (New York, University of Oxford Press, 1989).

174. *Report of the Working Group on Honours and Awards*, 8 February 1972, found in unnumbered file, "Honours and Awards, General," National Library and Archives, RG 24, Vol. 20152.

175. Christopher McCreery, *The Canadian Honours System* (Toronto, Dundurn Press, 2005), pp. 358-359.

INDEX

MEMBER OF SCABRINI GROUP

Québec, Canada
2006